ALL-TIME BAKING FAVORITES

Editor: JoAnne Alter
Art Director: Marsha J. Camera
Associate Editor: Lyle Lawson
Art Associate: Walter C. Schwartz
Production Manager: Norman Ellers

Cover photograph by Bill McGinn
How-to diagrams by Adolph Brotman
Illustrations by Oni

All recipes tested in Family Circle's Test Kitchens

A New York Times Company Publication

CONTENTS

Here are just a few of our All-Time Baking Favorites. From top, down: Burnt Sugar Cake; Grandmother's White Bread and Anadama Cheese Bread; Chocolate Chip Cookies, Oatmeal Crunchies, and Country Cherry Pie. Recipes for all are listed in the Index.

1

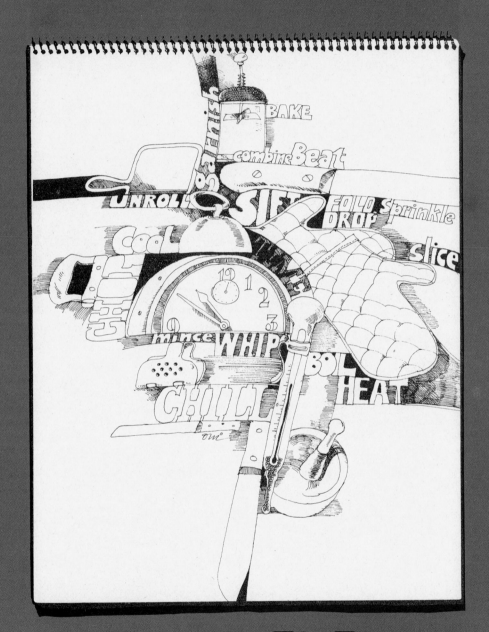

BAKING FACTS

Our first chapter is packed with baking basics! In it, you'll find helpful hints and how-to's—everything you need to know to bake, store, freeze and serve the best breads, rolls and baked desserts you ever made. You're sure to find it invaluable!

KINDS OF PANS

If you don't already have the following on hand, they're well worth the investment. (All new pans are stamped on the bottom, to indicate size):

Round pans—two 8-inch; two 9-inch
Square pans—two 8-inch; two 9-inch
Oblong pans—one 13x9x2-inch
Pie plates—two 9-inch
Loaf pans—two 9x5x3-inch
Jelly roll pan—one 15½x10½x1-inch
Bundt tube pan—one 9-inch cast aluminum, with nonstick coating
Spring-form pan—one 9-inch with removable bottom
Angel cake tube pan—one 10-inch with removable bottom
Muffin pans—two, 12 muffins each, 2½-in. diameter
Oven-proof custard cups (for popovers)—6 to 8
Cooky sheets—two; the biggest ones that will fit your oven, allowing at least one inch all around for proper circulation

The following aren't essential, but they're nice to have:

Ring mold—one 9¼x2¾-inch
Kugelhupf pan—one 10x4-inch
Fluted quiche pan—one 9-in. with removable bottom
Individual tart pans—6 to 8, fluted or plain
Small gem pan(s)—one or two, 12 small muffins each, 1¼-inch diameter
Heavy iron popover pan—one for 6 popovers
Madeleine pan—one for 12 cookies

Note: Round pans, square pans, small pie plates (7- to 8-inch), small loaf pans (8-inch) and small tart pans (3-inch) are generally available in reusable aluminum foil. You can buy them in department, hardware and variety stores.

ALTERNATE PAN CHART*

If your recipe calls for:	You may use:
Two 8x1½-inch round pans	18 to 24 (2½-inch) cupcake pan cups
Three 8x1½-inch round pans	Two 9x9x2-inch square pans; or one 13x9x2-inch oblong pan
Two 9x1½-inch round pans	Two 8x8x2-inch square pans; or one 13x9x2-inch oblong pan
One 9x5x3-inch loaf pan	One 9x9x2-inch square pan
Two 9x5x3-inch loaf pans	One 10x4-inch tube pan
One 8x4x3-inch loaf pan	One 8x8x2-inch square pan
One 9x3½-inch angel cake pan	One 10x3¾-inch bundt pan; or one 9x3½-inch fancy tube pan

*Note: This chart applies to butter cakes only. Chiffon, pound, sponge and angel food cakes are best baked in the pans specifically called for in recipes.

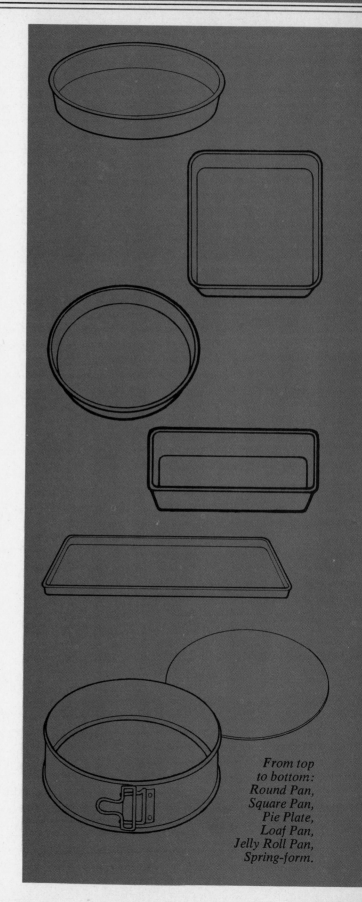

From top to bottom: Round Pan, Square Pan, Pie Plate, Loaf Pan, Jelly Roll Pan, Spring-form.

From top to bottom: Bundt Pan, Angel Cake Tube Pan, Muffin Pan, Ring Mold, Kugelhupf.

SPECIAL TIPS: Many pans are now available in either metal or glass. You can use either. But remember, ovenproof glass conducts heat more than metal does; so if you do use glass pans, always lower the oven temperature by *25 degrees*.

• Also, glass pans hold slightly less in volume than do metal pans. The difference isn't critical in most recipes, but you can expect your bread or cake to be slightly higher if you bake it in a glass pan.

OTHER EQUIPMENT YOU'LL WANT TO HAVE

Measuring and Mixing:

Flour sifter

Dry measuring cups—nested in sets from ¼ cup to 1 cup

Measuring spoons, also in sets, from ¼ teaspoon to 1 tablespoon

Liquid measuring cup—either one-, two- or four-cup size

Mixing bowls (small, medium, large)

Wooden spoons—set of three or four

Electric mixer—either standard or portable

Wire whisk—for combining and folding ingredients, keeping cooking mixtures smooth, and beating eggs

Pastry blender—for cutting shortening into flour, when making pastry. You can also use 2 knives, cutting in opposite directions next to each other.

Rubber scrapers—standard size and thin

18-inch ruler—for measuring pans and rolled-out dough

Small funnel

Rolling and Shaping:

Pastry board—for rolling and working with dough. Actually, any clean, dry, flat surface dusted with flour is fine.

Rolling pin

2-inch biscuit cutter (Try using an empty orange juice can.)

Kitchen scissors—for trimming pie crusts, cutting dried fruits, etc.

Cooky gun—metal tube with a variety of cut-out discs, to form cookies of different shapes

Cooky cutters—assorted shapes (For directions on how to trace and make your own cooky cutters, see pages 84 and 85.)

Cooking and Baking:

2- or 3-quart heavy saucepan

Double boiler

Kitchen timer—if your oven doesn't have one

Lifting and Cooling:

Wide spatula or pancake turner

Three wire racks for cooling cakes and cookies (You can also use your oven racks for cooling baked goods.)

Frosting and Decorating:

Straight-edged spatula—a must for frosting; also useful for leveling dry ingredients, lifting cookies, loosening cakes

Canvas pastry bag—for shaping eclairs, cream puffs, meringue layers; for decorating and garnishing cakes. (You can select tips to fit your pastry bag.) Also, for quick shaping of drop cookies.

Cake decorating set (metal tube plus assorted tips)—for decorating cakes and cookies. (For directions on how to make a disposable wax paper decorating bag to use with your own decorating tips, see page 13.)

ABOUT INGREDIENTS IN THIS BOOK

Butter and margarine: Either is fine. *Recipes in this book were tested with both.* Use only stick form, not whipped or diet.

Eggs: *All recipes were tested using large eggs.*

Flour: Important—All white flour (all-purpose and cake) must be sifted before measuring. Rye and whole wheat flour needn't be.
• All-purpose flour—milled from both hard and soft wheat; for all baking other than cakes.
• Cake flour—milled from soft wheat; for all cakes.
• Rye flour—used with other flours in making breads, e.g., with all-purpose flour for rye bread.
• Whole wheat flour—milled from hard wheat, with bits of whole grain remaining. Used with all-purpose flour to make whole wheat bread.

Leavening agents:
• Baking powder—principal leavening agent for quick breads. *All recipes in this book use double-action baking powder.*
• Baking soda—also called bicarbonate of soda; helps neutralize acids, such as brown sugar. Since baking soda loses its potency with age, it's a good idea to buy it in small cans.
• Cream of tartar—helps stabilize foams, such as meringues.
• Yeast—either active dry yeast (in granular form) or compressed yeast (in cake form) is fine. *Note:* You may want to use active dry yeast, however, since it lasts longer than compressed yeast and needs no refrigeration. In either case, always use yeast before its expiration date, to guarantee proper results.

Milk products:
• Buttermilk—whole, skim or nonfat milk that has been soured.
• Evaporated milk—whole milk from which 60% of the water has been removed.
• Heavy cream—contains between 36% and 40% butterfat.
• Light cream—contains between 18% and 30% butterfat.
• Milk (whole)—*Unless otherwise specified, used in all recipes calling for milk.*
• Sour cream—light cream that has been soured; contains between 18% and 20% butterfat.
• Sweetened condensed milk—whole milk with half the water removed and sugar added.

Shortening: Soft vegetable shortening comes in solid form; it's available in one-, two- and three-pound cans. Used in pastry, cookies and some cakes. *Unless otherwise specified, always grease pans with solid shortening.*

Sugars and syrups:
• Brown sugar (both light and dark)—the darker the color, the more the flavor of molasses. When measuring, be sure to pack firmly!
• Corn syrup (both light and dark)—for pies, some frostings.
• Granulated sugar—the kind in your sugar bowl. *Unless otherwise specified, used in all recipes calling for sugar.*
• Honey—used mainly in cookies and coffee cakes.
• Molasses—processed from sugar cane; used primarily in cookies and spice cakes.
• 10X (confectioners' or powdered) sugar—crushed sugar blended with cornstarch. Sometimes used instead of frosting; used in all butter cream frostings. (If your 10X sugar has gotten lumpy, sift before using.)

Thickening agents:
• Cornstarch—used to thicken pie and cake fillings; also used in dessert sauces.
• Tapioca—used to thicken fruit pies.

Vegetable oil: Any type (corn, peanut, safflower, etc.) is fine. Usually used in chiffon cakes and quick breads. Use only where specified.

GLOSSARY

Bake	To cook by means of dry heat, usually in an oven
Batter	A mixture of flour and liquid plus other ingredients; thin enough to drop or pour
Beat	To make a mixture smooth or to introduce air by using a vigorous, steady over-and-over motion
Blend	To gently, but thoroughly, mix two or more ingredients together
Boil	To cook a liquid or in a liquid in which bubbles break on surface (212° F. at sea level)
Caramelize	To heat sugar slowly until it becomes brown in color and caramel in flavor
Chop	To cut food into fine pieces with knife or mechanical chopper
Cream	To blend two or more foods, usually butter or margarine and sugar, until smooth and fluffy
Cut	To combine shortening or liquid with dry ingredients using pastry blender or two knives
Dissolve	To make a solution from a dry and a liquid ingredient
Dough	A mixture of flour and liquid plus other ingredients; stiff enough to knead or roll
Fold	To combine ingredients using an up-over-and-down motion

SPECIAL LOW-CALORIE TIPS

You can enjoy baked breads, cakes, cookies and pies, even if you're watching your weight! You'll find a number of sensational Low Calorie recipes in this book. In addition, the following tips, from _Family Circle's_ "Creative Low Calorie Cooking" series, by Barbara Gibbons, are some of the best ways to trim calories from almost any recipe:

- When recipes call for sour cream, try yogurt or buttermilk as a substitute, and eliminate four-fifths of the calories.

- Soy flour, which is slightly lower in calories and carbohydrates, but much richer in proteins than all-purpose flour, can be used to replace up to one-third of the flour in any recipe. You can find it in health food stores and some supermarkets.

- Use evaporated skim milk instead of heavy cream and cut calories by three-fourths.

- Any cake will be bigger and higher (which means more slices at fewer calories) if you separate the eggs and whip the whites stiff before adding them to the batter. Try it—even if the recipe doesn't call for this step.

- You can, in most cases, get chocolate flavor without chocolate calories by using cocoa in place of un-sweetened (baking) chocolate. Instead of one ounce of solid chocolate (143 calories), use 3 table-spoons unsweetened cocoa (60 calories). Better yet, instead of one tablespoon cocoa, use one tea-spoon chocolate extract (only 7 calories!)

- If, in addition to calories, you must watch your cholesterol level, substitute two egg whites, stiffly beaten and folded into cake batter, for each whole egg called for in the recipe.

- Pie crusts are the most calorific part of most pies. Chill the dough very well and roll crusts extra-thin, and you'll have fewer calories per portion.

- Sugar substitutes can really help to rescue a pie from the forbidden list. If you can't stand a pie totally made from sugar substitutes, use a mixture of half sugar, half substitute. This will drastically alter the calorie count without substantially chang-ing the taste.

- A well-fruited pie needs less thickener than does a skimpy one. Use cornstarch instead of flour to thicken any fruit pie. Both have 29 calories per tablespoon, but with cornstarch, you need only half as much!

- Spices add everything to a pie—except calories; so spice up any pie to suit your taste. A touch of vanilla can heighten the impression of sweetness, while such extracts as orange, lemon, brandy or rum are terrific flavor enhancers.

Knead	To work dough with the hands, using a pressing and folding motion until dough is smooth and elastic
Sift	To put dry ingredients through a sieve
Simmer	To cook a liquid or in a liquid at a temperature just below boiling. Bubbles form slowly and break just below the surface
Stir	To mix with a spoon, using circular motion
Whip	To beat rapidly to incorporate air and increase volume

HOW TO MEASURE INGREDIENTS

When measuring any ingredient, the key word to remember is "level".

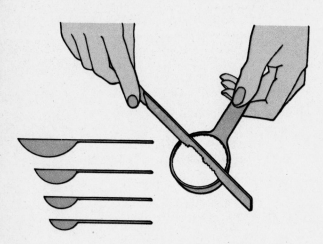

Make sure all dry ingredients measured in spoons or cups are leveled off at the top, with the edge of a knife, or with a straight-edged spatula.

Important: All white flour must be measured *after it has been sifted*. Spoon sifted flour lightly into measuring cup and level off. Do not tap the cup or in any way pack the flour down.

Brown sugar and solid shortening *should* be packed firmly in a measuring spoon or cup, then leveled off.

Measure liquids in a glass measuring cup, placed on a table or counter. Fill to the appropriate line, checking measurement at eye level.

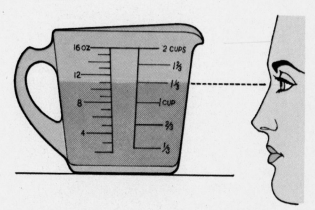

IMPORTANT MEASURES

1½ teaspoons	= ½ tablespoon
3 teaspoons	= 1 tablespoon
2 tablespoons	= 1 ounce
4 tablespoons	= ¼ cup
5 tablespoons plus 1 teaspoon	= ⅓ cup
8 tablespoons	= ½ cup
10 tablespoons plus 2 teaspoons	= ⅔ cup
12 tablespoons	= ¾ cup
16 tablespoons	= 1 cup (8 ounces)
2 cups	= 1 pint
2 pints	= 1 quart
4 quarts	= 1 gallon

EASY EQUIVALENTS

FOOD	EQUIVALENT
Eggs:	
Whole eggs, 1 cup	About 6 large
Egg yolks, 1 cup	11 to 12
Egg whites, 1 cup	7 to 8
Fruit:	
Apples, 1 pound	3 medium (3 cups sliced)
Lemon, 1 medium	2 teaspoons grated rind plus 2 tablespoons juice
Orange, 1 medium	4 teaspoons grated rind plus ⅓ cup orange juice
Strawberries, 1 quart	3½ cups hulled
Milk products:	
Butter or margarine	
1 pound	4 sticks or 2 cups
4 tablespoons	½ stick or ¼ cup
Heavy cream, 1 cup	2 cups, whipped
Ice cream, ½ gallon	4 pints
Milk, evaporated	
Small can (5⅓ ounces)	⅔ cup
Tall can (13 ounces)	1⅔ cups
Milk, sweetened condensed	
(14 ounces)	1⅔ cups
Nuts:	
Almonds, shelled, 1 pound	3½ cups
Peanuts, shelled, 1 pound	3 cups
Pecans, shelled, 1 pound	4 cups
Walnuts, shelled, 1 pound	4 cups
Starches:	
Flour, all-purpose, 1 pound	4 cups, sifted
Flour, cake, 1 pound	4½ cups plus 2 tablespoons, sifted
Graham crackers, 11 squares	1 cup crumbs
Sugars:	
Brown, 1 pound	2¼ cups, packed
Granulated, 1 pound	2 cups
10X (confectioners'), 1 pound	About 4 cups

SIMPLE SUBSTITUTIONS

INSTEAD OF	USE
Baking powder, 1 teaspoon	¼ teaspoon baking soda plus ⅝ teaspoon cream of tartar
Buttermilk, 1 cup	1 tablespoon lemon juice or vinegar plus sweet milk to equal 1 cup. (Let mixture stand for about 5 minutes.)
Chocolate, unsweetened 1 square, (1 ounce)	3 tablespoons cocoa plus 1 tablespoon fat.
Cornstarch, 1½ teaspoons	1 tablespoon flour
Corn syrup, 1 cup	1 cup sugar plus ¼ cup liquid
Egg, 1 whole	2 egg yolks
Honey, 1 cup	1¼ cups sugar plus ¼ cup liquid
Milk, skim, 1 cup	⅓ cup instant nonfat dry milk plus 1 cup minus 1 tablespoon water.
Milk, whole, 1 cup	½ cup evaporated milk plus ½ cup water.
Tapioca, 2 teaspoons	1 tablespoon flour

HIGH ALTITUDE TIPS

Unless you live at least 3,000 feet above sea level, you probably won't have to make any adjustments. Above that, you may wish to make the following changes:

Altitude	3,000 to 4,000 feet	4,000 to 6,000 feet	6,000 to 7,500 feet
Reduce Baking Powder For each teaspoon, decrease	⅛ tsp.	⅛ to ¼ tsp.	¼ tsp.
Reduce Sugar For each cup, decrease	1 Tbs.	1 to 2 Tbs.	3 to 4 Tbs.
Increase Liquid For each cup, add	1 to 2 Tbs.	2 to 4 Tbs.	3 to 4 Tbs.
Baking Temperature	Increase 25°	Increase 25°	Increase 25°

• For particularly rich butter or shortening cakes, try reducing the shortening by 1 or 2 tablespoons.

• If you live at an extremely high altitude, you may wish to increase the amount of egg in angel food, chiffon or sponge cakes.

• Only by experimenting will you find the right modifications for your needs. Try the smaller adjustments on any recipe the first time you make it; then, next time, if necessary, make the larger adjustment.

GETTING READY TO BAKE

1. Read recipe through. Make sure you have all ingredients on hand.
2. Assemble ingredients in one area; whenever possible, have all ingredients at room temperature.
3. Measure all ingredients accurately, (not over mixing bowl)!
4. Preheat oven at least 10 to 15 minutes before you plan to use it.
5. Be sure to follow recipe instructions, in the order they're given.

HOW TO PREPARE PANS

Use a generous coating of vegetable shortening (unless otherwise specified) and a light dusting of flour for an even, golden crust. Do *not* grease tube pans used for foam cakes (angel food, chiffon, sponge). The airy batter needs to cling to the sides of the pan as it expands.

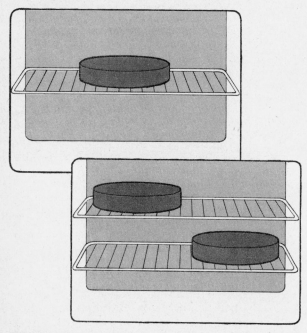

WHERE TO PUT PANS IN THE OVEN

Cake:
• When baking an oblong, or one layer, place pan on center of rack, in center of oven.
• When baking two layers, use two racks in center third of oven, layers in opposite corners.
• When baking three or four layers, use two racks in center third of oven. Stagger pans in opposite corners of both racks so they do not block heat circulation.
• For a tube cake, place pan on center of rack, in lower third of oven.
Cookies:
• Place cooky sheet in upper third of oven. If you're using two cooky sheets, place the other sheet on rack very close to the first one. Reverse sheets part way through baking, to assure even browning.
Breads and Rolls:
• Place two loaves or two pans of rolls on center rack, 2 inches apart. For more than two loaves or pans, stagger on 2 racks, for proper heat circulation.
Muffins, Biscuits, Cupcakes, Tea Loaves, Pies, Tarts:
• Follow same guidelines as for cakes: Place pans on center of rack, in center of oven. If you need more than one rack, stagger pans to assure proper heat circulation.

SPECIAL TIPS: It's generally a good idea to rotate items in the oven during baking time, to prevent uneven browning. Be sure to wait until the last five minutes to rotate cakes—otherwise they may fall.
• If a loaf of bread, a fruit cake or a two-crust pie is browning too rapidly, cover the top loosely with aluminum foil. That will prevent over-browning, without inhibiting baking.

ABOUT STORING

Cakes: Store in a cake keeper or on a serving plate covered by a large inverted bowl.
Cookies: Store in a canister, airtight box, or sealed in a plastic bag. Crisp cookies should be layered with plastic wrap, foil or wax paper, to keep them from breaking. Bar cookies can remain in their baking pan, tightly covered with foil.
Cupcakes: Store as you would cakes.
Pies: *All* pies should be covered with aluminum foil or plastic wrap and stored in the refrigerator.
Yeast Breads and Rolls: For maximum freshness, wrap in plastic bags or plastic wrap; refrigerate.

AND FREEZING

Cakes: Wrap unfrosted cakes in aluminum foil, plastic wrap, or in plastic bags; then freeze. For frosted cakes, place on a piece of cardboard or on a cooky sheet until firm. Wrap as above; freeze.
Cookies: For unbaked dough, drop on cooky sheet by teaspoonfuls; freeze. Then place frozen cooky balls in plastic bag, tied securely. Both bar and rolled cookies should be baked before freezing. Arrange carefully in single layers. Wrap tightly with aluminum foil or plastic wrap.
Cupcakes: Place side by side on cardboard; wrap as you would cakes.
Pies: *Unbaked* two-crust fruit pies should be frozen with *no* slits cut in the top crust. *Baked* fruit pies should be thoroughly cooled before wrapping and freezing. Wrap all fruit (and chiffon) pies in aluminum foil, plastic wrap or bags; then freeze. *Custard and cream pies should not be frozen.*
Yeast Breads and Rolls: You *can* freeze unbaked bread and rolls, but they will rise better if baked before freezing. Wrap in plastic bags; secure tightly.

HANDY FREEZING/SERVING CHART

BAKED ITEM	MAXIMUM STORAGE TIME AT 0° F.	TO PREPARE FOR SERVING
Breads, quick, loaf size:	1 to 2 months	Thaw 3 to 4 hours at room temperature
Breads, yeast:		
Sliced	2 weeks to 2 months	Thaw 15 minutes at room temperature or place, frozen, in toaster
Unsliced	3 to 6 months	Thaw 1 to 2 hours at room temperature
Rolls	2 weeks to 2 months	Heat at 250° to 300° F. for 15 minutes
Cakes:*		
Angel food or sponge	2 to 4 months	Thaw 2 hours at room temperature
Butter type		
frosted	1 to 2 months	Thaw 3 hours at room temperature
unfrosted	2 to 3 months	Thaw 1 to 2 hours at room temperature
Fruit, 1 pound	12 months	Thaw 2 hours at room temperature
Coffee cakes:	3 to 6 months	Heat at 250° to 300° F. for 30 minutes
Cookies:		
Baked	4 to 8 months	Thaw 1 hour at room temperature
Unbaked	4 to 6 months	Bake at 350° to 375° F. for 10 to 15 minutes
Cupcakes:	1 to 3 months	Thaw 1 hour at room temperature
Pies:**		
Baked	3 to 4 months	Thaw 8 hours at room temperature if served cold; or, heat at 450° F. for 30 to 50 minutes (depending upon size), if served warm.
Chiffon	2 weeks	Thaw 4 to 5 hours in 38° F. refrigerator; or 1 to 2 hours at room temperature
Shells, unbaked	2 months	Bake at 425° F. for 10 to 15 minutes; or thaw 30 minutes to one hour at room temperature
Unbaked, fruit	3 to 4 months	Bake at 450° F. for 15 to 20 minutes *on lowest shelf;* then reduce heat to 375° F. for an additional 45 minutes.

* Do not freeze cakes that are filled with custard, cream or fruit.
**Do not freeze custard or cream pies or those with meringue topping.

HOW TO MAKE A DISPOSABLE DECORATING BAG

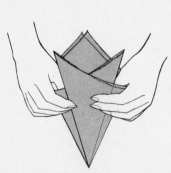  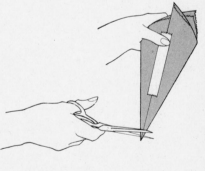

To make a disposable wax paper decorating bag, tear off a 12-inch square of wax paper. Fold in half to form a triangle. Pull opposite points around, to form a tight cone. (Cone should come to a point at the bottom.) Secure with tape; fill cone with frosting; snip off point to whatever size opening you wish.

Note: Try making a leaf tip by cutting an inverted "V" at the bottom of the unsnipped cone, or a notched tip by cutting the letter "M". The tips won't be as well-defined as those in a cake decorating set, but they will offer you some variation—and with only the snip of a scissors!

The chart below shows how many servings you can get from each cake or coffee cake you bake. The diagrams below demonstrate the easiest ways to cut the number of slices you want.

SPECIAL TIP: How many servings can you expect to get from a cake? Here's an idea:

9x5x3-inch loaf cake 8
8-inch square ....8 or 9
9-inch square 9
8-inch double layer ....10—12
9-inch double layer ....12—16
13x9x2-inch ....12—16
10-inch bundt or tube cake ....10—12
10-inch jelly roll 10

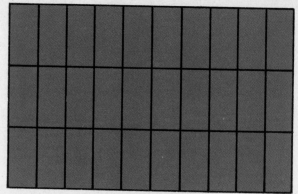

13x9x2-inch single-layer cake
30 servings

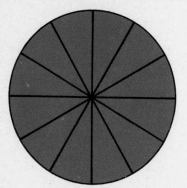

8- or 9-inch double-layer cake
12 servings

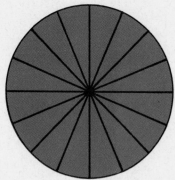

9-inch double-layer cake
16 servings (Good way to cut tortes.)

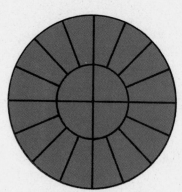

9-inch double-layer cake
20 servings (Good for very rich cakes.)

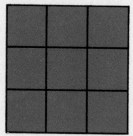

8- or 9-inch single-layer cake
9 servings

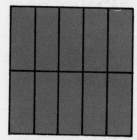

8- or 9-inch single-layer cake
10 servings

9-inch single-layer cake
16 servings (Good for cakes with
sweet, broiled toppings.)

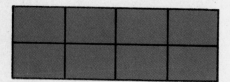

9x5x3-inch loaf
8 servings. (Good for coffee cakes.)

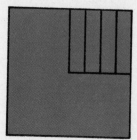

8- or 9-inch double-layer cake
16 servings (Note: Slice square double-layer
cake one quarter at a time, to keep
cake from collapsing.

9x5x3-inch loaf
8 servings (Note: To make 16 wedge-shaped slices,
for topping with ice cream, for example, cut each
of the eight slices in half, diagonally.)

Nutritious whole-grain breads:
Good tasting and good for you, too.
From top, down: High-protein Whole Wheat
Bread, Swedish Limpa, and our glazed,
round Swedish Limpa variation.
Recipes in Chapter 2.

Hot bread, fresh from the oven; what better way to say "Welcome"! Recipe for our inviting Anadama Cheese Bread in this chapter.

2

YEAST BREADS & ROLLS

Experience the sheer joy and satisfaction of baking wholesome and delicious yeast breads. Delight your family with savory, aromatic breads and rolls; warm, sweet coffee cakes and fragrant Danish. They're easy, and economical, too! And they're all in this chapter.

YEAST BREADS

SPECIAL TIPS: You don't have to be an experienced baker to make delicious bread. Here are some hints—to help you turn out perfect bread the first time, and every time you bake it.

• Make sure the water you dissolve your active dry yeast in is very warm. If you have a thermometer, it should register between 105° F. and 115° F. (about as hot as you'd want it for a bath—not burning, but not tepid, either). If you're using *compressed* yeast, however, the water should only be lukewarm—no hotter.

• To determine whether yeast is alive, you should always "proof" it: Dissolve yeast and a pinch of sugar in very warm water. The yeast, water and sugar mixture should bubble. If it doesn't, stop right there! Start again with new, fresh yeast.

• After the yeast is "proofed", be sure not to add any other hot liquids or other hot ingredients to the solution. Ingredients added after that point should be lukewarm.

• Don't worry about kneading dough too long. You can't hurt dough by over-kneading it; it's kneading *too little* that can prevent it from rising properly. Knead for the full amount of time specified, or until dough is soft and velvety. If you must stop during the kneading process, cover the dough with an inverted bowl. Then, as soon as possible, continue to knead for the remaining amount of time.

• Make sure the bowl you put the kneaded dough in is thoroughly greased, and that you turn the dough over in the bowl to cover all surfaces. If dough isn't properly greased (and the bowl completely covered), a crusty surface will form and you'll find pebble-like particles in your finished bread. If you'd prefer not to use cloth towels, you can cover your bowl or bowls loosely with plastic wrap.

• Let your dough rise in a *warm* place. Cold will inhibit proper yeast action. One of the best places to let dough rise is the oven of your gas or electric range. Place a pan of hot water on the shelf under the bowl of dough and close the door. If there is a pilot light, leave the door open.

• If you want a *glossy* crust on your bread, brush the top lightly with a mixture of either one whole egg, an egg yolk, or egg white, plus 1 or 2 tablespoons of water—immediately before baking. To insure a *soft* crust, brush lightly with melted butter or margarine as soon as you remove the bread from your oven.

• You'll notice that every bread recipe in this chapter indicates that you should test for doneness by tapping the top of the baked item with your knuckles, and listening for a hollow sound. That's important. You shouldn't go by color alone, particularly if you're using a glass loaf pan. A nice brown crust may be covering still unbaked bread. The sound is always the best clue!

• When you place baked breads and rolls on wire racks to cool, be sure to space them far enough apart to allow air circulation. Also, avoid drafts; otherwise the crusts may crack.

• To reheat bread, place loaves in a brown paper bag; sprinkle bag with a few drops of water; close tightly. Heat in moderate oven (350°) 10 minutes.

GRANDMOTHER'S WHITE BREAD

Golden crust, soft texture—delicious plain or toasted!

Bake at 400° for 40 minutes.
Makes 2 loaves.

> 1 envelope active dry yeast
> ½ cup very warm water
> 3 tablespoons sugar
> 2 cups milk
> 2 tablespoons butter or margarine
> 1 tablespoon salt
> 6 or 7 cups <u>sifted</u> unbleached all-purpose flour
> OR: 7 to 8 <u>cups</u> <u>sifted</u> all-purpose flour

1. Sprinkle yeast into very warm water in a 1-cup measure; stir in ½ teaspoon of the sugar. ("Very warm water" should feel comfortably warm when dropped on the wrist.) Stir until yeast dissolves. Let stand, undisturbed, to proof until bubbly and double in volume, about 10 minutes.
2. Combine remaining sugar, milk, butter and salt in a small saucepan; heat just until butter melts. Pour into large bowl; cool to lukewarm. Stir in yeast.
3. Stir in 3 cups of the flour; beat until smooth. Gradually stir in enough flour to make a soft dough (3 cups if you are using unbleached flour; 4 cups, if you are using all-purpose flour).
4. Turn out onto lightly floured surface; knead until smooth and elastic, about 10 minutes, using additional flour as needed to keep dough from sticking.
5. Place in a buttered bowl; turn to bring buttered side up. Cover with a towel. Let rise in a warm place, away from drafts, 1 hour, or until double in bulk.
6. Punch dough down; turn out onto lightly floured surface, knead a few times; invert the bowl over dough; let rest 10 minutes.
7. Divide dough in half and knead each half a few times. Shape into 2 loaves. Place loaves in two buttered 8½ x 4½ x 2½ -inch loaf pans.
8. Let rise again in a warm place, away from drafts, 1 hour, or until double in bulk.
9. Bake in a hot oven (400°) 40 minutes, or until golden brown and loaves sound hollow when tapped. If loaves are browning too quickly, cover loosely with foil. Remove from pans to wire racks to cool completely.

HIGH-PROTEIN WHOLE-WHEAT BREAD

This special bread is super-high in protein. Here's a great way to increase the nutritional value of bread.

Bake at 375° for 35 minutes.
Makes 2 loaves.

2 envelopes active dry yeast
3 tablespoons sugar
1½ cups very warm water
1 cup milk
2 tablespoons butter or margarine
1 tablespoon salt
⅔ cup instant nonfat dry milk powder
⅓ cup soya bean powder
3 tablespoons wheat germ
3 cups whole wheat flour
3 cups sifted unbleached all-purpose flour
Slightly beaten egg
Sesame seeds

1. Sprinkle yeast into ½ cup of the very warm water in a 1-cup measure; stir in 1 teaspoon of the sugar. ("Very warm water" should feel comfortably warm when dropped on wrist.) Stir until yeast dissolves. Let stand, undisturbed, to proof 10 minutes, or until bubbly and double in volume.
2. Combine remaining water and sugar with milk, butter or margarine and salt in a small saucepan; heat until butter melts. Pour into large bowl; cool to lukewarm. Stir in yeast.
3. Stir in dry milk powder, soya bean powder, wheat germ, 1½ cups of the whole wheat flour and 1 cup of all-purpose flour. Beat at medium speed with electric mixer, 3 minutes, scraping down side of bowl several times. Stir in remaining whole wheat flour and 1 cup all-purpose flour to make a stiff dough.
4. Turn out onto lightly floured surface. Knead until smooth and elastic, about 10 minutes, using the remaining all-purpose flour in order to keep the dough from sticking.
5. Place in a buttered large bowl; turn to bring buttered side up. Cover with a towel. Let rise in a warm place, away from drafts, 1 to 1½ hours, or until double in bulk.
6. Punch dough down; turn out onto lightly floured surface; knead a few times; invert bowl over dough; let rest about 10 minutes. Divide dough in half and knead each piece a few times; shape into 2 loaves. Place in two buttered 8½x4½x2½-inch loaf pans.
7. Let rise again in a warm place, away from drafts, 45 minutes, or until double in bulk. Brush tops with beaten egg; sprinkle with sesame seeds.
8. Bake in a moderate oven (375°) 35 minutes, or until golden and loaves sound hollow when tapped. Remove from pans to wire racks; cool completely.

Note: If you wish to make rolls, divide dough into 16 even pieces; shape into round balls for hamburger rolls, or 5-inch-long fingers for frankfurter rolls. Place, 3 inches apart, on greased large cooky sheet. Let rise 30 to 40 minutes, or until double in bulk. Brush tops with egg; sprinkle with sesame seeds. Bake in a hot oven (400°) 15 to 20 minutes, or until golden brown.

BUTTERMILK WHEAT BREAD

Creamy buttermilk blends with nutritious flour and crunchy cracked wheat.

Bake at 375° for 40 minutes.
Makes 2 loaves.

2 envelopes active dry yeast
½ cup very warm water
2 cups buttermilk
2 tablespoons vegetable shortening
¼ cup honey
1 tablespoon salt
½ teaspoon baking soda
3½ cups whole wheat flour
1 cup cracked wheat
2¼ cups sifted all-purpose flour

1. Sprinkle yeast into very warm water in a 1-cup measure; stir in 1 teaspoon of the honey. ("Very warm water" should feel comfortably warm when dropped on wrist.) Stir until yeast dissolves. Let stand undisturbed to proof until bubbly and double in volume, about 10 minutes.
2. Heat buttermilk with shortening, remaining honey and salt in small saucepan just to lukewarm; combine with yeast mixture in a large bowl.
3. Stir in baking soda, whole wheat flour and cracked wheat until smooth; beat in enough of the all-purpose flour to make a soft dough.
4. Turn out onto lightly floured surface. Knead until smooth and elastic, about 10 minutes, using only as much flour as needed to keep dough from sticking.
5. Place in a buttered bowl; turn to bring buttered side up. Cover with a towel. Let rise in a warm place, away from drafts, 1 hour, or until double in bulk.
6. Punch dough down; turn out onto lightly floured surface; knead a few times; invert a bowl over dough; let rest 10 minutes.
7. Divide dough in half and knead each half a few times. Roll each piece to an 18x9-inch rectangle. Roll up from short side, jelly roll fashion. Pinch ends together with fingers to seal. Place each loaf seam side down in a greased 9x5x3-inch pan.
8. Let rise again in a warm place, away from drafts, 40 minutes, or until double in bulk.
9. Bake in moderate oven (375°) 35 minutes, or until golden brown and loaves sound hollow when tapped. Remove from pans to wire racks to cool completely.

ANADAMA BREAD

Legend has it an old New England fisherman developed this bread from a cornmeal mush that his lazy wife, Anna, had been making for years. One day, so the story goes, the fisherman added yeast to her concoction, and, as he did so, supposedly yelled, "Anna, damn her!" The result of his efforts: A delicious new bread—"Anadama."

Bake at 375° for 50 minutes.
Makes 1 round loaf.

1½ **cups water**
 ½ **cup cornmeal**
  2 **teaspoons salt**
  6 **tablespoons butter or margarine**
 ½ **cup light molasses**
  2 **envelopes active dry yeast**
 ½ **cup very warm water**
  6 **cups** <u>sifted</u> **all-purpose flour**
    Cornmeal (for topping)

1. Heat water, cornmeal, salt, butter or margarine and molasses in a medium-size saucepan until thick and bubbly. Pour into a large bowl; cool to lukewarm, about 45 minutes.
2. Sprinkle yeast into ½ cup very warm water in a cup. ("Very warm water" should feel comfortably warm when dropped on wrist.) Stir until yeast dissolves, then blend into cooled cornmeal mixture.
3. Beat in 2 cups of the flour until smooth. Stir in 3 more cups of flour, 1 cup at a time, until dough is very stiff.
4. Turn out onto a lightly floured surface. Knead until elastic, about 10 minutes, using remaining cup of flour, as needed, to keep dough from sticking.
5. Place dough in a greased large bowl; turn to coat all over with shortening; cover with a towel. Let rise in a warm place, away from drafts, about 1½ hours, or until double in bulk.
6. Punch dough down; knead in bowl a few times. Shape into a ball. Press into a greased 10-cup baking dish. Brush top with soft shortening; sprinkle with cornmeal.
7. Let rise again, in a warm place, away from drafts, 1 hour, or until double in bulk.
8. Bake in a moderate oven (375°) 50 minutes, or until loaf is golden brown, and sounds hollow when tapped. Remove from pan to a wire rack; cool.

SPECIAL TIP: Both ANADAMA BREAD and ANADAMA CHEESE BREAD (recipe follows) are better the day after they're baked. When loaves have cooled, wrap in wax paper, foil or plastic wrap. Store overnight. The flavors will mellow, and ANADAMA BREAD will be easier to slice.

ANADAMA CHEESE BREAD

A variation of the cornmeal bread, baked as a cheesy loaf that breaks apart as small rolls.

Bake at 375° for 35 minutes.
Makes 2 loaves.

    Anadama Bread (recipe at left)
  8 **ounces process American cheese, shredded**
    Butter or margarine
    Cornmeal (for topping)

1. Follow recipe for ANADAMA BREAD adding cheese in Step 3.
2. To shape: After last rising, divide dough in half. Shape each half into 14 even-size balls, rolling each between palms of hands until smooth. Arrange balls in rows in two buttered 9x5x3-inch pans. Brush tops with melted butter; sprinkle with cornmeal.
3. Bake in moderate oven (375°) 35 minutes, or until loaves sound hollow when tapped. Remove from pans to wire racks; cool completely. Loaves will break apart into separate rolls for serving.

SOURDOUGH BREAD

Since the days of the gold rush in Alaska, people have been making a special type of bread that uses the yeast in the air as the leavening agent. The bread is called "sourdough" because of the particular flavor that the starter gives the bread. (Our starter takes about 7 days to make.) In the past, people used only the sourdough starter to raise their bread; rising took 24 hours. To quicken the process, we've added commercial yeast—but you'll still get that special old-fashioned flavor!

Bake at 400° for 40 minutes.
Makes 2 loaves.

  1 **envelope active dry yeast**
  1 **cup very warm water**
1½ **cups Sourdough Starter (recipe follows)**
  2 **tablespoons sugar**
  2 **teaspoons salt**
5½ **cups** <u>sifted</u> **all-purpose flour**
  1 **egg white**
  2 **tablespoons cold water**

1. Sprinkle yeast into very warm water in a large bowl. ("Very warm water" should feel comfortably warm when dropped on wrist.) Then stir in starter, sugar and salt.
2. Beat in 2 cups of the flour until smooth. Beat in enough of the remaining flour to make a soft dough.
3. Turn out onto a lightly floured surface. Knead until smooth and elastic, about 10 minutes, using only

HOMEMADE BREAD—THE EASY WAY

1.

Baking bread is a joy! And it's easy, too. Just follow these few simple steps.

1. While yeast is proofing, sift flour and measure onto wax paper; place heated milk and/or water, sugar or syrup, salt and butter or shortening called for in recipe in a large bowl; cool. Add proofed yeast to bowl.

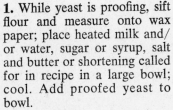
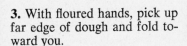

2. Stir in flour, according to recipe directions; beat with a wooden spoon until dough is smooth. Gradually add enough of remaining flour until dough forms a soft ball and no longer clings to side of bowl. Turn out onto a floured surface.

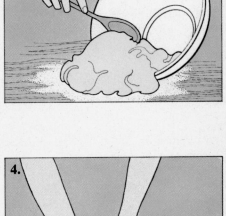

2.

4.

3. With floured hands, pick up far edge of dough and fold toward you.

4. Push into the dough, away from you, with heel of one hand, and at the same time, give the dough a quarter of a turn by pulling it toward you with the other hand. Repeat folding, pushing and turning this way, adding just enough flour to keep dough from sticking, until dough feels smooth and elastic.

3.

5. Place dough in large greased bowl; turn to bring greased side up. Cover and let rise according to recipe directions.

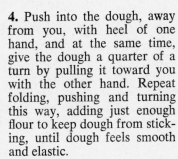

5.

6. When dough has doubled in bulk, press with two fingers; if indentations stay, dough is ready.

6.

7. Punch down dough with fist. Then, turn out onto a lightly floured surface and knead according to recipe directions.

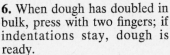
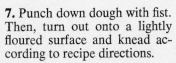
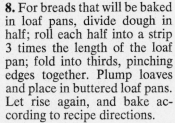

8. For breads that will be baked in loaf pans, divide dough in half; roll each half into a strip 3 times the length of the loaf pan; fold into thirds, pinching edges together. Plump loaves and place in buttered loaf pans. Let rise again, and bake according to recipe directions.

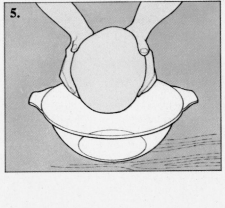

7.

8.

Breads from around the world, to add international flair to any meal. Top left: Irish Soda Bread (recipe, Chapter 3). Other breads shown: braided Challah, dark Scandinavian Rye Bread, saucer-shaped Armenian Breads and long Crusty French loaves. Recipes in this chapter.

as much flour as needed to keep dough from sticking.
4. Place in a greased, large bowl; turn to coat all over with shortening; cover with a clean towel. Let rise in a warm place, away from drafts, 1 hour, or until double in bulk.
5. Punch dough down; turn out onto lightly floured surface; invert bowl over dough; let rest 20 minutes.
6. Grease 2 cooky sheets; sprinkle with cornmeal.
7. Divide dough in half and knead each half a few times. Roll each half to a 15x10-inch rectangle. Roll up tightly from long side, jelly roll fashion; pinch long seams tightly to seal. Roll loaves gently back and forth with hands to taper ends. Place loaves diagonally on prepared cooky sheets.
8. Let rise again in a warm place, away from drafts, 45 minutes, or until double in bulk.
9. Make slits 2 inches apart on top of breads with a very sharp knife or razor blade. Beat egg white and cold water together in a small cup. Brush loaves.
10. Bake in a hot oven (400°) 40 minutes or until golden in color and loaves sound hollow when tapped. Remove from cooky sheets to wire racks; cool completely.

Sourdough Starter: Makes 4 cups.
    2 cups milk
    2 cups sifted all-purpose flour

Pour milk into a glass or ceramic bowl and cover bowl with cheesecloth. Let stand in the outdoors for 1 day. Stir in flour and re-cover bowl with cheesecloth. Place outside for 2 days. Place bowl in a sunny spot indoors and allow to stand until mixture bubbles and starts to sour, about 2 days. Spoon into a quart jar with a screw cap and store in refrigerator at least 1 day before using. (If top of starter should start to dry out at any time during this process, stir in a little lukewarm water.) When you remove 1½ cups of sourdough starter, simply combine ¾ cup milk and ¾ cup flour and stir into jar. Cover jar with cheesecloth and place in sunny spot for 1 day. Remove cheesecloth; cover jar and return to refrigerator.

TAOS BREAD

This Pueblo Indian bread is shaped in the form of the sun—to honor the Sun God.

Bake at 350° for 50 minutes.
Makes 3 loaves.

    1½ cups water
     3 tablespoons butter or margarine
     1 tablespoon sugar
     3 teaspoons salt
     2 envelopes active dry yeast
     ½ cup very warm water
    6½ cups sifted all-purpose flour

1. Combine water, butter or margarine, sugar and salt in a small saucepan. Heat slowly until butter or margarine melts; cool to lukewarm.
2. Sprinkle yeast into very warm water in a large bowl. ("Very warm water" should feel comfortably warm when dropped on wrist.) Stir until yeast dissolves; then stir in butter mixture.
3. Beat in 4 cups of flour until smooth. Beat in enough remaining flour to make a soft dough.
4. Turn out onto a lightly floured surface; knead until smooth and elastic, about 5 minutes, using only as much flour as needed to keep dough from sticking.
5. Place in a greased large bowl; turn to coat all over with shortening; cover with a clean towel. Let rise in a warm place, away from drafts, 1½ hours, or until double in bulk.
6. Punch dough down; turn out onto lightly floured surface; knead a few times; divide dough into 3 equal pieces. Shape each piece into a ball. Cover with a towel, let rest 10 minutes.
7. On the floured surface, roll each ball into a 9-inch circle. Fold each circle almost in half. Top circular edge should be about 1 inch from bottom circular edge. Place on greased cooky sheet. With kitchen scissors, make about 6 gashes in the dough, cutting from the circular edge about ⅔ the way inward to the folded edge. Spread the fingers of dough apart so they will not touch each other while baking. Do the same with the remaining 2 balls of dough. Let rise again in warm place, away from drafts, 1 hour, or until double in bulk.
8. Bake in moderate oven (350°) 50 minutes, or until breads are golden, and sound hollow when tapped. Remove from cooky sheet to wire racks; cool completely.

ARMENIAN BREAD

It looks like a flying saucer and makes a wonderful conversation piece, besides tasting so very good.

Bake at 350° for 30 minutes.
Makes 3 loaves.

     2 envelopes active dry yeast
    2¼ cups very warm water
     ¾ cup nonfat dry milk
     3 tablespoons sugar
     2 teaspoons salt
     3 tablespoons olive or vegetable oil
    6½ cups sifted all-purpose flour
     ¼ cup sesame seeds
     1 egg, beaten

1. Sprinkle yeast into very warm water in a large bowl. ("Very warm water" should feel comfortably warm when dropped on wrist.) Stir until yeast dissolves; then stir in dry milk, sugar, salt and oil.

2. Beat in 2 cups of the flour until smooth. Beat in enough of the remaining flour to make a soft dough.
3. Turn out onto lightly floured surface. Knead until smooth and elastic, about 10 minutes, using only as much flour as needed to keep dough from sticking.
4. Invert large bowl over dough; let rest 20 minutes.
5. Divide dough into 4 pieces. Divide one of these pieces into 3 pieces. Grease 3 cooky sheets with oil. Pat out one of the large pieces of dough to a 9-inch round on one of the cooky sheets. Make a 3-inch hole in center of round by pulling dough back with fingers. Pat a small piece of dough into a 3-inch round and place in center. Repeat to make 3 loaves. Cover each loaf with plastic wrap. Chill 2 to 6 hours.
6. Remove breads from refrigerator; remove plastic wrap. Let stand at room temperature 10 minutes.
7. Sprinkle sesame seeds in a shallow baking pan. Toast seeds in a moderate oven (350°), 5 minutes, or just until golden.
8. Brush breads with beaten egg and sprinkle with toasted sesame seeds.
9. Bake in moderate oven (350°) 30 minutes, or until breads are golden, and sound hollow when tapped. Remove from cooky sheets to wire racks; cool breads completely before serving.

CHALLAH

The serving of this golden egg bread traditionally marks the beginning of the Jewish Sabbath.

Bake at 350° for 30 minutes.
Makes 2 braided loaves.

1½ cups water
 ¼ cup sugar
  3 teaspoons salt
 ⅓ cup butter or margarine
  2 envelopes active dry yeast
 ½ cup very warm water
  3 eggs
7½ cups sifted all-purpose flour
  1 tablespoon water
  2 teaspoons poppy seeds

1. Combine water, sugar, salt and butter or margarine in a small saucepan. Heat slowly until butter or margarine melts; cool to lukewarm.
2. Beat eggs in a small bowl. Reserve 2 tablespoons for Step 8.
3. Sprinkle yeast into very warm water in a large bowl. ("Very warm water" should feel comfortably warm when dropped on the wrist.) Stir until the yeast dissolves; then stir in the water mixture and the eggs.
4. Beat in 4 cups of flour until smooth. Beat in enough remaining flour to make a soft dough.
5. Turn out onto a lightly floured surface; knead until smooth and elastic, about 5 minutes, using only

as much flour as needed to keep dough from sticking. The sticky soft dough will absorb flour as you knead it, and will become velvety-soft.
6. Place in a greased large bowl; turn to coat all over with shortening; cover with a clean towel. Let rise in a warm place, away from drafts, 1½ hours, or until double in bulk.
7. Punch dough down; let rise 30 minutes, or until almost double in bulk. Punch dough down again; turn out onto lightly floured surface; knead a few times; divide into 6 even pieces. Roll each into a rope about 15 inches long.
8. Place 3 ropes on a greased cooky sheet; plait into a braid; fasten securely at both ends. Repeat with remaining 3 ropes of dough. Let rise again in a warm place, away from drafts, 1 hour, or until double in bulk. Combine the reserved 2 tablespoons of egg and the 1 tablespoon water; brush over bread; sprinkle with poppy seeds.
9. Bake in moderate oven (350°) 30 minutes, or until braids are golden, and sound hollow when tapped. Place braids on wire racks; cool.

SCANDINAVIAN RYE BREAD

A traditional Northern European favorite, chock full of savory caraway seeds.

Bake at 400° for 35 minutes.
Makes 2 loaves.

  2 envelopes active dry yeast
2½ cups very warm water
 ¼ cup light molasses
  4 teaspoons salt
  2 tablespoons shortening
2½ cups rye flour
  1 tablespoon caraway seeds, crushed
5½ to 6 cups sifted all-purpose flour
   Cornmeal

1. Sprinkle yeast into ½ cup of the very warm water; stir in 1 teaspoon of the molasses. ("Very warm water" should feel comfortably warm when dropped on wrist.) Stir until yeast dissolves. Let stand, undisturbed, to proof until bubbly and double in volume, about 10 minutes.
2. Combine remaining water and molasses with salt and shortening in a large bowl; stir in yeast mixture, rye flour and caraway seeds; add enough all-purpose flour to make a soft dough.
3. Turn out onto a lightly floured surface. Knead until smooth and elastic, about 10 minutes, using enough of the remaining flour to keep dough from sticking.
4. Place in buttered large bowl; turn dough to bring buttered side up; cover with towel. Let rise in a warm place, away from drafts, 1 hour, or until double in bulk.

5. Butter a large cooky sheet. Sprinkle with cornmeal.
6. Punch dough down; turn onto lightly floured surface; knead a few times; invert bowl over dough; let rest 10 minutes; divide dough in half and knead each half a few times. Shape into 2 loaves. Place at least 4 inches apart on prepared cooky sheet.
7. Let rise again in a warm place, away from drafts, 45 minutes, or until double in bulk. Brush tops with water.
8. Bake in a hot oven (400°) 35 minutes, or until browned and loaves sound hollow when tapped. Remove from cooky sheet to wire rack; cool completely.

DOUBLE-WHEAT WHOLE WHEAT BREAD

Whole wheat bread at it's best; hearty flavor, golden color—with honey and wheat germ for extra goodness and nutrition.

Bake at 400° for 40 minutes.
Makes 2 loaves.

2 envelopes active dry yeast
1 cup very warm water
⅓ cup honey
2 cups milk
¼ cup (½ stick) butter or margarine
1½ tablespoons salt
5 cups whole wheat flour
¼ cup wheat germ
3 cups sifted all-purpose flour

1. Sprinkle yeast into very warm water in a 1-cup measure; stir in 1 teaspoon of the honey. ("Very warm water" should feel comfortably warm when dropped on wrist.) Stir until yeast dissolves. Let stand, undisturbed, to proof until bubbly and double in volume, about 10 minutes.
2. Combine remaining honey with milk, butter or margarine and salt in a small saucepan; heat until butter melts. Pour into large bowl; cool to lukewarm. Stir in yeast mixture.
3. Stir in whole wheat flour and wheat germ until smooth; add enough all-purpose flour to make a soft dough.
4. Turn out onto lightly floured surface. Knead until smooth and elastic, about 10 minutes, using only as much flour as needed to keep dough from sticking.
5. Place dough in a buttered large bowl; turn to bring buttered side up. Cover with towel. Let rise in a warm place, away from drafts, 1 hour, or until double in bulk.
6. Punch dough down; turn out onto lightly floured surface; knead a few times; invert bowl over dough; let rest about 10 minutes.
7. Divide dough in half and knead each half a few times; shape into 2 loaves. Place loaves in two buttered 9x5x3-inch loaf pans.

8. Let rise in a warm place, away from drafts, 45 minutes, or until double in bulk.
9. Bake in a hot oven (400°) 40 minutes, or until browned and loaves sound hollow when tapped. Remove from pans to wire racks to cool completely.

CRUSTY FRENCH LOAVES

Break off a chunk while warm and slather with butter; makes a "soup and salad" supper a hearty meal.

Bake at 400° for 30 minutes.
Makes 3 loaves.

1 envelope active dry yeast
2 cups very warm water
6 cups sifted all-purpose flour
2 tablespoons sugar
3 teaspoons salt
2 tablespoons vegetable shortening
Cornmeal
1 egg white
1 tablespoon cold water

1. Sprinkle yeast into very warm water in a large bowl. ("Very warm water" should feel comfortably warm when dropped on wrist.) Stir until the yeast dissolves.
2. Stir in 3 cups of the flour, sugar, salt and shortening; beat until smooth; slowly beat in enough of remaining 3 cups flour to make a stiff dough.
3. Turn out onto a lightly floured surface; knead 5 minutes, or until smooth and elastic, adding only enough extra flour to keep dough from sticking.
4. Place in a greased large bowl; turn to coat all over with shortening; cover with a clean towel. Let rise in a warm place, away from drafts, 45 minutes, or until double in bulk.
5. Punch dough down; cover. Let rise again 30 minutes, or until double in bulk.
6. Punch dough down again; knead 1 minute on a lightly floured surface; divide into 3 even pieces (dough will be sticky). Roll each piece to a 12x9-inch rectangle. Roll up from the short side, jelly roll fashion; tuck ends under.
7. Grease a large cooky sheet; sprinkle with cornmeal. Place loaves, seam-side down, 2 inches apart, on cooky sheet; cover. Let rise again 30 minutes, or until double in bulk.
8. Make several evenly spaced diagonal cuts in top of each loaf. Beat egg white slightly with cold water in a cup; brush over each loaf.
9. Place pan of hot water on bottom shelf in oven; place loaves on shelf above.
10. Bake in hot oven (400°) 30 minutes, or until loaves are golden brown and sound hollow when tapped. Remove from cooky sheet and cool on wire racks.

25

LITTLE DILL CHEESE LOAVES

Cottage cheese enhances the flavor of this simple-to-make batter bread.

Bake at 350° for 45 minutes.
Makes 6 individual loaves.

    1 package active dry yeast
    ½ cup very warm water
    1 cup (½ pound) cream-style cottage cheese
    2 tablespoons sugar
    1 tablespoon instant minced onion
    2 teaspoons dill weed
    1 teaspoon salt
    ¼ teaspoon baking soda
    1 egg
    2⅓ cups sifted all-purpose flour
       Butter or margarine

1. Sprinkle yeast into very warm water in a large bowl. ("Very warm water" should feel comfortably warm when dropped on wrist.) Stir; dissolve yeast.
2. Heat cheese just until lukewarm in small saucepan; stir into yeast mixture; add sugar, onion, dill weed, salt, baking soda, egg and 1⅓ cups flour. Beat with electric mixer at medium speed for 2 minutes. Stir in the remaining flour to make soft dough.
3. Cover with a towel. Let rise in a warm place, away from drafts, 1 hour, or until double in bulk.
4. Stir dough down; spoon evenly into six 6-ounce soufflé dishes or custard cups.
5. Let rise again in a warm place, away from drafts, 45 minutes, or until double in bulk.
6. Bake in moderate oven (350°) 30 minutes; cover with foil, then bake 15 minutes longer, or until loaves sound hollow when tapped. Brush tops with butter or margarine; remove from dishes to wire racks. Serve warm, or cool completely.

VIENNA CRESCENTS

This bread is made with the "sponge" method, which gives a fine texture inside and a beautiful crust outside. A sprinkle of poppy seeds adds a nice touch.

Bake at 450° for 10 minutes, then at 350° for 30 minutes.
Makes 2 crescents.

    2 envelopes active dry yeast
    1 cup very warm water
    4 teaspoons sugar
    6 cups sifted all-purpose flour
    1½ cups milk
    3 teaspoons salt
    1 egg, slightly beaten
       Poppy seeds

1. Make "sponge": Sprinkle yeast into very warm water in a large bowl. ("Very warm water" should feel comfortably warm when dropped on wrist.) Stir until yeast dissolves.
2. Stir in 1 teaspoon sugar and 2 cups of the flour; beat until smooth. Cover bowl with foil or plastic wrap. Let rise in a very warm place, away from drafts, 2½ to 3 hours, or until large bubbles appear on the surface.
3. Stir in milk, remaining sugar, salt and 2 cups flour; beat until smooth; slowly add remaining flour. Turn onto lightly floured surface; knead until smooth and elastic, about 5 minutes, using only as much flour as needed to keep dough from sticking.
4. Place in a greased large bowl; turn to coat all over with shortening; cover with clean towel. Let rise in warm place, away from drafts, 1 hour, or until double in bulk.
5. Punch dough down; turn out onto lightly floured surface; knead 1 minute; divide in half. Roll one half into a 30x24x24-inch triangle; roll up from long side to opposite point. Transfer to greased cooky sheet; shape into crescent. Repeat with other half. Cover; let rise again in a warm place, away from drafts, 45 minutes, or until double in bulk.
6. Brush tops with slightly beaten egg; sprinkle with poppy seeds.
7. Bake in a very hot oven (450°) 10 minutes; lower heat to 350° and bake 30 minutes longer or until bread sounds hollow when tapped. Remove from cooky sheets to wire racks; cool completely.

CURRANT BATTER BREAD

Mix this one up quickly; you'll have a fragrant warm loaf ready to enjoy in almost no time at all.

Bake at 350° for 40 minutes.
Makes 1 loaf.

    ¾ cup milk
    6 tablespoons sugar
    1 teaspoon salt
    5 tablespoons butter or margarine
    1 teaspoon grated orange rind
    ¼ cup very warm water
    1 envelope active dry yeast
    3 eggs, beaten
    3 cups sifted all-purpose flour
    1 cup dried currants
    ½ cup 10X (confectioners') sugar
    1 tablespoon orange juice

1. Heat milk, sugar, salt and butter or margarine in a small saucepan, just until butter is melted. Cool milk mixture to lukewarm. Stir in orange rind.
2. Measure very warm water into a large bowl; sprinkle in yeast. ("Very warm water" should feel

From one simple recipe, you can make any number of beautifully shaped rolls. Shown above: Cloverleaf Rolls, Crescents, Fantans and Knots. Recipe, plus easy shaping directions, in this chapter.

Crunchy Butterscotch-Nut Buns, swirled Sugar Buns and delicate Crumb Cake—all made from the same basic Sweet Yeast Dough. Recipes in this chapter.

comfortably warm when dropped on wrist.) Stir until dissolved. Add lukewarm milk mixture and eggs. Blend in flour, 1 cup at a time. Beat until smooth. Stir in currants. Turn into greased 6-cup baking dish.

3. Cover; let rise 45 minutes, or until double in bulk.

4. Bake in a moderate oven (350°) 40 minutes, or until loaf is golden brown and sounds hollow when tapped.

5. Cool a few minutes on wire rack; remove bread from baking dish. Blend 10X sugar and orange juice in a cup. While bread is still warm, drizzle with glaze.

PARMESAN GARLIC BREAD

Get a head start on your next Italian gala by baking this Parmesan Garlic Bread today and freezing it for later. (Don't freeze it all, though—there's enough for you to enjoy some right now!)

Bake at 400° for 40 minutes for large loaves; 30 to 35 minutes for medium-size and small loaves.
Makes 2 large loaves or 8 medium-size loaves or 14 small loaves.

    2 cups milk
    2 tablespoons sugar
    2 teaspoons salt
    2 envelopes active dry yeast
    2 cups very warm water
   10 cups sifted all-purpose flour
    1 cup grated Parmesan cheese
    2 tablespoons butter or margarine, melted
    1 clove garlic, crushed
      Grated Parmesan cheese

1. Heat milk with sugar and salt in small saucepan just to lukewarm.

2. Sprinkle yeast into very warm water in a large bowl. ("Very warm water" should feel comfortably warm when dropped on wrist.) Stir until yeast dissolves, then stir in cooled milk mixture.

3. Beat in 5 cups flour and 1 cup cheese until completely blended. Beat in remaining flour gradually to make a soft dough.

4. Turn out onto lightly floured surface; knead until smooth and elastic, adding only enough flour to keep dough from sticking.

5. Place in greased large bowl; turn to coat all over with shortening; cover with a clean towel. Let rise in warm place, away from drafts, 1 hour, or until double in bulk. Stir garlic into butter. Brush pans or casseroles with garlic butter.

6. Punch dough down; knead 1 minute on lightly floured surface, then shape this way: For large loaves, divide dough in half, divide each half in 7 even pieces, shape into rolls; place 6 rolls around edge of prepared pan and 1 in center. For medium-

size loaves: Divide dough into 16 even pieces; shape into rolls, place 2 rolls in each of 8 prepared ten-ounce casseroles or custard cups. For miniature loaves: Divide dough into 14 pieces; shape into loaves; place in prepared toy-size loaf pans; cover. Let rise again in warm place, away from drafts, 45 minutes, or until double in bulk. Brush tops with water; sprinkle lightly with extra Parmesan cheese.

7. Bake in very hot oven (400°) 40 minutes for large loaves, 30 to 35 minutes for small and medium loaves, or until breads sound hollow when tapped. Remove from pans to wire racks; cool completely.

SWEDISH LIMPA

This orange-scented whole rye and wheat bread has been a Scandinavian favorite for many generations.

Bake at 375° for 45 minutes.
Makes 2 loaves.

    2 envelopes active dry yeast
   2½ cups very warm water
    ¼ cup firmly packed brown sugar
    ⅓ cup molasses
    3 tablespoons vegetable shortening
    1 tablespoon salt
    2 tablespoons grated orange rind
    1 teaspoon anise seeds, crushed with hammer
    1 cup cracked wheat
   3½ cups whole rye flour
   3¾ to 4 cups sifted unbleached all-purpose flour

1. Sprinkle yeast into ½ cup of the warm water; stir in 1 teaspoon of the brown sugar. ("Very warm water" should feel comfortably warm when dropped on wrist.) Stir until yeast dissolves. Let stand, undisturbed, to proof until bubbly and double in volume, about 10 minutes.

2. Combine remaining water and sugar with molasses, shortening and salt in a small saucepan. Heat until shortening melts; cool to lukewarm.

3. Combine yeast mixture and molasses mixture in large bowl. Add orange rind, anise seeds, cracked wheat and rye flour. Beat with electric mixer at medium speed for 3 minutes. Gradually stir in enough all-purpose flour to make a soft dough.

4. Turn out onto lightly floured surface; knead until smooth and elastic, using remaining all-purpose flour to keep dough from sticking; add more flour, if needed.

5. Place in buttered large bowl; turn to bring greased side up; cover with a towel or plastic wrap. Let rise in a warm place, away from drafts, 1½ hours, or until double in bulk.

6. Punch dough down; turn out onto lightly floured surface; invert bowl over dough; allow to rest 10 minutes. Divide dough in half and knead each half

a few times, then shape each into an oval loaf. Place on buttered cooky sheets.

7. Let rise in a warm place, away from drafts, 40 minutes, or until double in bulk.

8. Bake in moderate oven (375°) 45 minutes, or until golden brown and loaves sound hollow when tapped. Cool loaves on wire racks.

Note: For an interesting variation, shape each half of dough into a round. Glaze by brushing tops with a mixture of 1 slightly beaten egg white plus 1 tablespoon cold water.

CUBAN BREAD

Crisp on the outside, even textured on the inside. Best to freeze the second loaf if you don't plan to serve it within two days.

Bake, starting in cold oven, at 400° for 40 minutes.
Makes 2 loaves.

> 1 envelope active dry yeast
> 2 cups very warm water
> 2 tablespoons sugar
> 3 teaspoons salt
> 6 cups sifted all-purpose flour
> Ice water

1. Sprinkle yeast into very warm water in a large bowl. ("Very warm water" should feel comfortably warm when dropped on wrist.) Stir until yeast dissolves, then stir in sugar and salt.

2. Beat in 2 cups of the flour until smooth. Beat in enough of the remaining flour to make a soft dough.

3. Turn out onto a lightly floured surface. Knead until smooth and elastic, about 5 minutes, using only as much flour as needed to keep dough from sticking.

4. Place in a greased large bowl; turn to coat all over with shortening; cover with a clean towel. Let rise in a warm place, away from drafts, 1 hour, or until double in bulk.

5. Punch dough down; turn onto lightly floured surface. Invert bowl over dough; let rest 10 minutes.

6. Divide dough in half and knead each piece a few times. Roll each to a 15x10-inch rectangle. Roll up tightly from long side, jelly roll fashion; pinch long seam tightly to seal. Roll loaf gently back and forth to taper ends. Place loaf diagonally on a large cooky sheet which has been greased and sprinkled with cornmeal.

7. Pat out second piece of dough to an 8-inch round and place on a second prepared cooky sheet.

8. Let rise again in a warm place, away from drafts, 45 minutes, or until double in bulk.

9. Make slits 2 inches apart on top of long loaf with a very sharp knife; make crisscross slits, 2 inches apart, on round loaf. Brush tops of both loaves with

ice water before placing in oven.

10. Place cooky sheets in cold oven.

11. Turn oven to hot (400°); bake 40 minutes, (brushing several times with ice water), or until bread sounds hollow when tapped. Remove from cooky sheets to wire racks; cool breads completely before serving.

TWO-TONE RYE TWIST

Light and dark rye, twisted together, are both made from the same basic dough.

Bake at 350° for 45 minutes.
Makes 2 loaves.

> 4 cups sifted all-purpose flour
> 4 cups whole rye flour
> 2 envelopes active dry yeast
> 2½ cups very warm water
> ¼ cup (½ stick) butter or margarine, melted
> ⅓ cup dark molasses
> 3 teaspoons salt
> 2 teaspoons caraway seeds, crushed
> 1 cup whole-bran cereal
> ¼ cup unsweetened cocoa powder
> 2 teaspoons instant coffee
> Cornmeal
> Butter or margarine, melted (for tops)
> 1 teaspoon cornstarch
> ½ cup cold water

1. Combine 3 cups of the all-purpose flour with rye flour in a medium-size bowl; blend well; reserve.

2. Sprinkle yeast into very warm water in a large bowl. ("Very warm water" should feel comfortably warm when dropped on wrist.) Stir until yeast dissolves; stir in butter or margarine, molasses, salt and caraway seeds. Pour one half of the mixture into a second large bowl.

3. To one half of the yeast mixture, add the bran, cocoa and coffee; mix well. Stir in enough of the flour mixture to make a soft dough (about 3 cups). Turn dough out onto a lightly floured surface. Knead until smooth and elastic, about 5 minutes, using only as much of the remaining all-purpose flour as needed to keep dough from sticking.

4. Place dough in a greased medium-size bowl; turn to coat all over with shortening; cover with clean towel. Let rise in a warm place, away from drafts, 45 minutes, or until double in bulk.

5. To remaining half of yeast mixture, stir in enough of the flour mixture, part at a time, to make a soft dough (about 3½ cups). Turn out onto a lightly floured surface; knead until smooth and elastic, about 5 minutes, adding only as much of the all-purpose flour as needed to keep dough from sticking. Let rise as in Step 4.

6. Grease 2 cooky sheets; sprinkle with cornmeal.

7. When both doughs have doubled, punch down; knead each a few times; divide each in half. Roll each of the four pieces on board, with hands, to form a thick rope 18 inches long. For each loaf: Twist light and dark rope together; pinch together at ends. Place loaf on cooky sheet; repeat with remaining 2 ropes.

8. Let rise again in a warm place, away from drafts, 45 minutes, or until double in bulk. Brush lightly with melted butter or margarine.

9. Bake in a moderate oven (350°) 45 minutes, or until loaves sound hollow when tapped.

10. While loaves are baking, combine cornstarch with cold water in small saucepan; stir until smooth. Cook, stirring constantly, until mixture thickens, and bubbles 1 minute. Brush mixture over baked loaves; return to oven; bake another 3 minutes. Remove from cooky sheets to wire racks; cool completely.

YEAST ROLLS

SUNDAY-BEST ONION ROLLS

Rapid mix method: Stir up dough the quick mixer way; then let it rise in the refrigerator until baking time. A trace of onion adds a zesty flavor to these golden-rich rolls.

Bake at 375° for 30 minutes.
Makes 32 rolls.

  6 to 7 cups <u>sifted</u> all-purpose flour
½ **cup sugar**
  2 tablespoons instant minced onion
  2 packages active dry yeast
1½ **teaspoons salt**
½ **cup (1 stick) butter or margarine, softened**
1½ **cups very hot water**
  2 eggs
    Vegetable oil

1. Measure 2 cups of the flour into a large bowl; stir in sugar, onion, yeast and salt. Add butter or margarine, then hot water, all at once.

2. Blend with electric mixer at low speed; then increase speed to medium and beat, 2 minutes, scraping down side of bowl several times. Add eggs and 1 cup more flour; blend, then beat at high speed, 1 minute, scraping down bowl once or twice.

3. Stir in just enough of the remaining flour to make a soft dough.

4. Turn out onto a lightly floured surface; knead 5 to 10 minutes, or until smooth and elastic, adding only enough flour to keep dough from sticking. Cover with plastic wrap, then a towel; let stand on surface 20 minutes.

5. Punch dough down; divide into quarters. Cut each quarter into 8 even pieces; shape each into a ball.

6. Measure 1 teaspoon vegetable oil into each of two 9x9x2-inch baking pans. Place 16 balls of dough in each pan, turning balls to coat with oil. Cover pans loosely with plastic wrap; chill from 2 to 24 hours.

7. When ready to bake, uncover; let stand at room temperature for 10 minutes.

8. Bake in moderate oven (375°) 30 minutes, or until rolls are golden. Remove from pans; cool a few minutes on a wire rack. If you prefer a softer crust, brush tops with butter or margarine. Serve warm.

Basic Recipe

FAVORITE YEAST ROLLS

Golden, butter-melting rolls to serve hot from the oven—at breakfast, or any time! Bake a batch and freeze in serving-size portions.

Bake at 375° for 20 minutes.
Makes about 5 dozen dinner-size rolls.

1½ **cups milk**
½ **cup (1 stick) butter or margarine**
¼ **cup sugar**
  2 teaspoons salt
  2 envelopes active dry yeast
½ **cup very warm water**
  2 eggs
  8 cups <u>sifted</u> all-purpose flour

1. Heat milk with butter, sugar and salt in a small saucepan until butter melts; cool to lukewarm.

2. Sprinkle yeast into very warm water in a large bowl. ("Very warm water" should feel comfortably warm when dropped on wrist.) Stir in 1 teaspoon sugar. Stir until yeast dissolves. Let stand until bubbly and double in volume, about 10 minutes.

3. Stir in cooled milk mixture and beat in eggs. Beat in enough flour to make a soft dough; turn out onto lightly floured surface. Knead until smooth and elastic, about 5 minutes, adding only enough of the flour to keep the dough from sticking.

4. Place dough in a greased large bowl; turn to bring greased side up. Cover bowl with clean towel. Let rise in a warm place, away from drafts, 1½ hours, or until double in bulk.

5. Punch dough down; divide into quarters, keeping dough covered with an inverted bowl until ready to shape. Shape rolls in knots, crescents, etc. according to directions that follow. Place shaped rolls in greased baking pans. Cover rolls with a clean towel; let rise again in a warm place, away from drafts, 45 minutes, or until double in bulk.

6. Bake in moderate oven (375°) 20 minutes, or until golden. Brush tops lightly with butter, if you wish. Serve hot.

Fantans: Makes 12 rolls.

**¼ recipe Favorite Yeast Rolls
2 tablespoons butter or margarine, melted**

Roll out dough to an 18x9-inch rectangle on a lightly floured surface. Cut into twelve 1½-inch wide strips. Brush with melted butter. Stack 6 strips on top of each other to make two stacks. Cut each stack into six 1½-inch wide pieces. Place each piece of the cut stack, cut-side down, into a greased muffin-pan cup.

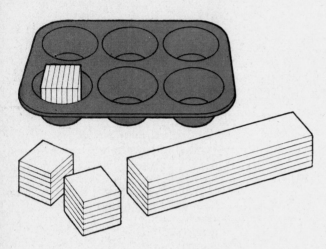

Crescent Rolls: Makes 16 or 24 rolls.

**¼ recipe Favorite Yeast Rolls
2 tablespoons butter or margarine, melted**

Divide dough in half; roll out each half on a lightly floured surface to an 8-inch round; cut into 8 or 12 wedges. Brush wedges with melted butter. Roll up each wedge, starting at the large end; place, pointed-side down on an ungreased cooky sheet, curving the ends of the rolls slightly in order to shape as crescents.

Knots: Makes 16 rolls.

¼ recipe Favorite Yeast Rolls

Divide dough into 16 equal pieces. Roll each piece with palms of hands to a 6-inch rope on lightly floured surface. Tie a simple knot; form a loop; bring one end through. Place knots on greased cooky sheet 2 inches apart.

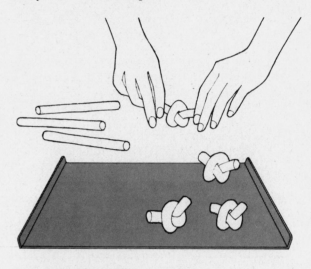

Cloverleaf Rolls: Makes 12 rolls.

**¼ recipe Favorite Yeast Rolls
2 tablespoons butter or margarine, melted**

Divide dough into quarters and divide each quarter into 9 pieces to make 36 small pieces of dough. Shape dough into marble-size balls and place, 3 at a time, into greased muffin-pan cups; brush generously with butter.

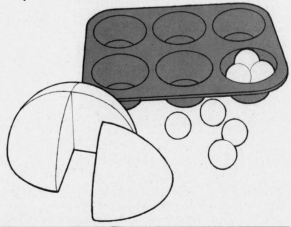

SPECIAL TIPS: To serve frozen baked yeast rolls, place on a cooky sheet and heat in a slow oven (300°) 15 minutes, or just until hot.
• To freshen and reheat rolls that aren't frozen, place in a large brown paper bag; sprinkle bag with a few drops of water; close tightly. Heat in moderate oven (350°) 10 minutes.

Make our basic Danish Pastry dough and create this lovely Mayor's Braid, plus a dozen of the beautiful individual pastries shown on page 39. Recipes for all in this chapter.

DANISH PASTRY

Basic Recipe

DANISH PASTRY DOUGH

Makes 2 large pastries, or about 24 individual pastries, or makes 1 large pastry and 12 individual pastries.

    2 envelopes active dry yeast
    ½ cup very warm water
    ⅓ cup sugar
    ¾ cup cold milk
    2 eggs
 4¼ cups <u>sifted</u> all-purpose flour
    1 teaspoon salt
    1 pound (4 sticks) butter or margarine
      Flour

1. Sprinkle yeast into very warm water in a 1-cup measure. ("Very warm water" should feel comfortably warm when dropped on wrist.) Stir in ½ teaspoon of the sugar. Stir until yeast dissolves. Let stand, undisturbed, until bubbly and double in volume, about 10 minutes.
2. Combine remaining sugar, milk, eggs, 3 cups of the flour, salt and the yeast mixture in large bowl. Beat, with electric mixer at medium speed, for 3 minutes (or beat with spoon, 3 minutes). Beat in remaining flour with a wooden spoon until dough

is shiny, elastic and soft. Scrape down sides of bowl. Cover with plastic wrap. Refrigerate 30 minutes.
3. Place the sticks of butter or margarine 1 inch apart, between 2 sheets of wax paper; roll out to a 12-inch square *(see Photo 1)*. Chill on a cooky sheet until ready to use.
4. Sprinkle working surface heavily with flour, about ⅓ cup; turn dough out onto flour *(see Photo 2)*; sprinkle flour on top of dough. Roll out to an 18x13-inch rectangle. Brush off excess flour with a soft pastry brush.
5. Peel off top sheet of wax paper from butter;

place butter, paper side up on one end of dough to cover two-thirds of the dough; peel off remaining sheet of wax paper. For easy folding, carefully score butter lengthwise down center, without cutting into dough. Fold uncovered third of dough over middle third (see Photo 3); brush off excess flour; then fold remaining third of dough over middle third to enclose butter completely. Turn dough clockwise so open side is away from you.

6. *Roll out to a 24x12-inch rectangle using enough flour to keep dough from sticking. Fold ends in to meet on center (see Photo 4); then fold dough in half to make 4 layers. Turn again so open side is away from you (see Photo 5).

*Repeat rolling and folding this way 2 more times. Keep the dough to a perfect rectangle by rolling straight up and down and from side to side. When it is necessary, chill the dough between rollings. [Note: If using margarine, which is of a softer consistency than butter, refrigerate 20 minutes between each rolling.] Clean off the working surface each time and dust lightly with flour. Refrigerate dough 1 hour or more (even overnight, if you wish, to relax dough and firm up butter layers). Cut dough in half (see Photo 6), you can see the buttery layers, which when baked, become flaky and crisp. Work with only half the dough at a time. Keep the other half refrigerated until ready to use (see Photo 7).

SPECIAL TIPS: Here are some helpful how-to's for making and baking delicious Danish:

• Before you begin to make Danish, be sure you have a working surface large enough to roll dough to 30 inches.

• Use more flour on your rolling surface than you would when rolling out other types of dough. Be sure you brush off excess flour with a soft pastry brush immediately before folding and filling, so excess flour won't build up in pastry.

• It is important to keep butter enclosed in dough, while rolling Danish. If butter oozes out, immediately sprinkle with flour. Also, if dough becomes too sticky to handle, it's probably because butter has softened. In both cases, chill for 30 minutes before continuing rolling and folding.

• For freezing unbaked Danish: Place shaped Danish on cooky sheets. Don't brush with egg or sprinkle with toppings. Cover with plastic wrap; freeze.

• To bake: Remove Danish from freezer the night before you plan to bake it, and place in refrigerator. Next morning, arrange on cooky sheets, 2 inches apart. Let rise, according to recipe instructions, until double in volume. Then brush with egg; sprinkle with topping; bake following individual recipes.

• For refrigerating unbaked Danish: Place shaped Danish on cooky sheets; cover; refrigerate.

• To bake: Next day, remove Danish from refrigerator; let rise and bake, as above.

ALMOND CRESCENTS (Mandelhorn)

Easy to shape; delicious to eat—almond flavor inside and out.

Pre-heat oven to 400°; bake at 350° for 20 minutes. Makes 12 individual pastries.

½ **Danish Pastry Dough (recipe page 34)**
Almond Filling (recipe page 37)
Slightly beaten egg
Sugar
Sliced Almonds

Roll pastry on floured surface to a 20x15-inch rectangle; trim edges evenly. With a sharp knife, cut into twelve 5-inch squares. Spoon an equal amount of filling onto one corner of each square. Roll pastry dough around filling; continue rolling to opposite corner. Place pastries point down, 2 inches apart on cooky sheet. Curve into crescent shapes. Let rise in a warm place in your kitchen, until double in bulk, about 30 minutes. (*Not* in your oven, or over hot water, as with other yeast breads; the extra heat will melt the butter and ruin the texture of the Danish pastry.) Brush with egg; sprinkle with sugar and almonds. Place in a hot oven (400°); lower heat immediately to 350°; then bake 20 minutes, or until puffed and golden. Remove to wire rack; cool.

COCKSCOMBS (Hanekam)

Distinctively shaped pastries with an almond filling.

Preheat oven to 400°; bake at 350° for 20 minutes. Makes 12 individual pastries.

½ **Danish Pastry Dough (recipe page 34)**
Almond Filling (recipe page 37)
Slightly beaten egg
Sugar

Roll and cut dough as in ALMOND CRESCENTS. Spoon an equal amount of filling onto the center of each square. Spread filling parallel to one edge; brush edges lightly with egg, then fold opposite edge over; press edges together to seal. Make 4 or 5 slits in sealed edge; place on cooky sheets, curving pastries slightly to resemble a cockscomb. Let rise in a warm place in your kitchen, until double in bulk, about 30 minutes. (*Not* in your oven, or over hot water, as with other yeast breads; the extra heat will melt the butter and ruin the texture of the Danish pastry.) Brush with egg; sprinkle generously with sugar. Place in a hot oven (400°); lower heat immediately to 350°. Bake 20 minutes, or until puffed and golden brown. Remove pastries to wire rack; cool completely.

FRUIT-FILLED DANISH (Svedske Konvolut)

Light, flaky Danish bursting with fruit. Use prune filling, as indicated, or try canned cherry or apple pie filling, or apricot preserves for interesting variations.

Preheat oven to 400°; bake at 350°, 25 minutes.
Makes 12 individual pastries.

½ **Danish Pastry Dough (recipe page 34)**
1 **can (12 ounces) prune filling**
   OR: **1 jar (8 ounces) Lekvar**
   OR: **1 can (about 1 pound, 5 ounces) other fruit filling**
   OR: **Apricot preserves**
   Slightly beaten egg
½ **cup corn syrup**

Roll dough and cut into squares as in ALMOND CRESCENTS. Spoon a rounded tablespoon of prune or other fruit filling onto center of each square; bring 2 opposite corners over filling to overlap about 1 inch. Place on a cooky sheet 2 inches apart; let rise in a warm place in your kitchen, until double in bulk, about 30 minutes. (*Not* in your oven, or over hot water, as with other yeast breads; the extra heat will melt the butter and ruin the texture of the Danish pastry.) Brush with beaten egg. Place in a hot oven (400°); lower heat to 350° immediately, then bake 20 minutes. Warm corn syrup slightly in a small saucepan; brush over pastries; bake 5 minutes longer. Remove to wire rack; cool.

ELEPHANT EARS (Elefantører)

Try these classic pastries swirled with Sugar Icing. The recipe follows.

Preheat oven to 400°; bake at 350°, 20 minutes.
Makes 12 individual pastries.

½ **Danish Pastry Dough (recipe page 34)**
   Cinnamon-Pecan Filling (recipe page 37)
   Slightly beaten egg
   Sugar
   Coarsely chopped pecans

Roll pastry to a 12x12-inch square; spread filling evenly over pastry; roll up jelly roll fashion. With a sharp knife, cut into 1-inch pieces, then carefully cut each piece in half, but not all the way through. Spread out the 2 halves, leaving them attached in the center; place 2 inches apart on cooky sheets. Let rise in a warm place in your kitchen until double in bulk, about 30 to 45 minutes. (*Not* in your oven or over hot water, as with other yeast breads; the extra heat will melt the butter and ruin texture of the Danish pastry.) Brush with egg; sprinkle

with sugar and pecans. Place in a hot oven (400°); lower heat immediately to 350°. Bake 20 to 25 minutes, or until puffed and golden brown. Remove to wire rack; cool.

Sugar Icing: Combine ½ cup 10X (confectioners') sugar with 1 tablespoon warm water. Drizzle over baked Danish with the top of a teaspoon.

APRICOT BOW TIES (Abrikos Sløjfe)

A walnut topping and sweet apricot filling combine for a delectable taste treat.

Preheat oven to 400°; bake at 350°, 20 minutes.
Makes 12 individual pastries.

½ **Danish Pastry Dough (recipe page 34)**
   Apricot preserves
   Slightly beaten egg
2 **tablespoons chopped walnuts mixed with 2 tablespoons sugar**

Roll and cut dough as in ALMOND CRESCENTS. Place 1 teaspoon of the apricot preserves along one of the edges of the pastry ½ inch in from edge. Fold over opposite edge; press edges together to seal. With a sharp knife, make a lengthwise slit in folded pastry to within 1 inch of each end. Slip one end under and pull it through the slit. Place pastries 2 inches apart on cooky sheets. Let rise in a warm place in your kitchen, until double in bulk, 30 to 45 minutes. (*Not* in your oven, or over hot water, as in other yeast breads; the extra heat will melt the butter and ruin the texture of the Danish pastry.) Brush with egg; sprinkle with walnut mixture. Place in a hot oven (400°); lower heat immediately to 350°. Bake 20 minutes or until golden. Cool on wire racks.

CHEESE DANISH (Spandauer)

Bright cherry glaze adds a colorful finishing touch to these coffee-time favorites.

Preheat oven to 400°; bake at 350°, 20 minutes.
Makes 12 individual pastries.

½ **Danish Pastry Dough (recipe page 34)**
   Cheese Filling (recipe page 37)
   Cherry preserves
   Slightly beaten egg
½ **cup corn syrup**

Roll and cut dough as in ALMOND CRESCENTS. Spoon equal amounts of CHEESE FILLING onto the center of each square; fold in all 4 corners to meet and overlap slightly in center, to enclose filling completely; press points down with fingertip. Place 2 inches apart on cooky sheet; let rise in a warm place in your kitchen, until double in bulk, about 30 minutes. (*Not* in your oven, or over hot water, as with other yeast breads; the extra heat will melt the butter and ruin the texture of the Danish pastry.) Press down points again and fill center with a teaspoon of cherry preserves. Brush pastry with egg. Place in a hot oven (400°); lower heat immediately to 350°. Bake 20 minutes, or until puffed and golden brown. Heat corn syrup just until warm; brush over pastries. Remove to wire rack; cool. Add more preserves after pastries are baked, if you wish. Pastries will open up as they bake.

MAYOR'S BRAID (Borgmestor Krans)

Large, almond-and-sugar sprinkled. A Danish delight!

Preheat oven to 400°, then bake at 350° for 40 minutes.
Makes one 10-inch round pastry.

> ½ **Danish Pastry Dough (recipe page 34)**
> **Almond Filling (recipe follows)**
> **Slightly beaten egg**
> **Sugar**
> **Sliced almonds**

Roll dough on a floured surface to a 30x9-inch rectangle; cut lengthwise into 3 strips. Spread equal amounts of filling down the center of each strip. Fold edges of strips over filling to enclose filling completely. Press ends of the 3 filled strips together; braid; press other ends together. Ease braid onto an ungreased cooky sheet; join ends together to make a ring, about 9 inches in diameter. Let rise in a warm place in your kitchen, about 45 minutes, or until double in bulk. (*Not* in your oven, or over a bowl of hot water, as with other yeast breads; the extra heat will melt the butter and ruin the texture of the Danish pastry.) Brush with egg; sprinkle generously with sugar and almonds. Place in a hot oven (400°); lower heat immediately to 350°. Bake 40 minutes or until puffed and golden; remove to a wire rack; cool. Cut into wedges to serve. This pastry is rich and will spread when baked. You may wish to place a collar of foil around the pastry just before baking to keep it more compact.

Almond Filling: Makes 1 cup.

Beat ½ of an 8-ounce package or can of almond paste (4 ounces), 4 tablespoons softened butter or margarine and ¼ cup sugar in a small bowl until smooth and well blended.

Cheese Filling: Makes 1 cup.

Combine 1 cup pot cheese, 1 egg yolk, ¼ cup sugar, and 1 teaspoon grated lemon rind in container of electric blender; whirl until smooth.

Cinnamon-Pecan Filling: Makes 1 cup.

Beat 4 tablespoons softened butter or margarine, ½ cup sugar, ½ teaspoon ground cinnamon and ½ teaspoon ground cardamom in a small bowl until smooth. Stir in ½ cup coarsely chopped pecans and ¼ cup currants.

SWEET COFFEE CAKES AND BUNS

Basic Recipe

SWEET YEAST DOUGH

From this sweet and simple recipe, you can make 24 buns; 2 crumb cakes; or 12 buns and one crumb cake.

> ½ **cup milk**
> ½ **cup sugar**
> 1 **teaspoon salt**
> ⅔ **cup vegetable shortening**
> 2 **envelopes active dry yeast**
> ½ **cup very warm water**
> 4 **eggs, beaten**
> 4½ **cups sifted all-purpose flour**

1. Combine milk, sugar, salt and shortening in saucepan. Heat just until shortening is melted; cool to lukewarm.
2. Sprinkle yeast into very warm water in a large bowl. ("Very warm water" should feel comfortably warm when dropped on wrist.) Add lukewarm milk mixture, eggs and 2 cups of the flour; beat until smooth. Add just enough of remaining flour to make soft dough.
3. Turn out onto lightly floured surface; knead until smooth and elastic, about 5 minutes, using only as much flour as needed to keep dough from sticking.
4. Place in large greased bowl; turn to bring greased side up. Cover. Let rise in warm place, away from drafts, 1 to 1½ hours, or until double in bulk.
5. Punch dough down; knead a few times; let rest 5 minutes. Shape into BUTTERSCOTCH-NUT BUNS, SUGAR BUNS or CRUMB CAKES or BUNS.

BUTTERSCOTCH-NUT BUNS

Tender buns with a buttery-caramel coating; as pretty as they are delicious.

Bake at 375° for 25 minutes.
Makes 12 buns.

> ¾ **cup firmly packed brown sugar**
> ½ **cup light corn syrup**

¼ cup (½ stick) butter or margarine
½ cup walnut or pecan halves
½ recipe Sweet Yeast Dough (recipe page 37)
2 tablespoons butter or margarine, softened
⅓ cup granulated sugar
½ teaspoon ground cinnamon
½ cup raisins

1. Combine brown sugar, corn syrup and the ¼ cup butter or margarine in a small saucepan; simmer 2 minutes. Pour into a 9x9x2-inch baking pan. Sprinkle with nuts.
2. Roll out SWEET YEAST DOUGH to a 15x8-inch rectangle on a lightly floured surface. Spread entire surface of the dough with the soft butter or margarine.
3. Combine granulated sugar, cinnamon and raisins; sprinkle over dough. Roll up, jelly roll fashion, beginning with the long side. Pinch to seal seam. Cut into 12 equal slices. Place, cut side down, in prepared pan. Cover. Let rise in warm place, away from drafts, 1 hour, or until double in bulk.
4. Bake in moderate oven (375°) 25 minutes, or until golden brown. Turn upside down on plate. Leave pan in place 5 minutes to allow topping to run over buns; lift off pan.
5. To serve: Separate buns with two forks; serve warm with coffee or tea.

SUGAR BUNS

Sugary roll-ups swirled with icing.

Bake at 375° for 25 minutes.
Makes 12 buns.

½ recipe Sweet Yeast Dough (recipe page 37)
2 tablespoons butter or margarine, softened
⅓ cup sugar
½ teaspoon ground cinnamon
½ cup raisins
½ cup 10X (confectioners') sugar
2 teaspoons milk

1. Roll out SWEET YEAST DOUGH to a 15x8-inch rectangle on a lightly floured surface. Spread entire surface of the dough evenly with the softened butter or margarine.
2. Combine sugar, cinnamon and raisins; sprinkle over dough. Roll up, jelly roll fashion, beginning with the long side. Pinch to seal seam. Cut into 12 equal slices. Place cut side up, in a greased 9-inch square pan. Cover. Let rise 1 hour, or until dough is double in bulk.
3. Blend 10X sugar and milk in a small bowl to make a thin icing.
4. Bake in a moderate oven (375°) 25 minutes, or until golden brown. Turn out on wire rack. Turn right side up. While warm, drizzle icing over tops.

CRUMB CAKE

This yummy crumb-topped cake makes good eating with a mug of steaming coffee.

Bake at 375° for 25 minutes.
Makes one 13x9x2-inch cake.

½ recipe Sweet Yeast Dough (recipe page 37)
½ cup (1 stick) butter or margarine, softened
⅓ cup firmly packed brown sugar
1 cup sifted all-purpose flour
¼ teaspoon ground nutmeg
½ teaspoon ground cinnamon

1. Press dough evenly into a greased 13x9x2-inch baking pan. Brush top with part of the softened butter or margarine. Let rise in a warm place, away from drafts, 1 hour, or until double in bulk.
2. Combine remaining butter or margarine, brown sugar, flour, nutmeg and cinnamon in a small bowl. Sprinkle over dough.
3. Bake in moderate oven (375°) 25 minutes, or until golden brown. Remove from oven; cool 5 minutes; loosen cake in pan. Remove from pan this way: Press a sheet of foil lightly over top of cake to hold crumbs in place; turn upside down and lift off pan; turn right side up. Remove to wire rack; cool completely. Sprinkle with 10X sugar, if you wish.

Crumb Buns: Cut dough in pan in 16 sections with a sharp knife dipped in melted butter or margarine. Let rise, top with crumbs and bake as in CRUMB CAKE.

APPLE KUCHEN

Delicious German coffee cake with a moist apple topping, dripped with butter and brown sugar.

Bake at 375° for 30 minutes.
Makes one 13x9x2-inch cake.

½ recipe Sweet Yeast Dough (recipe page 37)
3 medium-size tart cooking apples
¼ cup firmly packed light brown sugar
½ teaspoon ground cinnamon
¼ teaspoon ground cloves
¼ teaspoon ground allspice
¼ cup (½ stick) butter or margarine
⅓ cup apple jelly

1. Press dough evenly into a greased 13x9x2-inch baking pan. Cover with towel; let rise in a warm place, away from drafts, 30 minutes, or until dough is almost double in bulk.
2. Meanwhile, pare, quarter and core apples; cut into very thin slices. Mix brown sugar, cinnamon, cloves and allspice in a small bowl. Melt butter or margarine in a small saucepan.

Cheese Danish

Cockscomb

Apricot Bow Tie

Elephant Ears

Almond Crescent

Prune Danish

Glazed apples and moist coffee cake combine to make a company-perfect Apple Kuchen. Recipe in this chapter.

3. Arrange apple slices over dough in an overlapping pattern. Sprinkle with sugar mixture; drizzle with butter.
4. Bake in a moderate oven (375°) 30 minutes, or until a wooden pick inserted in center comes out clean. Remove from oven.
5. Melt apple jelly in a small saucepan. Brush over apples to glaze. Cool kuchen in pan on wire rack at least 30 minutes before cutting. Serve with pour cream or ice cream, if you wish.

Basic Recipe

SWEET COFFEE-CAKE BATTER

Whip up this basic batter and make 2 coffee cakes—one to freeze; one to serve at breakfast tomorrow!

    2 envelopes active dry yeast
1½ cups very warm water
    1 cup sugar
½ teaspoon salt
½ cup (¼ stick) butter or margarine, softened
    4 eggs
5¾ cups sifted all-purpose flour

1. Sprinkle yeast into very warm water in a large bowl. ("Very warm water" should feel comfortably warm when dropped on wrist.) Stir until yeast dissolves, then stir in sugar, salt, butter or margarine, eggs and 2½ cups of the flour. Beat with electric mixer at low speed for ½ minute; then beat 4 minutes at medium speed.
2. Stir in remaining flour until dough is thick and elastic. Cover with towel. Let rise in a warm place, away from drafts, 1½ hours, or until double in bulk.
3. Follow directions for individual coffee cakes for shaping and baking.

ORANGE BUTTER STREUSEL COFFEE CAKE

The fresh taste of grated orange rind atop a buttery coffee cake. What better way to brighten your morning?

Bake at 350° for 45 minutes.
Makes one 9-inch square.

    Butter or margarine
½ recipe Sweet Coffee-Cake Batter (recipe above)
¼ cup (½ stick) butter or margarine
½ cup sugar
    1 tablespoon grated orange rind

1. Butter a 9x9x2-inch baking pan.
2. Beat SWEET COFFEE-CAKE BATTER 25 strokes; spoon into prepared pan.

3. Cover pan with towel. Let rise in a warm place, away from drafts, 1 hour, or until double in bulk.
4. Make streusel topping: Mix butter or margarine, sugar and orange rind in a small bowl, until crumbs form.
5. Poke little dents in the top of the cake. Sprinkle topping into dents and all over top of cake.
6. Bake in a moderate oven (350°) 45 minutes, or until golden brown. Remove from pan to wire rack; cool.

KUGELHUPF

Use your fanciest 8-cup mold to bake this delightful, almond-covered Bavarian coffee cake.

Bake at 350° for 45 minutes.
Makes 1 coffee cake.

    2 tablespoons butter or margarine
½ cup almonds, sliced
½ recipe Sweet Coffee-Cake Batter (recipe at left)
½ cup golden raisins
    10X (confectioners') sugar

1. Grease an 8-cup fancy tube mold generously with butter or margarine; sprinkle surface evenly with almonds.
2. Beat SWEET COFFEE-CAKE BATTER 25 strokes; stir in raisins. Spoon batter into prepared pan.
3. Cover pan with towel. Let rise in a warm place, away from drafts, 1 hour, or until double in bulk.
4. Bake in moderate oven (350°) 45 minutes, or until golden brown and cake sounds hollow when tapped. Remove from pan to wire rack; cool. Sprinkle with 10X sugar.

POTECA

This tender sour-cream coffee cake from Yugoslavia has a walnut filling that is just out of this world.

Bake at 350° for 40 minutes.
Makes 2 coffee cakes.

    1 cup dairy sour cream
¼ cup milk
¾ cup sugar
    1 teaspoon salt
    2 envelopes active dry yeast
    1 teaspoon sugar
½ cup very warm water
    6 cups sifted all-purpose flour
    4 egg yolks
½ cup (1 stick) very soft butter or margarine
    Walnut Filling (recipe follows)
    Honey

1. Combine sour cream, milk, the ¾ cup sugar and salt in a medium-size saucepan. Heat slowly, stirring constantly, just until mixture begins to bubble and sugar dissolves; pour into a large bowl to cool.

2. Dissolve yeast and 1 teaspoon sugar in very warm water in a small bowl. ("Very warm water" should feel comfortably warm when dropped on wrist.) Stir until well blended and allow to stand 10 minutes, or until mixture begins to bubble.

3. Stir yeast into cooled sour cream mixture; beat in 3 cups of flour until very smooth. Cover bowl with a clean cloth. Let rise in a warm place, away from drafts, 45 minutes; beat mixture down.

4. Beat egg yolks until well blended in a medium-size bowl; beat in *very soft* butter or margarine until smooth.

5. Beat egg-butter mixture and enough of remaining flour into yeast mixture to make a soft dough. Turn out onto a lightly floured surface and knead 10 minutes, or until dough is smooth and elastic.

6. Place dough in a greased large bowl; turn over to bring greased side up. Cover; let rise in a warm place, away from drafts, 1 hour, or until double in bulk. Punch dough down; knead a few times; let rest 5 minutes.

7. Divide dough in half; roll out one half on a lightly floured surface, to a 26x10-inch rectangle. Spread half the WALNUT FILLING over dough. Roll up jelly roll fashion, starting with the long end. Place, seam side down, in a well-greased 10-inch bundt pan or a 9-inch angel cake tube pan; press ends together to seal.

8. Repeat with remaining dough and filling to make a second cake. Cover pans with a clean towel; let rise in a warm place, away from drafts, 45 minutes, or until almost double in bulk.

9. Bake in a moderate oven (350°) 40 minutes, or until cakes are golden. Cool in pans on wire racks for 15 minutes; loosen around edges of pans; invert onto wire racks to cool.

10. To serve: Brush cakes with honey and garnish with walnut halves and candied red cherries, if you wish.

Walnut Filling: Makes enough for 2 coffee cakes.
  1 package (1 pound) shelled walnuts
  4 egg whites
  ¾ cup sugar
  1 teaspoon grated lemon rind
  Dash of salt

1. Chop walnuts, about 1 cup at a time, until very fine on a wooden board. (It is essential that the nuts be very fine, so that the cake will cut neatly.)

2. Just before the dough is ready to be spread, beat egg whites in a large bowl until foamy white and double in volume; beat in sugar, 1 tablespoon at a time, until meringue forms firm peaks; gradually fold in chopped nuts, lemon rind and salt until mixture is well blended.

CHRISTMAS STOLLEN

Lemon-scented, buttery, fruit-filled coffee cake that deserves its place as the No. 1 favorite at Christmas.

Bake at 375° for 30 minutes.
Makes 2 loaves.

  1 envelope active dry yeast
  ¼ cup very warm water
  ½ cup sugar
  ¾ cup milk
  ½ teaspoon salt
  ¾ cup (1½ sticks) butter or margarine
  1 teaspoon almond extract
  1 tablespoon grated lemon rind
  2 eggs
  5 to 5½ cups sifted all-purpose flour
  1 cup mixed candied fruits, chopped
  1 cup raisins
  ½ cup citron, chopped
  ½ cup candied red cherries
  ½ cup almonds, chopped
  10X (confectioners') sugar

1. Sprinkle yeast into very warm water in a 1-cup measure. ("Very warm water" should feel comfortably warm when dropped on wrist.) Stir in ¼ teaspoon of the sugar. Stir until yeast dissolves. Let stand until bubbly and double in volume, about 10 minutes.

2. Heat milk with remaining sugar, salt and 10 tablespoons of the butter or margarine in a small saucepan until lukewarm; combine with yeast mixture in a large bowl.

3. Stir in almond extract, lemon rind and eggs. Beat in enough flour to make a soft dough; turn out onto lightly floured surface. Knead until smooth and elastic, about 10 minutes, using enough of remaining flour to keep dough from sticking.

4. Place in a buttered bowl; turn to bring buttered side up. Cover with a towel. Let rise in a warm place, away from drafts, 1 hour, or until double in bulk.

5. Punch dough down; turn out onto lightly floured surface; knead a few times. Invert bowl over dough; let rest 10 minutes. Knead candied fruits, raisins, citron, cherries and almonds into dough until evenly distributed. Divide in half; roll each to a 12x8-inch oval; fold in half by bringing one side of oval over to within ½ inch from edge of other side. Place on one large or two small buttered cooky sheets.

6. Let rise again in a warm place, away from drafts, 45 minutes, or until double in bulk.

7. Bake in moderate oven (375°) 20 minutes; brush with remaining butter or margarine. Bake 10 minutes longer, or until loaves are golden brown and sound hollow when tapped. Remove to wire racks; cool completely. Just before serving, sprinkle with 10X sugar. Or, combine ¼ cup 10X sugar with enough water to make a thin glaze; drizzle over tops.

PANETTONE

Golden Italian fruit bread—chock full of raisins, candied citron and pine nuts.

Bake at 350° for 45 minutes.
Makes one 8-inch round loaf.

- ½ cup milk
- ½ cup granulated sugar
- 1 teaspoon salt
- 10 tablespoons (1¼ sticks) butter or margarine
- 1 envelope active dry yeast
- ¼ cup very warm water
- 2 eggs
- 2 egg yolks
- 4½ cups <u>sifted</u> all-purpose flour
- 1 tablespoon grated lemon rind
- 1 cup golden raisins
- 1 container (4 ounces) candied citron, chopped
- ½ cup pine nuts (pignolias)
- 10X (confectioners') sugar

1. Combine milk, granulated sugar, salt and 8 tablespoons (1 stick) of the butter or margarine in a small saucepan. Heat slowly, stirring constantly, just until butter melts; cool to lukewarm.
2. Sprinkle yeast into very warm water in a large bowl. ("Very warm water" should feel comfortably warm when dropped on wrist.) Stir until yeast dissolves, then beat in cooled milk mixture, eggs, and egg yolks.
3. Beat in 2 cups of the flour until smooth; stir in lemon rind, raisins, citron and nuts. Stir in 2 cups more flour to make a soft, sticky dough.
4. Turn out onto a lightly floured surface; knead until smooth and elastic, adding only enough extra flour to keep dough from sticking. Place in a greased, large bowl; turn to coat all over with shortening; cover with towel. Let rise in a warm place, away from drafts, 1½ hours, or until double in bulk.
5. While dough rises, grease an 8-inch round layer-cake pan. Tear off a strip of foil long enough to fit around pan with a 2-inch overlap; fold in quarters lengthwise. Place around inside edge of pan; hold in place with a paper clip. (Foil will make a collar 1½ inches above edge of pan.)
6. Punch dough down and knead in bowl several times; shape into a ball. Press into prepared pan; cover. Let rise again in a warm place, away from drafts, 1½ hours, or until double in bulk. Lightly cut a shallow cross in top of dough with a sharp knife.
7. Melt remaining 2 tablespoons butter or margarine in a small saucepan. Brush part over dough.
8. Bake in a moderate oven (350°) 20 minutes; brush with remaining melted butter or margarine. Bake 25 minutes longer, or until loaf sounds hollow when tapped. Remove from pan to a wire rack; cool. Sprinkle top with 10X sugar. Slice into wedges; serve.

HOT CROSS BUNS

"One a penny, two a penny," sang street vendors selling these warm Lenten buns in 18th Century England. Today, a popular breakfast treat—to serve year 'round, anywhere.

Bake at 350° for 30 minutes.
Makes 32 buns.

- 2 envelopes active dry yeast
- ½ cup very warm water
- ½ cup (1 stick) butter or margarine
- 1 small can (⅔ cup) evaporated milk
- ½ cup sugar
- 1 teaspoon salt
- 2 eggs
- ½ cup currants
- ½ cup citron, chopped
- 4½ cups <u>sifted</u> all-purpose flour
- ¼ teaspoon ground cinnamon
- ¼ teaspoon ground nutmeg
- Sugar Icing (recipe follows)

1. Sprinkle yeast into very warm water in large bowl. ("Very warm water" should feel comfortably warm when dropped on wrist.) Stir until yeast dissolves.
2. Heat butter, evaporated milk, sugar and salt in a small saucepan until butter is melted. Cool to lukewarm. Stir into yeast mixture.
3. Beat eggs in small bowl; measure 2 tablespoons into a cup; set aside for Step 8. Stir remaining egg into yeast mixture, then stir in currants and citron.
4. Sift 2 cups of the flour, cinnamon and nutmeg over yeast mixture; beat until smooth; stir in remaining 2½ cups flour to make a soft dough.
5. Turn out onto lightly floured surface; knead until smooth and elastic, adding only enough flour to keep dough from sticking.
6. Place in greased bowl; brush top lightly with butter; cover with clean towel. Let rise in warm place, away from drafts, 1 hour, or until double in bulk.
7. Punch dough down; turn out onto lightly floured surface; divide in half. Cut each half into 16 equal-size pieces; shape each lightly into a smooth round. Arrange 16 buns in each of two well-greased 9x9x2-inch baking pans. Buns should be almost touching.
8. Cover with clean towel; let rise in warm place, away from drafts, 45 minutes, or until double in bulk. Cut shallow cross on top of each bun with tip of scissors. Brush tops lightly with reserved egg.
9. Bake in moderate oven (350°) 30 minutes, or until golden brown; remove from pans; cool on wire racks.
10. Drizzle SUGAR ICING from tip of teaspoon on top of buns to make crosses.

Sugar Icing: Blend 1 cup unsifted 10X (confectioners') sugar with 2 tablespoons milk and ¼ teaspoon vanilla until smooth in small bowl. Makes about ½ cup.

KOLACHE

The Czech way with yeast rolls—sweet and shapely, plump with prune filling.

Bake at 350° for 15 minutes.
Makes 2 dozen rolls.

- ½ cup milk
- 2 envelopes active dry yeast
- ½ cup very warm water
- ¾ cup (1½ sticks) butter or margarine
- ½ cup sugar
- 1 teaspoon salt
- 4 egg yolks
- 4½ cups <u>sifted</u> all-purpose flour
  Prune Filling (recipe follows)
- 1 egg

1. Heat milk in a small saucepan until lukewarm.
2. Sprinkle yeast into very warm water in a large bowl. ("Very warm water" should feel comfortably warm when dropped on wrist.) Stir; dissolve yeast.
3. Beat butter or margarine with sugar, salt and egg yolks in large bowl with electric mixer, until light and fluffy. Stir in yeast mixture, cooled milk, and 2 cups of the flour. Beat 5 minutes at medium speed or 300 strokes by hand.
4. Stir in remaining flour to make a very soft dough; cover with a towel. Let rise in a warm place, away from drafts, 1 hour, or until double in bulk.
5. Stir dough down; turn onto lightly floured surface. Knead several minutes, adding only enough flour to keep dough from sticking; divide in half.
6. Roll out one half to a 12x9-inch rectangle; cut into twelve 3-inch squares. Place 1 tablespoon PRUNE FILLING in center of each. To shape each roll, fold one point over filling to cover, then fold opposite point over top; press to seal. (Filling will show at both ends.) Place, 2 inches apart, on a greased large cooky sheet; cover.
7. Cut remaining dough into 12 even pieces; shape each into a smooth, even ball; place, 2 inches apart, on a second greased cooky sheet; cover.
8. Let all dough rise again 45 minutes, or until double in bulk.
9. Press large hollows in centers of round rolls with fingertips; place a tablespoon of PRUNE FILLING in each. Beat egg with a tablespoon water. Brush over tops of rolls.
10. Bake all in a moderate oven (350°) 15 minutes, or until golden. Remove from cooky sheets; cool on wire racks.

Prune Filling: Chop 1 package (12 ounces) pitted prunes; combine with 2 cups water and 2 tablespoons sugar in a medium-size saucepan. Cook slowly, stirring constantly, 15 minutes, or until very thick; cool. Stir in 2 teaspoons grated orange rind. Makes 1¾ cups; enough for 2 dozen rolls.

KING'S CAKE

Traditional for the Mardi Gras celebration in New Orleans. The person who gets the bean in his or her portion becomes king or queen for a day or a week (until the next party).

Bake at 375° for 30 minutes.
Makes one 12-inch ring.

- ½ cup (1 stick) butter or margarine
- 1 small can (⅔ cup) evaporated milk
- ½ cup granulated sugar
- 2 teaspoons salt
- 5 eggs
- 2 envelopes active dry yeast
- ⅓ cup very warm water
- 1 tablespoon grated lemon rind
- 1 tablespoon grated orange rind
- 5½ cups <u>sifted</u> all-purpose flour
- 1 dry bean
- 1 cup 10X (confectioners') sugar
- 2 tablespoons water
  Candied citron slices
  Tiny candy decorettes
  Gold and silver dragees

1. Combine butter or margarine, evaporated milk, granulated sugar and salt in a small saucepan. Heat slowly; melt butter or margarine; cool to lukewarm.
2. Beat 4 of the eggs in a large bowl; stir in milk mixture.
3. Sprinkle yeast into very warm water in a cup. ("Very warm water" should feel comfortably warm when dropped on wrist.) Stir; dissolve yeast. Add to egg mixture; blend well. Add lemon and orange rinds.
4. Beat in flour, about 1 cup at a time, to make a stiff dough. Turn onto lightly floured surface; knead until smooth and elastic, about 10 minutes, adding only enough flour to keep dough from sticking.
5. Place in a greased large bowl; bring greased side up; cover with a towel. Let rise in a warm place, away from drafts, 1 hour, or until double in bulk.
6. Punch dough down; knead a few times; divide in half. Using palms of hands, roll half into a rope about 20 inches long; lift ends, and, twisting loosely one or two times, place on a greased large cooky sheet in half circle; repeat with second half of dough, pinching ends of ropes together to form a large ring. Lift ring slightly at one side and push the bean about 1 inch into the dough from the bottom. Cover with towel; let rise again in warm place, away from drafts, about 45 minutes, or until double in bulk.
7. While dough rises, beat remaining egg in a small bowl. Brush over dough.
8. Bake in moderate oven (375°) 30 minutes, or until deep golden brown. Slide onto wire rack; cool.
9. Before serving, mix 10X sugar with water in a cup until smooth. Drizzle over ring, then decorate ring with candied citron, decorettes, and dragees.

Here are three festive coffee cakes to brighten any holiday table. From left to right, top: Panettone, and Poteca. Bottom: Christmas Stollen. Recipes for all are in this chapter.

Butter-melting Blueberry Muffins from a
bountiful basket. Also shown: Corn
Muffins and Whole Wheat Muffins. Recipes
in this chapter.

Photographer: Bill McGinn

3

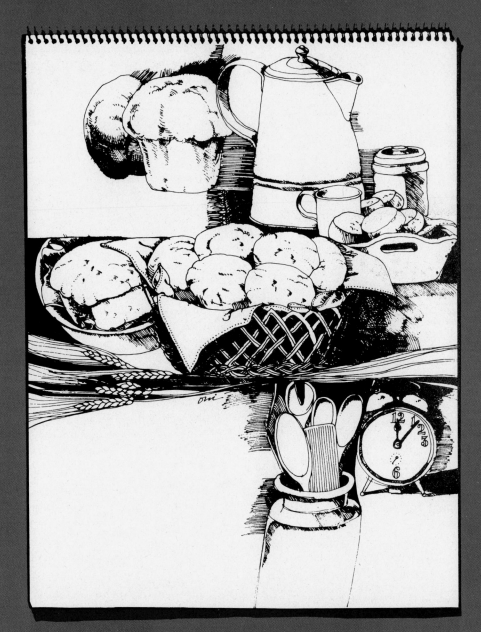

QUICK BREADS

If you've wanted to bake butter-melting biscuits, mouth-watering muffins, or tempting tea loaves, but didn't think you had the time, rejoice! The quickest of Quick Breads are in this chapter, including the beauty on our cover—Classic Strawberry Shortcake.

BISCUITS AND MUFFINS

BAKING POWDER BISCUITS

Flaky, light buttered biscuits to serve with Sunday dinner. Or try one of our biscuit variations, for a tea-time snack.

Bake at 450° for 12 minutes.
Makes 12 biscuits.

> **2 cups sifted all-purpose flour**
> **3 teaspoons baking powder**
> **½ teaspoon salt**
> **¼ cup vegetable shortening**
> **¾ cup milk**

1. Sift flour, baking powder and salt into a large bowl.
2. Cut in shortening with a pastry blender until mixture resembles cornmeal.
3. Add milk; stir lightly with a fork until a soft puffy dough forms.
4. Turn out onto a lightly floured surface. Knead lightly about 20 turns.
5. Roll or pat dough to a ½-inch thickness. Cut into 2-inch rounds with a floured biscuit cutter, working neatly from rim to middle so there will be few scraps to reroll. Place biscuits on an ungreased cooky sheet 1 inch apart.
6. Bake in a hot oven (450°) 12 minutes or until golden brown.

SPECIAL TIP: If you want your biscuits to have soft sides, bake them with sides touching.

Drop Biscuits: Prepare BAKING POWDER BISCUITS increasing the milk to 1 cup. Drop by spoonfuls, 1 inch apart on ungreased cooky sheet. Bake following biscuit directions.

Sesame Butter Fingers: Turn oven to hot (450°). Melt ¼ cup butter or margarine in a 9x9x2-inch pan. Put ½ cup sesame seeds on a large plate. Prepare BAKING POWDER BISCUITS. Roll or pat dough to an 8-inch square on a lightly floured surface. Cut square in half. Cut each half into nine 4-inch strips. Dip each strip into the melted butter, then dip one side into sesame seeds. Arrange strips in 2 rows in the baking pan. Bake 15 minutes or until golden brown.

Scones: Prepare BAKING POWDER BISCUITS recipe, but do not add milk. Add 3 tablespoons sugar, 1 teaspoon grated orange rind and ½ cup raisins to dry mix. Beat 1 egg with ⅓ cup milk; pour into dry ingredients. Stir and knead as in biscuits. Divide dough in half. Pat each half to an 8-inch circle. Cut each circle into 6 wedges. Brush tops with milk; sprinkle with sugar. Place wedges, 1 inch apart on ungreased cooky sheet. Bake in a very hot oven (450°) 10 minutes or until golden brown.

POPOVERS

Giant airy puffs with hot crispy shells, just waiting to be buttered and eaten.

Bake at 425° for 40 minutes.
Makes 8 popovers.

> **2 eggs**
> **1 cup milk**
> **1 tablespoon butter or margarine, melted**
> **1 cup sifted all-purpose flour**
> **½ teaspoon salt**

1. Butter generously eight 5-ounce custard cups; place on a jelly-roll pan. If you have cast-iron popover pans, heat in oven, then brush cups with melted butter before pouring in batter.
2. Beat eggs in a large bowl; add milk and butter or margarine. Beat until blended. Add flour and salt; beat until batter is quite smooth. Ladle into prepared cups filling each about half full.
3. Bake in a hot oven (425°) 35 minutes. Cut slit in side of each popover to allow steam to escape. Bake 5 minutes longer, or until popovers are deep brown and very crisp. Serve at once.

Yorkshire Pudding: Spoon 2 tablespoons of roast beef pan drippings into each of two 8x1½-inch round layer pans. Place in oven as it heats to 450°. Divide POPOVER batter between the two pans. Bake in a very hot oven (450°) 15 minutes. Lower temperature to 350°; bake 20 minutes longer or until puddings are puffed and brown.

CLASSIC STRAWBERRY SHORTCAKE

Luscious, juicy strawberries, tender buttery biscuit and cool rich cream—all add up to one of the favorite American desserts of all time.

Makes one 8-inch cake.

> **1 quart strawberries**
> OR: **1 package (16 ounces) frozen strawberry halves***
> **½ cup granulated sugar**
> **3 cups sifted all-purpose flour**
> **3½ teaspoons baking powder**
> **½ teaspoon salt**
> **1 tablespoon granulated sugar**
> **½ cup vegetable shortening**
> **1 cup milk**

½ cup 10X (confectioners') sugar
¼ cup (½ stick) butter or margarine, softened
1 cup heavy cream, plain or whipped

1. Wash, hull and halve berries; combine with granulated sugar in a large bowl. Stir lightly, crushing a few of the berries. Let stand 30 minutes or until juices run freely.
2. Sift flour, baking powder, salt and sugar into a large bowl. Cut in shortening with pastry blender until mixture resembles cornmeal.
3. Add milk; stir lightly with fork just until blended.
4. Turn out onto lightly floured surface; knead, about 20 turns.
5. Divide dough in half. Put each half into a greased 8x1½-inch layer pan; or, for a more textured biscuit, pat both halves into 8-inch rounds on a large cooky sheet.
6. Bake in a very hot oven (450°) 20 minutes, or until golden brown.
7. Mix 10X sugar and butter in a small bowl until smooth.
8. Spread bottom layer with butter mixture and half the strawberries and cream.
9. Top with remaining layer, strawberries and cream.

*Omit sugar when using frozen syrup-packed berries.

Basic Recipe

FAVORITE MUFFINS

Light, tender, melt-in-your-mouth muffins—delicious plain, super with cheese or bacon. Either way, simple to make.

Bake at 400° for 25 minutes.
Makes 12 medium-size muffins.

    2 cups sifted all-purpose flour
    2 tablespoons sugar
    2 teaspoons baking powder
    1 teaspoon salt
    1 egg, beaten
    1 cup milk
    ¼ cup (½ stick) butter or margarine, melted and cooled

1. Sift flour, sugar, baking powder and salt into a medium-size bowl. Make a well in the center of dry ingredients.
2. Combine egg, milk and melted, cooled butter or margarine in a small bowl; add all at once to flour mixture; stir lightly, just until liquid is absorbed. (Batter will be lumpy.)
3. Spoon into 12 greased medium-size muffin-pan cups, filling each ⅔ full.
4. Bake in a hot oven (400°) 25 minutes or until golden brown. Serve hot.

Jelly Muffins: Spoon part of batter into cups; add a dab of jelly; top with remaining batter.

Cheese Muffins: Add ½ cup shredded Cheddar cheese to dry ingredients.

Bacon Muffins: Add 4 slices of crumbled, crisp-cooked bacon to dry ingredients.

SPECIAL TIPS: Avoid over-mixing and you'll avoid the most common mistake people make when preparing muffin batter. Mix the batter just until it becomes moist. (The batter *should* be lumpy!) Too much mixing will cause toughness and uneven texture.
• Use an ice cream scoop to measure batter; you'll save time, and muffins will be uniform in size.

APPLE STREUSEL MUFFINS

Mouth-watering muffins chock full of apples and sprinkled with walnuts for the perfect topping.

Bake at 425° for 20 minutes.
Makes 12 muffins.

    2 cups sifted all-purpose flour
    ½ cup sugar (for batter)
    3 teaspoons baking powder
    1 teaspoon salt
    ½ cup (1 stick) butter or margarine
    1 medium-size tart apple, pared, quartered, cored, and diced (1 cup)
    2 teaspoons grated lemon rind
    1 egg
    ⅔ cup milk
    ¼ cup walnuts, chopped
    2 tablespoons sugar (for topping)

1. Sift flour, the ½ cup sugar, baking powder and salt into a large bowl. Cut in butter or margarine with a pastry blender until mixture is crumbly. Measure out ½ cup for topping; reserve. Stir apple and 1 teaspoon of the lemon rind into mixture in bowl.
2. Beat eggs in a small bowl; stir in milk. Add all at once to apple mixture; stir lightly just until moist. (Batter will be lumpy.) Spoon into 12 greased medium-size muffin-pan cups, filling each ⅔ full.
3. Blend reserved crumb mixture with remaining lemon rind, walnuts, and the 2 tablespoons of sugar; sprinkle over batter in each cup.
4. Bake in a hot oven (425°) 20 minutes, or until golden and tops spring back when pressed with fingertip. Remove from cups to a wire rack. Serve warm with butter or margarine and jelly, if you wish.

SPECIAL TIP: To refresh stale muffins, slice, butter, wrap in foil and place on a cooky sheet in a slow oven (325°) for 15 minutes.

BLUEBERRY MUFFINS

Golden, sweet muffins spilling over with blueberries. Come berry season, use fresh ones instead of the frozen variety called for here.

Bake at 425° for 20 minutes.
Makes 12 medium-size muffins.

   2 cups <u>sifted</u> all-purpose flour
   ⅓ cup sugar (for batter)
   3 teaspoons baking powder
   1 teaspoon salt
   1 egg, well beaten
   1 cup milk
   ¼ cup (½ stick) butter or margarine, melted and cooled
   1 cup frozen quick-thaw blueberries, drained (from a 10-ounce package)
   1 tablespoon sugar (for topping)
   1 teaspoon grated lemon rind

1. Sift flour, the ⅓ cup sugar, baking powder and salt into a large bowl. Mix egg, milk and melted, cooled butter or margarine in a small bowl; add all at once to flour mixture; stir lightly with a fork just until liquid is absorbed. (Batter will be lumpy.) Fold in blueberries.
2. Spoon into greased medium-size muffin-pan cups, filling each ⅔ full. Sprinkle with a mixture of the 1 tablespoon sugar and lemon rind.
3. Bake in a hot oven (425°) 20 minutes, or until golden; remove from pans. Serve hot.

CORN MUFFINS

Buttermilk plus cornmeal equals country goodness and sunny "wake-up" flavor.

Bake at 400° for 20 minutes.
Makes 12 medium-size muffins.

   1 cup <u>sifted</u> all-purpose flour
   3 tablespoons sugar
   1½ teaspoons baking powder
   ½ teaspoon baking soda
   ½ teaspoon salt
   1 cup yellow or white corn meal
   1 egg, well beaten
   ⅔ cup buttermilk
   ¼ cup vegetable shortening, melted and cooled

1. Sift flour, sugar, baking powder, baking soda, and salt into a large bowl; stir in corn meal.
2. Mix egg, buttermilk and melted, cooled shortening in a 1-cup measure; add all at once to flour mixture; stir lightly with a fork just until liquid is absorbed. (Batter will be lumpy.)

3. Spoon into greased medium-size muffin-pan cups, filling each ⅔ full.
4. Bake in hot oven (400°) 20 minutes, or until golden. Serve hot.

WHEAT GERM MUFFINS

Doubly rich with old-fashioned molasses and nut-sweet wheat germ—and good for you, too!

Bake at 400° for 30 minutes.
Makes 12 medium-size muffins.

   1½ cups <u>sifted</u> all-purpose flour
   ¼ cup sugar
   2 teaspoons baking powder
   1 teaspoon salt
   1 cup wheat germ (from a 12-ounce jar)
   1 egg, well beaten
   ¾ cup milk
   ¼ cup (½ stick) butter or margarine, melted and cooled
   ¼ cup molasses

1. Sift flour, sugar, baking powder and salt into medium-size bowl; stir in wheat germ.
2. Combine egg, milk, melted and cooled butter or margarine, and molasses in small bowl; add all at once to flour mixture; stir lightly just until liquid is absorbed. (Batter will be lumpy.)
3. Spoon into 12 greased medium-size muffin-pan cups, filling each ⅔ full.
4. Bake in hot oven (400°) 30 minutes, or until richly browned; remove from pan at once; serve hot with butter or margarine and your favorite jelly, jam, marmalade, or preserves.

WHOLE WHEAT MUFFINS

Vitamin-rich whole wheat gives these tasty morning muffins a nutrition boost.

Bake at 400° for 25 minutes.
Makes 12 medium-size muffins.

   1 cup <u>sifted</u> all-purpose flour
   2 teaspoons baking powder
   1 teaspoon salt
   1 cup unsifted whole wheat flour
   ¼ cup molasses
   1 egg, beaten
   1 cup milk
   ¼ cup (½ stick) butter or margarine, melted and cooled

1. Sift all-purpose flour, baking powder and salt into a medium-size bowl; stir in whole wheat flour

and make a well in center of ingredients.

2. Combine molasses, egg, milk and melted, cooled butter or margarine in a small bowl; add all at once to flour mixture; stir lightly just until liquid is absorbed. (Batter will be lumpy.)

3. Spoon into 12 greased medium-size muffin-pan cups, filling each ⅔ full.

4. Bake in a hot oven (400°) 25 minutes or until golden brown and springy to the touch. Serve hot.

LOAF QUICK BREADS

BANANA-NUT BREAD

The luscious bananas and crunchy nuts in this classic loaf make a moist bread with great texture.

Bake at 325° for 1 hour and 20 minutes.
Makes one 9x5x3-inch loaf.

2⅔ cups sifted all-purpose flour
  3 teaspoons baking powder
  1 teaspoon salt
  ¼ teaspoon baking soda
  ½ cup (1 stick) butter or margarine
  1 cup sugar
  3 eggs
  2 medium-size ripe bananas, peeled and mashed (about 1 cup)
  ¾ cup pecans, finely chopped
  2 teaspoons grated orange rind

1. Grease a 9x5x3-inch loaf pan, line bottom with wax paper; grease paper.

2. Sift flour, baking powder, salt and baking soda onto a sheet of wax paper.

3. In a large bowl, cream butter or margarine with sugar, until fluffy. Beat in eggs, one at a time, until fluffy again.

4. Stir in flour mixture, alternately with mashed bananas; fold in pecans and orange rind. Pour into prepared pan.

5. Bake in a slow oven (325°) 1 hour and 20 minutes, or until golden, and a wooden pick inserted in the center comes out clean. Cool in pan on a wire rack 10 minutes. Loosen around edges with a knife; turn out onto rack; peel off waxed paper. Let cool completely. Wrap and store overnight.

SPECIAL TIPS: It's a good idea to bake any tea loaf the day before you plan to serve it. The flavors improve with overnight standing and loaves are easier to slice the next day. After your loaf has cooled completely, store it in an airtight container.

• Because of the consistency of loaf breads, it's best to test them for doneness by inserting a wooden

pick in the center of the loaf. If the wooden pick comes out clean, the bread is done; if not, bake an additional 5 minutes and check again.

COUNTRY CORN BREAD

Warm and golden, this Southern favorite is absolutely delicious spread with soft butter and homemade jelly.

Bake at 450° for 25 minutes.
Makes two 8x8x2-inch breads.

1½ cups yellow cornmeal
  2 cups sifted all-purpose flour
  2 tablespoons sugar
  4 teaspoons baking powder
  1 teaspoon salt
  2 eggs
  2 cups milk
  4 tablespoons bacon drippings or shortening

1. Combine cornmeal, flour, sugar, baking powder and salt in a large bowl. Add eggs and milk. Stir to make a smooth batter; stir in bacon drippings.

2. Pour into two greased 8x8x2-inch baking pans.

3. Bake in hot oven (450°) 25 minutes, or until crusty and golden brown. Cool slightly in pans on wire racks; serve warm.

BRIDIE'S IRISH SODA BREAD

This bread, which many consider the Irish soda bread, is usually served at high teas and other important occasions.

Bake at 400° for 40 minutes.
Makes 1 round loaf.

  4 cups sifted all-purpose flour
  1 tablespoon sugar
1½ teaspoons salt
  1 teaspoon baking soda
  1 cup dried currants
1½ cups buttermilk

1. Sift flour, sugar, salt and baking soda into a large bowl; stir in currants to coat with flour.

2. Stir in buttermilk, just until flour is moistened. Knead dough in bowl with lightly floured hands 10 times.

3. Turn dough out onto lightly floured cooky sheet and shape into an 8-inch round. Cut a cross into the top with a floured knife.

4. Bake in hot oven (400°) 40 minutes, or until loaf turns golden and sounds hollow when tapped. Cool completely on a wire rack before slicing.

SPECIAL TIP: Irish Soda Bread *can* be served the day you bake it, with flavors already fully developed. Just be sure the bread has cooled completely before you slice it.

CRANBERRY-PECAN BREAD

No need to ice this cranberry filled bread; chopped pecans sprinkled into the pan before baking make the interesting crust.

Bake at 350° for 1 hour and 10 minutes.
Makes one 9-inch round loaf.

1½ **cups chopped pecans**
1½ **cups cranberries, coarsely ground**
1¼ **cups sugar**
 3 **cups** sifted **all-purpose flour**
4½ **teaspoons baking powder**
 ½ **teaspoon salt**
 ½ **cup vegetable shortening**
 2 **teaspoons grated lemon rind**
 2 **eggs**
 1 **cup milk**

1. Grease a 9-inch angel cake pan; sprinkle half of the pecans evenly over bottom.
2. Mix cranberries and ¼ cup of the sugar in a small bowl; let stand while preparing batter.
3. Sift flour, the remaining 1 cup sugar, baking powder and salt in a large bowl; cut in shortening with a pastry blender until mixture resembles cornmeal. Stir in remaining 1 cup pecans and lemon rind.
4. Beat eggs well in a small bowl; stir in milk. Add all at once to flour mixture; stir just until moist. (Batter will be lumpy.) Spread in prepared pan.
5. Bake in a moderate oven (350°) 1 hour and 10 minutes, or until a wooden pick inserted near center comes out clean. Cool in pan on a wire rack 10 minutes. Loosen around edges and center with a knife; turn out onto rack. Cool loaf completely.
6. Wrap loaf in foil or plastic wrap. Store overnight.

OUR BEST GINGERBREAD

Dark, spicy gingerbread—a treat for all seasons! Try topping it with a mound of fresh whipped cream.

Bake at 350° for 30 minutes.
Makes one 13x9x2-inch cake.

2½ **cups** sifted **all-purpose flour**
1½ **teaspoons baking soda**
 1 **teaspoon ground ginger**
 1 **teaspoon ground cinnamon**
 ½ **teaspoon salt**
 ½ **cup vegetable shortening**
 ½ **cup sugar**
 ¾ **cup molasses**
 1 **egg**
 1 **cup hot water**

1. Sift flour, baking soda, ginger, cinnamon and salt onto wax paper.
2. In a large bowl, beat shortening with sugar, until fluffy; beat in molasses and egg.
3. Stir in flour mixture, half at a time, just until blended; beat in hot water until smooth. Pour into a well-greased 13x9x2-inch baking pan.
4. Bake in a moderate oven (350°) 30 minutes or until center springs back when lightly pressed with fingertip.
5. Leave in pan to cool on a wire rack, or let cool 10 minutes, then loosen around edge with a knife and turn out onto rack.

QUICK APPLE CAKE

Serve this easy-to-make cake whenever you're expecting guests. Equally good for a weekday kaffeeklatsch or a Sunday brunch.

Bake at 350° for 45 minutes.
Makes one 9-inch coffee cake.

 2 **cups** sifted **all-purpose flour**
 2 **teaspoons baking powder**
 ½ **teaspoon salt**
 ¼ **teaspoon pumpkin-pie spice**
 1 **cup firmly packed light brown sugar**
 ½ **cup (1 stick) butter or margarine**
 ¼ **cup dried currants**
 2 **eggs**
⅔ **cup (1 small can) evaporated milk**
 1 **large tart apple, pared, cored and sliced thin**
 2 **tablespoons granulated sugar**

1. Sift flour, baking powder, salt and pumpkin-pie spice into a large bowl; stir in brown sugar.
2. Cut in 6 tablespoons of the butter or margarine with a pastry blender until the mixture is crumbly. Measure out ½ cup and set aside for topping; stir currants into remainder.
3. Beat eggs slightly in a small bowl; stir in evaporated milk. Stir egg mixture into flour mixture until well-blended. Spoon into a greased 9-inch pie plate.
4. Arrange apple slices, overlapping, in 2 circles on top. Sprinkle with the ½ cup reserved crumb mixture; dot with remaining 2 tablespoons butter or margarine; sprinkle top evenly with granulated sugar.
5. Bake in a moderate oven (350°) 45 minutes, or until center springs back when lightly pressed with fingertip. Cool 10 minutes on a wire rack; cut in wedges. Serve warm.

Our Best Gingerbread served with a glass of milk: perfect for after school. Recipe in this chapter.

Swirls of frosting and glistening bits of
candied orange peel add the finishing touches
to the best Orange-Nut Cake ever created!
Recipe in this chapter.

Photographer: George Nordhausen

4

CAKES AND FROSTINGS

Bake our basic butter, white or chocolate cake, add a fabulous frosting and a great garnish, and you can create any of dozens of simply sensational cakes. And that's not all! You'll find dozens more cake recipes in this chapter, plus an entire section on cake decorating.

The silver Lady and golden Lord Baltimore—a classic cake "couple" often baked together, since "the Lady" requires egg whites, "the Lord," egg yolks—and both share the same basic frosting. Recipes in this chapter.

George Nordhausen

BUTTER AND POUND CAKES

SPECIAL TIPS: Here are some helpful hints to make your cake—and cupcake—baking a snap:
• When making a cake, *never* use vegetable oil or melted shortening unless the recipe specifically calls for it; otherwise, your cake will turn out heavy and tough, and may sink in the middle.
• The easiest way to tell if a cake is done is to touch it lightly in the center. If it springs back, it's done. Another test is to insert a wooden pick in the center of the cake. If batter or crumbs cling to the pick, bake cake for an additional five minutes; then test it again.
• Always leave cakes in pans on wire racks for at least 10 minutes, to cool. Then loosen sides with a knife or spatula, invert each cake on wire rack or plate, and *immediately* turn cake right side up on wire rack to complete cooling.
• Most butter cake recipes will make between 24 and 36 medium-size cupcakes. To make cupcakes, place pleated muffin-pan liners in muffin-pan cups. Fill each ⅔ full with batter. Bake in a moderate oven (375°) 20 minutes, or until centers spring back when lightly pressed with fingertip.

Basic Recipe

GOLDEN BUTTER CAKE

Here's a basic double-layer yellow cake to be filled or frosted with any filling or frosting you choose. The possibilities are almost limitless!

Bake at 350° for 30 minutes.
Makes two 9-inch layers, or about 24 cupcakes.

      3 cups <u>sifted</u> cake flour
   2½ teaspoons baking powder
    ½ teaspoon salt
    ¾ cup (1½ sticks) butter or margarine, softened
   1⅔ cups sugar
      2 eggs
      2 teaspoons vanilla
   1⅓ cups milk

1. Grease two 9x1½-inch round layer-cake pans. Dust lightly with flour; tap out excess.
2. Sift flour, baking powder and salt onto wax paper.
3. Beat butter or margarine, sugar, eggs and vanilla in a large bowl with electric mixer at high speed, 3 minutes. (Finish mixing cake by hand.)
4. Add flour mixture alternately with milk, beating after each addition until batter is smooth. Pour into prepared pans.
5. Bake in a moderate oven (350°) 30 minutes, or until centers of layers spring back when lightly pressed with fingertip.

6. Cool layers in pans on wire racks 10 minutes. Loosen around edges with knife; turn out onto wire racks; cool completely.
7. Put layers together with CHOCOLATE BUTTER CREAM FROSTING, BURNT SUGAR FROSTING, or any frosting you prefer. Make any of the frosting patterns shown on page 77, or try your hand at one of the easy-to-make garnishes shown on pages 76 through 78.

BANANA-NUT CAKE

The cake layers have nuts baked inside. The finished, frosted cake has nuts outside; there's banana through and through!

Bake at 350° for 30 minutes.
Makes one 9-inch double-layer cake.

   2⅓ cups <u>sifted</u> cake flour
   2½ teaspoons baking powder
    ½ teaspoon baking soda
    ½ teaspoon salt
    ½ teaspoon ground cinnamon
      1 cup mashed ripe bananas (2 medium-size)
    ½ cup buttermilk
    ½ cup (1 stick) butter or margarine
   1¼ cups sugar
      2 eggs
    ¼ teaspoon vanilla
    ¾ cup chopped walnuts
         Rum Butter Cream Frosting (recipe page 73)

1. Grease two 9x1½-inch round layer-cake pans; dust lightly with flour; tap out excess.
2. Sift flour, baking powder, baking soda, salt, and cinnamon onto wax paper. Stir buttermilk into mashed bananas in a small bowl.
3. Beat butter or margarine, sugar, and eggs in large bowl with electric mixer at high speed, 3 minutes. (Finish mixing cake by hand.)
4. Stir in flour mixture alternately with banana-milk mixture, beating after each addition until batter is smooth. Stir in the ¼ teaspoon vanilla and ¼ cup of the chopped nuts; pour the cake batter into prepared pans.
5. Bake in moderate oven (350°) 30 minutes, or until centers spring back when lightly pressed with fingertip.
6. Cool layers in pans on wire racks 10 minutes; loosen around edges with a knife; turn out onto wire racks; cool completely.
7. Put layers together with RUM BUTTER CREAM FROSTING; frost side and top with remaining frosting. Press remaining ½ cup chopped nuts on sides of cake. Garnish top of cake with banana slices, if you wish. (Dip slices in orange or pineapple juice to keep them white.)

OLD-TIME NUT CAKE

Use a fancy bundt pan to bake this buttery nut cake.

Bake at 350° for 1 hour and 5 minutes.
Makes one 9-inch tube or 10-inch bundt cake.

2¾ cups sifted cake flour
  2 teaspoons baking powder
  1 teaspoon salt
  1 cup (2 sticks) butter or margarine
1¾ cups sugar
  4 eggs
 ⅔ cup milk
  2 teaspoons vanilla
  1 cup nuts, very finely chopped (use hickory nuts, walnuts, or pecans)
   Rum Butter Cream Frosting (recipe page 73)

1. Grease a 9-inch angel cake or 10-inch bundt pan; dust lightly with flour; tap out excess.
2. Sift flour, baking powder, and salt onto wax paper.
3. Beat butter or margarine, sugar, and eggs in large bowl with electric mixer at high speed, 3 minutes. (Finish mixing cake by hand.)
4. Stir in dry ingredients alternately with milk, beating after each addition, until batter is smooth.
5. Stir in vanilla and nuts. Pour batter into pan.
6. Bake in moderate oven (350°) 1 hour and 5 minutes, or until top springs back when lightly pressed with fingertip.
7. Cool in pan on wire rack 10 minutes; loosen cake around tube and outside edge with a knife; turn out onto wire rack; cool completely.
8. Frost top and side of cake with RUM BUTTER CREAM FROSTING. Sprinkle with nuts if you wish.

STRAWBERRIES AND CREAM CAKE

There's whipped cream in the cake batter, to make the layers light as air. The dreamy strawberry frosting finishes the cake beautifully.

Bake at 350° for 30 minutes.
Makes one 9-inch double-layer cake.

2⅔ cups sifted cake flour
1½ cups sugar
  2 teaspoons baking powder
 ¼ teaspoon salt
1⅓ cups heavy cream
  4 eggs
1½ teaspoons vanilla
   Strawberry Butter Cream Frosting (recipe page 73)

1. Grease two 9x1½-inch round layer-cake pans; dust lightly with flour; tap out excess.

2. Measure flour, sugar, baking powder, and salt into a sifter.
3. Beat cream in a medium-size bowl until stiff.
4. Beat eggs in a small bowl until very thick and light; beat in vanilla; fold into reserved whipped cream. Sift dry ingredients over cream mixture; gently fold in until batter is smooth; pour batter into prepared pans.
5. Bake in moderate oven (350°) 30 minutes, or until centers spring back when lightly pressed with fingertip.
6. Cool layers in pans on wire racks 10 minutes; loosen aronud edges with a knife; turn out onto wire racks; cool completely.
7. Put layers together with STRAWBERRY BUTTER CREAM FROSTING; frost side and top with remaining frosting; garnish with strawberries, if you wish.

LADY BALTIMORE CAKE (Silver Cake)

The Lord and Lady Baltimore Cakes—they're perfect to make together, and both are perfectly beautiful. The Lady Baltimore layers can be used as a Basic White Cake, any time.

Bake at 350° for 30 minutes.
Makes one 9-inch double-layer round cake.

2⅔ cups sifted cake flour
1½ cups sugar
  4 teaspoons baking powder
  1 teaspoon salt
 ⅔ cup vegetable shortening
1¼ cups milk
  1 teaspoon vanilla
  4 egg whites
   Pink Mountain Cream Frosting (recipe page 74)
   Lady Baltimore Filling (recipe follows)

1. Grease bottoms of two 9x1½-inch round layer-cake pans; line pans with wax paper; grease and flour paper; tap out excess.
2. Combine flour, sugar, baking powder, salt, shortening, ¾ cup of the milk, and vanilla in a large bowl. Beat at low speed with electric mixer until blended, then beat at high speed for 2 minutes. Add remaining ½ cup milk and egg whites; continue beating at high speed, 2 minutes longer, scraping down side of bowl often; pour cake batter into prepared pans.
3. Bake in moderate oven (350°) 30 minutes, or until centers spring back when lightly pressed with fingertip.
4. Cool layers in pans on wire racks, 10 minutes; loosen around edges with a knife; turn out onto wire racks; remove wax paper; cool completely.

5. Put layers together with LADY BALTIMORE FILLING; frost side and top with PINK MOUNTAIN CREAM FROSTING. Decorate with whole or sliced maraschino cherries, if you wish.

Lady Baltimore Filling: Makes enough to fill two 9-inch layers.

    ½ **cup pecans, finely chopped**
    ⅓ **cup dried figs, cut-up**
    ⅓ **cup raisins, chopped**
    3 **tablespoons maraschino cherries, chopped**
    2 **tablespoons grated orange rind**
    1½ **cups Pink Mountain Cream Frosting (recipe page 74)**

1. Combine pecans, figs, raisins, cherries and orange rind in a medium-size bowl; toss to mix well.
2. Fold in PINK MOUNTAIN CREAM FROSTING until well blended.

SPECIAL TIP: You'll note that baking pans are lined with wax paper. This helps to make it easier to remove the delicate cake. It's also a good idea to use wax paper for a particularly large cake—to help keep it from breaking when removed.

LORD BALTIMORE CAKE (Gold Cake)

The Lord Baltimore is the golden member of this pair, baked in square pans, and covered with white frosting.

Bake at 350° for 30 minutes.
Makes one 8-inch double-layer square cake.

    2 **cups sifted cake flour**
    2½ **teaspoons baking powder**
    ¾ **teaspoon salt**
    1 **cup sugar**
    ⅓ **cup vegetable shortening**
    4 **egg yolks**
    1 **teaspoon vanilla**
    1 **cup milk**
       White Mountain Cream Frosting (recipe page 74)
       Lord Baltimore Filling (recipe follows)

1. Grease two 8x8x2-inch layer-cake pans; dust lightly with flour; tap out excess.
2. Sift flour, baking powder and salt onto wax paper.
3. Beat sugar, shortening, egg yolks, and vanilla in large bowl with electric mixer at high speed, 3 minutes. (Finish mixing cake by hand.)
4. Stir in flour mixture alternately with milk, beating well with wooden spoon, after each addition, until batter is smooth. Pour batter into prepared pans.
5. Bake in moderate oven (350°) 30 minutes,

or until centers spring back when lightly pressed with fingertip.
6. Cool layers in pans on wire racks 10 minutes; loosen around edges with a knife; turn out onto wire racks; cool completely.
7. Put layers together with LORD BALTIMORE FILLING; frost side and top with remaining WHITE MOUNTAIN CREAM FROSTING. Decorate with pecan halves and cherry halves, if you wish.

Lord Baltimore Filling: Makes enough to fill two 8-inch layers.

    ½ **cup flaked coconut, toasted**
    ½ **cup pecans, finely chopped**
    ⅓ **cup candied red cherries, chopped**
    2 **teaspoons grated orange rind**
    1 **teaspoon almond extract**
    1½ **cups White Mountain Cream Frosting (recipe page 74)**

1. Combine coconut, pecans, cherries, orange rind, and almond extract in a medium-size bowl.
2. Fold in WHITE MOUNTAIN CREAM FROSTING until well blended.

ALMOND POUND CAKE

Crumbled almond paste provides the nut-like flavor in this smooth pound cake.

Bake at 325° for 45 minutes.
Makes one 10-inch bundt or 9-inch tube cake.

    2½ **cups sifted cake flour**
    1 **teaspoon baking powder**
    ½ **cup almond paste (from an 8-ounce can or package)**
    ⅔ **cup butter or margarine, softened**
    1¼ **cups sugar**
    4 **eggs**
    ½ **cup milk**

1. Grease a 10-inch bundt or a 9-inch angel cake tube pan. Dust lightly with flour; tap out excess.
2. Sift flour and baking powder onto wax paper.
3. Crumble almond paste into butter or margarine in a large bowl. Beat with electric mixer until creamy and smooth. Slowly add sugar, beating until fluffy. Add eggs, one at a time, beating well after each addition.
4. Add the flour mixture alternately with milk, beating after each addition until batter is smooth. (Use low speed on mixer.) Pour into pan.
5. Bake in slow oven (325°) 45 minutes, or until top springs back when lightly pressed with fingertip. Cool in pan on wire rack, 10 minutes; loosen around edges with a knife; turn out onto wire rack; cool completely. Serve with ice cream, if you wish.

LEMON POUND CAKE

A light, lemony pound cake—just right with coffee, after a heavy meal.

Bake at 350° for 1 hour.
Makes one 10-inch bundt or 9-inch tube cake.

> 2⅓ cups <u>sifted</u> cake flour
> 1 teaspoon baking powder
> ½ teaspoon salt
> ⅔ cup butter or margarine, softened
> 1¼ cups sugar
> 3 eggs
> ½ cup milk
> 1 teaspoon grated lemon rind
> 1 tablespoon lemon juice

1. Grease a 10-inch bundt or 9-inch angel cake tube pan. Dust lightly with flour; tap out excess.
2. Sift flour, baking powder, and salt onto wax paper.
3. Combine butter or margarine, sugar and eggs in a large bowl; beat with electric mixer at high speed, 3 minutes. (Finish mixing cake by hand.)
4. Combine milk, lemon rind and juice in a cup. Stir flour mixture into batter alternately with milk mixture, beating after each addition, until batter is smooth. Pour into prepared pan.
5. Bake in moderate oven (350°) 1 hour, or until top springs back when lightly pressed with fingertip. Cool in pan on wire rack 10 minutes; loosen around edge and tube with a knife; turn out onto wire rack; cool completely. Sift 10X (confectioners') sugar over cake, if you wish.

COCONUT LAYER CAKE

Our version of this popular cake calls for Lemon Filling between the layers. The coconut is sprinkled over the frosting.

Bake at 350° for 30 minutes.
Makes one 8-inch triple-layer cake, or one 9-inch double-layer cake.

> 3 cups <u>sifted</u> cake flour
> 2 teaspoons baking powder
> ½ teaspoon salt
> 1 cup (2 sticks) butter or margarine, softened
> 2 cups sugar
> 4 eggs
> 1 teaspoon vanilla
> 1 cup milk
> Lemon Filling (recipe page 74)
> Fluffy 7-Minute Frosting (recipe page 75)
> 1 can (3½ ounces) flaked coconut

1. Grease three 8x1½-inch or two 9x1½-inch round layer-cake pans; dust with flour; tap out excess.
2. Sift flour, baking powder and salt onto wax paper.
3. Beat softened butter or margarine, sugar, eggs and vanilla in a large bowl with electric mixer at high speed, 3 minutes.
4. Beat in flour mixture alternately with milk, at low speed with electric mixer. Scrape side of bowl with rubber scraper after each addition. Pour batter into prepared pans.
5. Bake in moderate oven (350°) 30 minutes, or until centers spring back when lightly touched with fingertip.
6. Cool layers in pans on wire racks 10 minutes; loosen around edges with a knife; turn out onto wire racks; cool completely.
7. Spread LEMON FILLING between layers. Frost side and top with FLUFFY 7-MINUTE FROSTING. Sprinkle generously with coconut.

ORANGE-NUT CAKE

This beautiful cake combines the fresh taste of orange, smooth frosting and the crunch of walnuts.

Bake at 350° for 30 minutes.
Makes one 9-inch double-layer cake.

> 2¾ cups <u>sifted</u> cake flour
> 3 teaspoons baking powder
> ½ teaspoon salt
> ¾ cup vegetable shortening
> 1½ cups sugar
> 2 eggs
> 1 tablespoon grated orange rind
> 1¼ cups milk
> ½ cup walnuts, finely chopped
> Rich Orange Butter Cream Frosting (recipe page 73)
> Candied Orange Peel (recipe page 76)
> Walnut halves

1. Grease two 9x1½-inch round layer-cake pans; dust lightly with flour; tap out excess.
2. Sift flour, baking powder, and salt onto wax paper.
3. Combine shortening, sugar, eggs, and orange rind in a large bowl. Beat with electric mixer at high speed, 3 minutes. (Finish mixing cake by hand.)
4. Stir in flour mixture alternately with milk, beating after each addition, until batter is smooth. Pour batter into prepared pans.
5. Bake in a moderate oven (350°) 30 minutes, or until tops spring back when lightly pressed with fingertip.
6. Cool layers in pans on wire racks 10 minutes; loosen around edges with a knife; turn out onto wire racks; cool completely.
7. Put layers together with part of RICH ORANGE BUTTER CREAM FROSTING. Frost side and top with

remaining frosting. Decorate with CANDIED ORANGE PEEL and walnut halves.

PINEAPPLE-APRICOT UPSIDE-DOWN CAKE

Apricot joins pineapple in our version of the grand-daddy of all upside-down cakes.

Bake at 350° for 45 minutes.
Makes one 9-inch square cake.

¼ cup (½ stick) butter or margarine
¼ cup firmly packed brown sugar
6 pineapple slices packed in juice (from a 1 pound, 4 ounce can), drained
1 can (8 ounces) apricot halves, drained
   Maraschino cherries
1¼ cups sifted all-purpose flour
2 teaspoons baking powder
¼ teaspoon salt
1 cup sugar
¼ cup vegetable shortening
¾ cup milk
1 teaspoon vanilla
1 egg

1. Melt butter or margarine; pour into a 9x9x2-inch baking pan. Sprinkle brown sugar over butter. Arrange pineapple slices and apricot halves in butter-sugar mixture; fill centers of pineapple slices with cherries.
2. Sift flour, baking powder, salt and sugar into large bowl. Add shortening and milk. Beat 2 minutes at medium speed with electric mixer, scraping down side of bowl several times. Add vanilla and egg; beat 2 minutes longer. Pour over the fruit in baking pan.
3. Bake in moderate oven (350°) 45 minutes, or until center springs back when lightly pressed with fingertip.
4. Invert cake on serving plate; leave baking pan in place 2 minutes. Lift off pan. Serve warm with whipped cream or dessert topping, if you wish.

CHOCOLATE CAKES

SPECIAL TIPS: To keep cocoa and chocolate cakes brown on the outside, grease pans and dust with cocoa, instead of flour.
• BUSY DAY CHOCOLATE CAKE makes delicious cupcakes. Here's how to make them: Line muffin-pan cups with pleated muffin-pan liners. Fill ⅔ full batter. Bake in a moderate oven (375°) 20 minutes, or until centers of cupcakes spring back when lightly pressed with fingertip.

BUSY DAY CHOCOLATE CAKE

A nice, easy chocolate cake made with buttermilk; covered, while still warm, with a chocolate glaze.

Bake at 350° for 30 minutes.
Makes one 13x9x2-inch cake, or about 30 cupcakes. (For cupcakes, bake at 375° for 20 minutes.)

3 squares unsweetened chocolate, melted
2 cups sifted all-purpose flour
1 teaspoon baking soda
½ teaspoon salt
½ cup (1 stick) butter or margarine
1½ cups firmly packed light brown sugar
3 eggs
1 teaspoon vanilla extract
1 cup buttermilk
   Chocolate Glaze (recipe page 74)

1. Grease a 13x9x2-inch baking pan. Dust lightly with flour; tap out excess.
2. Melt chocolate in small saucepan over very low heat; cool.
3. Sift flour, baking soda and salt onto wax paper.
4. Beat butter or margarine, sugar, eggs and vanilla in a large bowl with electric mixer at high speed, 2 minutes until light and fluffy. Add chocolate.
5. Add flour mixture alternately with buttermilk, starting and ending with flour. Scrape down side of bowl frequently to blend all ingredients.
6. Pour into prepared pan, spreading mixture evenly.
7. Bake in a moderate oven (350°) 30 minutes, or until center springs back when lightly pressed with fingertip. Cool in pan on wire rack. Top with CHOCOLATE GLAZE.

BURNT SUGAR CAKE

A rich, extra-special triple-layer dessert.

Bake at 350° for 40 minutes.
Makes one 8-inch triple-layer cake.

2½ cups sifted cake flour
½ cup unsweetened cocoa
1½ teaspoons baking soda
½ teaspoon salt
1 tablespoon vinegar
   Milk
1 cup vegetable shortening
1½ cups sugar
2 eggs
½ cup hot water
1 teaspoon vanilla
   Burnt Sugar Frosting (recipe page 75)

1. Grease three 8x1½-inch round layer-cake pans.

Dust with flour; tap out excess.

2. Sift flour, cocoa, baking soda and salt onto wax paper. Measure vinegar into a 1-cup measure. Fill cup to 1-cup mark with milk. Let stand 5 minutes to sour.

3. Beat shortening, sugar and eggs in a large bowl with electric mixer at high speed, 3 minutes. (Finish mixing cake by hand.)

4. Stir in dry ingredients alternately with soured milk, beating after each addition, until batter is smooth. Stir in hot water and vanilla; pour batter into prepared cake pans.

5. Bake in moderate oven (350°) 40 minutes, or until centers spring back when lightly pressed with fingertip.

6. Cool layers in pans on wire racks 10 minutes; loosen around edges with a knife; turn out onto wire racks; cool completely.

7. Put layers together with BURNT SUGAR FROSTING; frost side and top with remaining frosting; drizzle with reserved syrup.

CHOCOLATE NUT UPSIDE-DOWN CAKE

Fudgy and crunchy and topped with nuts. So good when served warm with either whipped or pour cream.

Bake at 350° for 45 minutes.
Makes one 10-inch bundt cake.

10 tablespoons butter or margarine
¼ cup firmly packed light brown sugar
⅔ cup light corn syrup
¼ cup heavy cream
1 cup broken walnuts
1¾ cup sifted cake flour
2 teaspoons baking powder
¼ teaspoon salt
1½ cups granulated sugar
2 eggs, separated
3 squares unsweetened chocolate, melted
1 teaspoon vanilla
1 cup milk

1. Melt 4 tablespoons of the butter or margarine in a small saucepan; stir in brown sugar; heat until bubbly. Stir in corn syrup and cream; heat, stirring constantly, just to boiling. Add nuts; pour into a generously greased 10-inch bundt pan. (Mixture will be thin.) Let stand while preparing cake batter.

2. Sift flour, baking powder and salt onto wax paper.

3. Beat remaining butter or margarine in large bowl, until soft. Gradually beat in granulated sugar until well blended. Beat in egg yolks, chocolate and vanilla until thoroughly blended.

4. Add flour mixture alternately with milk, beginning and ending with flour. Beat egg whites in a small bowl, until stiff; fold into cake batter.

Spoon batter evenly over nut mixture in pan.

5. Bake in moderate oven (350°) 45 minutes, or until wood pick inserted in the center of the cake comes out clean.

6. Loosen cake from edges with a small knife; cover pan with serving plate; invert; shake gently, then lift off pan. Scoop out any nuts and syrup clinging to pan onto cake with a rubber scraper.

MOCHA CHERRY CAKE

Frosted mocha cake, covered with red cherries.

Bake at 350° for 35 minutes.
Makes one 9-inch double-layer cake.

3 squares unsweetened chocolate
2 tablespoons instant coffee
1 cup firmly packed brown sugar
⅓ cup water
2⅓ cups sifted cake flour
2 teaspoons baking powder
½ teaspoon baking soda
½ cup vegetable shortening
1 cup granulated sugar
3 eggs
1 cup milk
1 teaspoon vanilla
1 can (1 pound, 5 ounces) cherry pie filling
Chocolate Butter Cream Frosting (recipe page 75)

1. Grease two 9x1½-inch round layer-cake pans. Dust lightly with flour; tap out excess.

2. Combine chocolate, coffee, brown sugar and water in the top of a double boiler. Heat over simmering water, stirring several times, until chocolate melts; remove from heat; cool.

3. Sift flour, baking powder and baking soda onto wax paper.

4. Combine shortening, granulated sugar and eggs in a large bowl; beat at high speed with electric mixer, 2 minutes, or until light and fluffy. Slowly beat in chocolate mixture, until smooth.

5. Beat in flour mixture, alternately with milk, at low speed, until blended. Pour into prepared pans.

6. Bake in moderate oven (350°) 35 minutes, or until centers spring back when lightly pressed with fingertip. Cool in pans on wire racks, 10 minutes. Loosen around edges with a knife; turn out onto wire racks; cool completely.

7. Stir vanilla into cherry pie filling in a small bowl. Spread about 1 cupful over one cake layer; place layer on a serving plate; top with second layer.

8. Prepare CHOCOLATE BUTTER CREAM FROSTING. Spread over side of cake and in a 1-inch wide ring around top edge; spread remaining cherry pie filling in center, up to edge of frosting.

DEVIL'S FOOD CAKE

Here's a classic light Devils' Food—deep, dark chocolate cake and fluffy white frosting. Use chocolate layers with any frosting for a superb basic double-layer chocolate cake.

Bake at 350° for 35 minutes.
Makes one 9-inch double-layer cake.

> **3 squares unsweetened chocolate**
> **2¼ cups <u>sifted</u> cake flour**
> **2 teaspoons baking soda**
> **½ teaspoon salt**
> **½ cup (1 stick) butter or margarine**
> **2¼ cups firmly packed light brown sugar**
> **3 eggs**
> **1½ teaspoons vanilla**
> **1 cup dairy sour cream**
> **1 cup boiling water**
> **Fluffy 7-Minute Frosting (recipe page 75)**

1. Melt chocolate in a small bowl over hot, not boiling, water; cool.
2. Grease two 9x1½-inch round layer-cake pans. Dust lightly with flour; tap out excess.
3. Sift flour, baking soda and salt onto wax paper.
4. Beat butter or margarine in a large bowl until soft. Add brown sugar and eggs; beat with electric mixer at high speed, until light and fluffy, about 5 minutes. Beat in vanilla and cooled, melted chocolate.
5. Stir in dry ingredients alternately with sour cream, beating well with a wooden spoon after each addition, until batter is smooth. Stir in boiling water. (Batter will be thin.) Pour cake batter at once into prepared pans.
6. Bake in moderate oven (350°) 35 minutes, or until centers spring back when lightly pressed with fingertip.
7. Cool layers in pans on wire racks, 10 minutes; loosen around edges with a knife; turn out onto wire racks; cool completely.
8. Fill and frost with FLUFFY 7-MINUTE FROSTING.

SPONGE AND CHIFFON CAKES

SPECIAL TIPS: With all "foam" cakes, it's particularly important to have eggs at room temperature. That way, you'll get the maximum volume when you beat them.
• Butter cakes, as you have already seen, are always cooled on wire racks, to allow air to circulate around the hot layers. The reason you cool "foam" cakes upside down, over a funnel or bottle, is to keep the cake high and light, until the walls are cool and strong enough to support the weight of the cake once it is turned right side up.

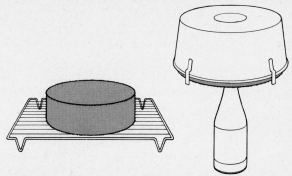

• Use the funnel or bottle method, rather than relying on the "feet" of the pan, particularly if the cake has risen higher than the "feet". That way, you won't mash the cake down. (Don't worry, if you've baked the cake the full amount of time specified in the recipe, it won't fall out of the pan.)
• The best way to cut a sponge or chiffon cake is to use a cake breaker, or a long serrated knife. If you use the knife, cut with a sawing motion.

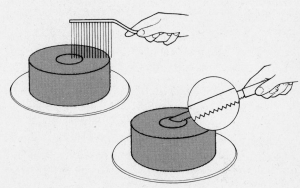

• Don't throw out stale sponge cake. You can make a super dessert with it. Soak pieces in rum, then mix into a thick vanilla pudding. Cover with whipped cream or decorate with slivered almonds, or garnish with canned fruit and syrup.

OLD-FASHIONED SPONGE CAKE

High and light, this is the perfect accompaniment to ice cream or fruit for dessert.

Bake at 325° for 1 hour.
Makes one 9-inch tube cake.

> **1 cup <u>sifted</u> cake flour**
> **1 teaspoon baking powder**
> **½ teaspoon salt**
> **6 eggs, separated**
> **1 cup sugar**
> **1 teaspoon grated lemon rind**

1. Sift flour, baking powder, and salt onto a piece of wax paper.

2. Beat egg whites in a large bowl with electric mixer at high speed, until foamy white and double in volume. Gradually beat in ½ cup of the sugar, until meringue stands in soft peaks.
3. Beat egg yolks in small bowl with electric mixer at high speed, until thick and lemon-colored. Gradually beat in remaining ½ cup sugar until mixture is very thick and fluffy. Beat in lemon rind.
4. Fold flour mixture, one third at a time, into egg yolk mixture with rubber scraper until completely blended.
5. Fold flour-egg yolk mixture into meringue until no streaks of yellow or white remain. Pour into ungreased 9-inch angel cake tube pan.
6. Bake in a slow oven (325°) 1 hour, or until top springs back when lightly pressed with fingertip.
7. Invert pan, placing tube over a funnel or quart-size soft-drink bottle; let cake cool completely. Loosen cake around the tube, and down the side with a spatula. Remove from pan. Sift 10X sugar over top, if you wish, and serve with fruit.

COFFEE CHIFFON CAKE

Light-as-a-cloud chiffon cake topped with a mocha glaze; sure to be a treat for your family and friends.

Bake at 325° for 1 hour and 10 minutes.
Makes one 10-inch tube cake.

2⅓ cups sifted cake flour
1⅓ cups sugar
 3 teaspoons baking powder
 ½ teaspoon salt
 ½ cup vegetable oil
 5 egg yolks
 ¾ cup cold water
 1 tablespoon instant coffee
 1 cup (7 to 8) egg whites
 ½ teaspoon cream of tartar
   Mocha Glaze (recipe page 74)

1. Sift flour, 1 cup of the sugar, baking powder, and salt into a medium-size bowl. Make a well and add, in order: oil, egg yolks, water and coffee; beat with a spoon until smooth.
2. Beat egg whites and cream of tartar in large bowl with electric mixer, until foamy white and double in volume. Gradually beat in remaining ⅓ cup sugar, until meringue stands in firm peaks.
3. Gradually pour egg yolk mixture over beaten whites, gently folding until no streaks of white remain. Spoon into ungreased 10-inch angel cake tube pan.
4. Bake in slow oven (325°) 1 hour and 10 minutes, or until top of cake springs back when lightly pressed with fingertip.

5. Invert pan, placing tube over a funnel or quart-size soft drink bottle; let cake cool completely. When cool, loosen cake around outside edge and tube and down sides with a spatula. Remove from pan. Drizzle MOCHA GLAZE over top of cake, letting it run down the side.

CARIOCA CHOCOLATE ROLL

Coffee cream filling on inside, and a rich chocolate frosting on top—this roll will certainly please lovers of both flavors.

Bake at 375° for 12 minutes.
Makes one 10-inch jelly roll.

 1 cup sifted cake flour
 ¼ cup unsweetened cocoa
 1 teaspoon baking powder
 ¼ teaspoon salt
 3 eggs
 1 cup granulated sugar
 ⅓ cup cold coffee
 1 teaspoon vanilla
   10X (confectioners') sugar
   Coffee Cream Filling (recipe page 73)
   Carioca Chocolate Frosting (recipe page 75)

1. Grease a 15x10x1-inch jelly roll pan; line bottom with wax paper; grease paper.
2. Sift flour, cocoa, baking powder and salt onto a fresh piece of wax paper.
3. Beat eggs in a medium-size bowl with an electric mixer, until thick and creamy. Gradually add sugar, beating constantly until mixture is very thick. Stir in coffee and vanilla. Fold in flour mixture. Spread batter evenly in prepared pan.
4. Bake in a moderate oven (375°) 12 minutes or until center springs back when lightly pressed with fingertip.
5. Loosen cake around edges with a knife; invert pan onto a clean towel dusted with 10X sugar; peel off wax paper. Trim ¼-inch from all 4 sides for easy rolling. Starting at short end, *roll up cake and towel together*. Place, seam side down, on wire rack; cool completely.
6. When cake is cool, unroll carefully.
7. Spread evenly with COFFEE CREAM FILLING. To start rerolling, lift cake with end of towel. Place, seam side down on serving plate.
8. Spread roll evenly with CARIOCA CHOCOLATE FROSTING, or sprinkle with 10X sugar. Refrigerate.

Chocolate Cream Roll: Follow recipe for CARIOCA CHOCOLATE ROLL through Step 6. Spread cooled cake with 1 cup heavy cream, whipped. Reroll; sprinkle with 10X sugar or spread with CHOCOLATE GLAZE (recipe page 74). Refrigerate.

Here's a trio of sugar-sprinkled jelly rolls with luscious fillings inside. Top, left to right: Spicy Prune Roll and Strawberry Roll. Bottom: Chocolate Cream Roll. Recipes in this chapter.

George Nordhausen

Everybody's favorite—Chocolate!
Baked in moist Chocolate-Nut
Upside Down Cake, delicate Burnt
Sugar Cake (recipes in this
chapter), and in Our Best-Ever
Brownies (recipe, Chapter 5);
swirled atop Chocolate Eclairs
(recipe, Chapter 7) and cooled
in Black Bottom Pie
(recipe, Chapter 6).

Cocoa
mix ½ c. fine sugar
with ¼ c. plus 2 tbls.
pure, dark cocoa
... a dash of salt
a bit of ground
cinnamon + add
4 c. fresh milk
a bit at a time....
cook until about to boil

These Happy Birthday cupcakes are made from our Golden Butter Cake and Busy Day Chocolate Cake recipes. They're topped with Vanilla, Strawberry and Chocolate Butter Cream frostings. Recipes, plus suggestions for easy cupcake garnishes, in this chapter.

HOT-MILK SPONGE CAKE

This sponge cake uses fewer eggs than does traditional sponge cake, and relies on milk to provide part of the liquid. Layers add extra versatility.

Bake at 350° for 25 minutes.
Makes two 8-inch layers.

    1 cup sifted cake flour
    1 teaspoon baking powder
    ¼ teaspoon salt
    3 eggs
    1 cup sugar
    ¼ cup hot milk
    1 teaspoon vanilla

1. Grease two 8x1½-inch round layer-cake pans. Dust lightly with flour; tap out excess.
2. Sift flour, baking powder and salt onto a piece of wax paper.
3. Beat eggs in a large bowl with electric mixer at high speed, until thick and fluffy; slowly beat in sugar until mixture is almost double in volume and is very thick. Turn speed to low; beat in hot milk and vanilla. (Finish mixing cake by hand.)
4. Fold in flour mixture, one third at a time, just until blended. Pour into prepared pans.
5. Bake in moderate oven (350°) 25 minutes, or until centers spring back when lightly pressed with fingertip. Cool in pans on wire racks, 10 minutes; loosen carefully around edges with a knife; turn out onto racks; cool completely. Serve with fresh fruit, or well-drained canned fruit, if you wish.

SPICY PRUNE ROLL

A thick, flavorful prune filling rolled up in a moist, rich, golden-brown cake.

Bake at 375° for 12 minutes.
Makes one 10-inch jelly roll.

    ¾ cup sifted cake flour
    1 teaspoon baking powder
    ½ teaspoon ground cinnamon
    ¼ teaspoon salt
    4 eggs
    ¾ cup granulated sugar
    1 teaspoon vanilla
      10X (confectioners') sugar
      Prune Filling (recipe follows)

1. Grease a 15x10x1-inch jelly roll pan; line with wax paper; grease paper.
2. Measure flour, baking powder, cinnamon and salt into a sifter.
3. Beat eggs in a medium-size bowl until foamy; gradually beat in granulated sugar until mixture is very thick and light. *(This step is very important!)* Stir in vanilla.
4. Sift dry ingredients over egg mixture; gently fold in until no streaks of flour remain. Spread batter evenly in prepared pan.
5. Bake in a moderate oven (375°) 12 minutes, or until center springs back when lightly pressed with fingertip.
6. Loosen cake around edges, with a knife; invert pan onto clean towel dusted with 10X sugar; peel off wax paper. Trim ¼-inch from all 4 sides for easy rolling. Starting at short end, *roll up cake and towel together*. Place, seam side down, on wire rack. Cool completely.
7. When cake is cool, unroll carefully. Spread with PRUNE FILLING. To start rerolling, lift end of cake with towel. Place roll, seam side down, on serving plate. Sprinkle with 10X sugar.

Prune Filling: Makes about 1⅔ cups.

    2 cups pitted prunes
    1 cup water
    2 tablespoons sugar
    1 tablespoon lemon juice
    ½ teaspoon ground cinnamon

1. Combine prunes with water in a small saucepan; simmer, covered, 25 minutes.
2. Purée prune with remaining cooking liquid, part at a time, in blender (or press through sieve).
3. Stir in sugar, lemon juice and cinnamon. Chill.

PINEAPPLE SPONGE ROLL

This jelly roll has a sunny fruit filling already baked in the pan.

Bake at 375° for 12 minutes.
Makes one 10-inch jelly roll.

    ¼ cup (½ stick) butter or margarine
    ¾ cup firmly packed light brown sugar
    1 can (about 14 ounces) crushed pineapple, well-drained
    1 cup sifted cake flour
    1 teaspoon baking powder
    ¼ teaspoon salt
    3 eggs
    1 cup granulated sugar
    ¼ cup water
    1 teaspoon vanilla
      10X (confectioners') sugar
      Whipped cream

1. Melt butter or margarine in a small saucepan; stir in brown sugar and pineapple. Spread evenly in a 15x10x1-inch jelly roll pan.

2. Sift flour, baking powder, and salt onto a piece of wax paper.

3. Beat eggs in a medium-size bowl, until foamy; slowly beat in granulated sugar until mixture is thick and fluffy. Stir in water and vanilla.

4. Fold in flour mixture until no streaks of white remain. Spread over pineapple mixture in pan.

5. Bake in moderate oven (375°) 12 minutes, or until center of cake springs back when lightly pressed with fingertip.

6. Cool cake in pan on a wire rack several minutes, then loosen around edges with a knife; invert onto a towel sprinkled with 10X sugar. Starting at one end, roll up, jelly roll fashion; cool. Cut in slices; serve warm or cold with whipped cream.

Basic Recipe

JELLY ROLL

There are as many variations of jelly rolls as there are fillings and frostings. First, you might wish to try the variations we suggest—then why not experiment on your own.

Bake 375° for 12 minutes.
Makes one 10-inch jelly roll.

- 1 cup <u>sifted</u> cake flour
- 1 teaspoon baking powder
- ¼ teaspoon salt
- 3 eggs
- ¾ cup granulated sugar
- ⅓ cup water
- 1 teaspoon vanilla
- 10X (confectioners') sugar
- ¾ cup raspberry, strawberry or currant jelly

1. Grease a 15x10x1-inch jelly roll pan; line bottom with wax paper; grease paper.

2. Sift flour, baking powder and salt onto a fresh piece of wax paper.

3. Beat eggs in a medium-size bowl, with an electric mixer, until thick and creamy. Gradually add sugar, beating constantly, until mixture is very thick. Stir in water and vanilla. Fold in flour mixture. Spread batter evenly in prepared pan.

4. Bake in a moderate oven (375°) 12 minutes or until center of cake springs back when lightly pressed with fingertip.

5. Loosen cake around edges with a knife; invert pan onto clean towel dusted with 10X sugar; peel off wax paper. Trim ¼-inch from all 4 sides for easy rolling. Starting at short end, *roll up cake and towel together.* Place roll, seam side down, on wire rack; cool completely. When cool, unroll carefully.

6. Spread evenly with jelly. To start rerolling, lift end of cake with towel. Place roll, seam side down on serving plate. Sprinkle with 10X sugar.

Strawberry Roll: Follow recipe for JELLY ROLL through Step 5. Spread cake with 1 cup heavy cream, whipped, and 1 cup sliced strawberries. Reroll; refrigerate. Decorate with additional strawberries and whipped cream, if you wish.

Lemon Roll: Follow recipe for JELLY ROLL through Step 5. Spread cake with cooled LEMON FILLING (recipe page 74). Reroll; refrigerate.

SPECIAL TIP: Here's an easy way to cut jelly roll slices: Slip a piece of sewing thread, about 18 inches long, under the roll. Crisscross the string on top of the jelly roll; pull quickly and evenly, to cut. Repeat for each slice.

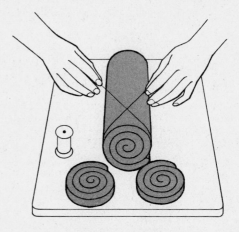

FRUIT AND SPICE CAKES

RIBBON SPICE CAKE

Brown sugar frosting provides the perfect finish to this golden brown spice cake.

Bake at 350° for 35 minutes.
Make one 9-inch triple-layer cake.

- 3½ cups <u>sifted</u> cake flour
- 3 teaspoons baking powder
- 1 teaspoon salt
- 1 cup (2 sticks) butter or margarine, softened
- 2½ cups sugar
- 4 eggs
- 1 cup milk
- 1 teaspoon vanilla
- 3 tablespoons molasses
- ¾ teaspoon ground cinnamon
- ¼ teaspoon ground cloves
- Fluffy Brown Sugar Frosting (recipe page 75)

1. Grease three 9x1½-inch round layer-cake pans. Dust lightly with flour; tap out excess.

2. Sift flour, baking powder, and salt onto a piece of wax paper.

3. Beat butter or margarine, sugar and eggs in a large bowl with electric mixer at high speed, 3 minutes. (Finish mixing cake by hand.)

4. Stir in flour mixture alternately with milk and vanilla, beating after each addition, until smooth.

5. Pour one third of batter into each of two prepared pans. Stir molasses, cinnamon and cloves into remaining batter; pour into third prepared pan.

6. Bake in moderate oven (350°) 35 minutes, or until centers of layers spring back when lightly pressed with fingertip.

7. Cool layers in pans on wire racks 10 minutes; loosen around edges with knife; turn out onto wire racks; cool completely.

8. Put layers together with FLUFFY BROWN SUGAR FROSTING; frost side and top of the cake with remaining frosting.

SPECIAL TIP: Fruitcakes mellow and improve with time. If you want to make your cake ahead, and keep it for the holidays, here's how: Sprinkle cake with brandy or rum, if you wish. Wrap cake securely in heavy foil. Cakes may be kept at room temperature at least one week; in the refrigerator one month; or in the freezer, three months. Glaze and garnish cake the day you wish to use it.

PLANTATION FRUIT CAKE

Golden peaches are an unusual and pleasing ingredient in this very dark fruitcake. See the Special Tip above, for the easiest way to prepare and store fruitcakes for holiday giving, or for your own family to enjoy—whenever you want to serve it.

Bake at 300° for 2 hours.
Makes one 10-inch bundt or 9-inch tube cake.

    2 cups seedless raisins
    1 can (1 pound) cling peaches, drained and chopped
    1 cup vegetable shortening
    1 cup firmly packed brown sugar
    ½ cup cream sherry or orange juice
    1 jar (1 pound) mixed candied fruits
    2 cups walnuts, chopped
    4 eggs, beaten
    2½ cups sifted all-purpose flour
    1 teaspoon baking powder
    1½ teaspoons salt
    1 teaspoon ground cinnamon
    ½ teaspoon ground cloves

1. Grease a 10-inch bundt or 9-inch angel cake tube pan. Dust with flour; tap out excess.

2. Combine raisins, peaches, shortening, brown sugar and sherry or orange juice in a medium-size saucepan; heat just to boiling. Cool.

3. Add candied fruits and nuts to cooled mixture; stir in beaten eggs.

4. Sift flour, baking powder, salt, cinnamon and cloves together on wax paper; stir into fruit mixture. Turn into prepared pan.

5. Bake in a slow oven (300°) 2 hours, or until center springs back when lightly pressed with fingertip. Cool in pan on wire rack 15 minutes; turn out onto wire rack; cool completely. Decorate with marzipan, candied fruits, or nuts, if you wish.

AUNT SAL'S CARROT CAKE

Every once in a while, we come across a slightly different version of what more and more seems to be an American original—Carrot Cake. This recipe makes a particularly big cake that is moist and spicy, and keeps very well. It's equally good sliced for dessert, or thin-sliced and buttered as a snack for those hungry after-school hours.

Bake at 350° for 1 hour and 15 minutes.
Makes one 10-inch tube cake.

    4 eggs
    1½ cups sugar
    1½ cups vegetable oil
    3¼ cups whole wheat flour
    2 teaspoons baking powder
    2 teaspoons baking soda
    ½ teaspoon salt
    1 teaspoon ground cinnamon
    1 can (8 ounces) juice-packed crushed pineapple, drained
    2 cups finely grated carrots (about 1 pound)
    1 cup chopped pecans
    1 cup chopped dates

1. Grease a 10-inch angel cake tube pan; line bottom of the pan with wax paper.

2. Beat eggs in a large mixing bowl. Gradually beat in the 1½ cups sugar. Stir in oil.

3. Combine the whole wheat flour with the baking powder, baking soda, salt and cinnamon on wax paper. Stir into egg mixture. Add drained pineapple and grated carrots; mix well.

4. Stir in chopped pecans and dates. Turn mixture into the prepared angel cake tube pan.

5. Bake in a moderate oven (350°) 1 hour and 15 minutes, or until top springs back when lightly pressed with fingertip.

6. Cool cake in pan on wire rack about 15 minutes. Remove cake from pan; peel off wax paper. Cool completely before cutting. Wrap tightly in foil or plastic wrap to store.

APPLESAUCE CAKE

Here's a fragrant, spicy cake with raisins and nuts inside; delicious plain or with ice cream.

Bake at 350° for 40 minutes.
Makes one 13x9x2-inch cake.

    3 cups <u>sifted</u> cake flour
 1½ cups sugar
 1½ teaspoons baking soda
    ½ teaspoon salt
    ½ teaspoon ground cinnamon
    ¼ teaspoon ground allspice
    ¼ teaspoon ground cloves
    ¾ cup vegetable shortening
 1½ cups applesauce
    2 eggs
    1 teaspoon vanilla
    1 cup seedless raisins, chopped
    ½ cup walnuts, chopped

1. Grease a 13x9x2-inch baking pan. Dust lightly with flour; tap out excess.
2. Sift flour, sugar, baking soda, salt, cinnamon, allspice, and cloves into a large bowl. Add shortening and applesauce. Beat with electric mixer at medium speed, 2 minutes. Add eggs and vanilla. Beat at medium speed, 1 minute.
3. Stir in raisins and nuts until well blended; pour into prepared pan.
4. Bake in moderate oven (350°) 40 minutes, or until center springs back when lightly pressed with fingertip.
5. Cool cake in pan on wire rack 10 minutes; loosen around edges with a knife; turn out onto wire rack; cool completely.
6. Cut into squares and serve with whipped cream or ice cream, if you wish.

DIAMOND HEAD FRUITCAKE

Tropical fruits and nuts combine to make a lush golden fruitcake for the holidays and throughout the rest of the year.

Bake at 275° for 1 hour and 15 minutes.
Makes one 9x5x3-inch loaf.

    3 jars (4 ounces each) candied pineapple, chopped
    3 jars (4 ounces each) candied orange peel, chopped
    1 can (3½ ounces) flaked coconut
 1½ cup golden raisins
    1 cup pecans or macadamia nuts, chopped
 2½ cups <u>sifted</u> cake flour
    1 teaspoon baking powder

    ½ teaspoon salt
    ½ cup (1 stick) butter or margarine
    1 cup sugar
    4 eggs
    ½ cup pineapple juice
      Red and green candied cherries
      Pecan halves

1. Grease a 9x5x3-inch loaf pan. Dust lightly with flour; tap out excess.
2. Combine fruit and nuts in a large bowl.
3. Sift flour, baking powder and salt onto wax paper.
4. Beat butter or margarine, sugar and eggs in large bowl with electric mixer at high speed, 3 minutes, or until light and fluffy.
5. Stir in flour mixture alternately with pineapple juice, beating after each addition, until the batter is quite smooth.
6. Pour batter over fruits and nuts and fold just until blended. Spoon batter into prepared pan.
7. Bake in a very slow oven (275°) 1 hour and 15 minutes, or until center springs back when lightly pressed with fingertip.
8. Cool cake in pan or wire rack 15 minutes; loosen around edges with a knife; turn out onto a wire rack; cool completely.
9. Decorate with candied fruits and nuts.

DUNDEE CAKE

A traditional light fruit-filled cake. The cake slices thinly and neatly for serving at Christmas or other festive gatherings.

Bake at 325° for 1 hour and 45 minutes.
Makes one 10-inch tube cake.

    1 package (15 ounces) raisins
    1 package (11 ounces) currants
    1 jar (4 ounces) candied mixed fruits
    4 cups <u>sifted</u> all-purpose flour
    2 teaspoons baking powder
    1 teaspoon salt
    1 teaspoon ground cinnamon
    ¼ teaspoon ground nutmeg
 1½ cups (3 sticks) butter or margarine
 1½ cups sugar
    6 eggs
    6 tablespoons brandy or orange juice
    1 tablespoon grated lemon rind
    2 tablespoons lemon juice
      Whole blanched almonds

1. Grease a 10-inch angel cake tube pan. Dust lightly with flour; tap out excess.
2. Combine raisins, currants and mixed fruit in a large bowl.

3. Sift flour, baking powder, salt, cinnamon and nutmeg onto wax paper.

4. Beat butter or margarine, sugar and eggs in a large bowl with electric mixer at high speed, 3 minutes, or until light and fluffy.

5. Stir in flour mixture alternately with the brandy, lemon rind and juice, beating well until batter is smooth. Add fruit; stir just until well blended. Spoon batter into prepared pan. Arrange almonds in a pattern on top.

6. Bake in a slow oven (325°) 1 hour and 45 minutes, or until a wooden pick inserted near center comes out clean.

7. Cool cake in pan on wire rack 15 minutes. Loosen around edges with a knife; turn out onto wire rack; cool completely.

FROSTINGS AND FILLINGS

SPECIAL TIPS: You can choose any frosting you wish, for almost any double-layer cake! Here's how to tell the difference between the basic frostings:
• Butter Cream: Uncooked frosting made with butter, 10X (confectioners') sugar, flavoring, and a little bit of liquid; *smooth* consistency.
• 7-Minute (Double-Boiler): Cooked frosting, made with egg whites, corn syrup and water, beaten at high speed; *fluffy* consistency.
• Mountain Cream: Also cooked; similar consistency to 7-Minute, but a bit heavier. Can be used interchangeably with 7-Minute frosting.
• Royal: Hardened by an acid, such as lemon juice; almost always used for decorating. Not cooked.

Basic Recipe

VANILLA BUTTER CREAM FROSTING

Makes enough to fill and frost two 8- or 9-inch cake layers.

    ½ cup (1 stick) butter or margarine
    1 package (1 pound) 10X (confectioners') sugar
    4 tablespoons milk
    2 teaspoons vanilla

Beat butter or margarine in a medium-size bowl with electric mixer, until soft. Beat in 10X sugar alternately with milk and vanilla, until smooth and spreadable.

Lemon Butter Cream Frosting: Follow Basic Recipe but: Omit vanilla, add ½ teaspoon grated lemon rind and substitute 3 tablespoons lemon juice for 3 tablespoons of the milk.

Rum Butter Cream Frosting: Follow Basic Recipe but: Substitute 1½ teaspoons rum extract for vanilla, or 2 tablespoons rum for 2 tablespoons of the milk, and omit vanilla.

Rich Orange Butter Cream Frosting: Follow Basic Recipe but: Omit vanilla. Beat 1 egg yolk with the butter. Add 2 teaspoons grated orange rind and substitute orange juice for the milk.

Strawberry Butter Cream Frosting: Follow Basic Recipe but: Omit vanilla and milk. Mash enough fresh, washed and hulled strawberries to measure ⅓ cup. Add mashed strawberries and 10X sugar alternately with butter.

SPECIAL TIP: There's no reason why you can't use frostings or glazes for different size cakes. Here's how to tell if you'll have enough: If a frosting recipe makes enough for two 8- or 9-inch layers, you'll have enough to frost any 13x9x2-inch cake, or between 24 and 36 cupcakes, depending on their size.
• To help lend a more professional look to your cake decorating, cut triangles of wax paper and arrange them, overlapping, to form a circle on the serving plate. Place bottom layer on top of circle. When you've finished frosting the cake, pull pieces of wax paper out, one at a time. You'll be left with a spotless plate.
• Frosting will be much easier if you occasionally dip your spatula in warm water. The water also adds a nice, glossy look to the frosting, and swirls are easier to make.
• For an easy way to frost cupcakes, twirl the top of each in a bowl of fluffy-type frosting (7-Minute or Mountain Cream). You'll get pretty swirls, in only a couple of seconds.
• Here's a super-quick way to frost cupcakes: Place a piece of milk chocolate, or semisweet chocolate, on the top of each warm cupcake; spread with a knife or spatula, as chocolate melts.

COFFEE CREAM FILLING

Makes about 2 cups; enough for one 15x10x1-inch jelly roll; or for any two 8- or 9-inch cake layers, split in half, to make a torte.

    1 cup heavy cream
    1 tablespoon instant coffee
    ½ cup sifted 10X (confectioners') sugar

1. Combine cream, instant coffee and 10X sugar in a medium-size bowl.
2. Beat ingredients with electric mixer, until stiff. Chill until ready to use.

WHITE MOUNTAIN CREAM FROSTING

Make enough to fill and frost two 8- or 9-inch cake layers.

   1 cup granulated sugar
   ⅓ cup light corn syrup
   ¼ cup water
   ¼ teaspoon salt
   4 egg whites
   ⅛ teaspoon cream of tartar
   ½ teaspoon vanilla

1. Combine sugar, corn syrup, water, and salt in a small saucepan; cover. Heat to boiling; uncover; boil gently, until mixture registers 242° on a candy thermometer, or until a small amount of the hot syrup falls, thread-like, from spoon.
2. While syrup cooks, beat egg whites with cream of tartar in a large bowl until stiff peaks form when beaters are removed. Pour hot syrup onto egg whites in a very thin stream, beating all the time at high speed, until frosting is stiff and glossy. Beat in the ½ teaspoon vanilla.

Pink Mountain Cream Frosting: Follow Basic Recipe for WHITE MOUNTAIN CREAM FROSTING, using ¼ cup maraschino cherry liquid in place of water; add a few drops red food coloring together with the ½ teaspoon vanilla to tint frosting a delicate pink. Add more red food coloring if you prefer a deeper shade.

LEMON FILLING

Makes 1½ cups: enough to fill one 8-inch torte, one 8-inch triple-layer cake, or one 15x10x1-inch jelly roll.

   ⅔ cup granulated sugar
   3 tablespoons cornstarch
   ⅔ cup water
   2 egg yolks, slightly beaten
   1 tablespoon butter or margarine
   2 teaspoons grated lemon rind
   ¼ cup lemon juice

1. Combine sugar and cornstarch in small saucepan. Stir in water.
2. Cook, stirring constantly, until mixture thickens and bubbles, 1 minute. Remove from heat.
3. Beat half the hot sugar-cornstarch mixture into beaten egg yolks; stir back into saucepan. Cook 1 minute longer.
4. Stir in butter, lemon rind and juice. Place piece of plastic wrap directly on filling to prevent skin from forming. Chill until ready to use.

SUGAR ICING

Makes ½ cup; enough to drizzle over a 10-inch tube or 9-inch bundt cake, or over 3 dozen bar cookies or 8-dozen 1-inch cookies.

   1 cup 10X (confectioners') sugar
   2 tablespoons milk
   ½ teaspoon vanilla

Blend sugar, milk and vanilla in a small bowl until very smooth.

Lemon Glaze: Follow Basic Recipe substituting 1 tablespoon lemon juice for 1 tablespoon milk.

Rum Glaze: Follow Basic Recipe substituting 2 tablespoons rum for the milk.

CHOCOLATE GLAZE

Makes about 1 cup; enough for one 13x9x2-inch cake, or 6 dozen bar cookies.

   2 squares unsweetened chocolate
   3 tablespoons butter or margarine
   2 cups sifted 10X (confectioners') sugar
   ¼ cup boiling water

1. Melt butter or margarine and chocolate over low heat in a small saucepan. Cool.
2. Combine chocolate mixture with 10X sugar and boiling water in a medium-size bowl. Beat with wire whisk or rotary beater until smooth. (Mixture will be thin, but will thicken upon standing.) Spread, while still warm, on cooled cake.

MOCHA GLAZE

Makes ½ cup; enough glaze to drizzle over one 10-inch tube cake, or over 3 dozen bar cookies, or 8 dozen 1-inch cookies.

   2 tablespoons butter or margarine
   2 squares unsweetened chocolate
   1 teaspoon instant coffee
   ⅛ teaspoon ground cinnamon
   1 cup sifted 10X (confectioners') sugar
   2 tablespoons hot water

1. Melt butter or margarine with chocolate in a small, heavy saucepan over very low heat; stir until blended.
2. Remove from heat; gradually stir in the coffee and cinnamon.
3. Add sugar alternately with hot water, beating until smooth.

CHOCOLATE BUTTER CREAM FROSTING

Makes enough to fill and frost two 8- or 9-inch cake layers.

4 squares unsweetened chocolate
½ cup (1 stick) butter or margarine
½ cup milk
1 package (1 pound) 10X (confectioners') sugar
2 teaspoons vanilla

1. Melt chocolate and butter or margarine in a small saucepan over low heat.
2. Stir milk into sugar in a large bowl until smooth. Stir in chocolate-butter mixture and vanilla. Beat with wooden spoon until mixture is thick and spreadable. To hasten thickening, put bowl in pan of ice and water while stirring, or refrigerate frosting until it begins to thicken.

CARIOCA CHOCOLATE FROSTING

Makes about 1½ cups; enough to cover one 10-inch jelly roll; or one 8- or 9-inch round or square cake layer.

¼ cup (½ stick) butter or margarine
2 squares unsweetened chocolate
2 cups sifted 10X (confectioners') sugar
1 teaspoon instant coffee
¼ cup milk

1. Melt chocolate and butter or margarine in a small, heavy saucepan over very low heat.
2. Combine 10X sugar, instant coffee and milk in a medium-size bowl. Slowly beat in chocolate mixture until frosting is smooth and spreadable.

BURNT SUGAR FROSTING

Makes enough to frost three 8-inch layers or two 9-inch layers.

¾ cup granulated sugar
¾ cup boiling water
1 cup (2 sticks) butter or margarine
2 egg yolks
1 package (1 pound) 10X (confectioners') sugar

1. Spread granulated sugar in a large heavy skillet; heat very slowly until sugar melts and starts to turn a deep golden color; add water slowly; stirring constantly. Continue heating, until melted sugar dissolves completely in water. Boil syrup rapidly, (there should be about ¾ cup). Cool completely.

2. Beat butter or margarine in a medium-size bowl until smooth; add yolks; blend well.
3. Reserve 2 tablespoons of the cooled syrup for decorating cake; add remaining syrup alternately with 10X sugar to butter mixture; beat until smooth and spreadable.

ROYAL FROSTING (For Decorating)

Makes about 2½ cups.

3 egg whites
½ teaspoon cream of tartar
1 package (1 pound) sifted 10X (confectioners') sugar

1. Beat egg whites and cream of tartar in a small bowl, until foamy.
2. Slowly beat in 10X sugar until frosting stands in firm peaks and is stiff enough to hold a sharp line when cut through with a knife. (Keep bowl of frosting covered with damp paper toweling while working, to keep frosting from drying out. Store any leftover frosting in a tightly covered jar in the refrigerator for another day's baking.)

Note: For ½ recipe, use two egg whites, ½ teaspoon cream of tartar and 3 cups *sifted* 10X sugar.

Basic Recipe

FLUFFY 7-MINUTE FROSTING
(Double-Boiler Frosting)

Makes enough to fill and frost two 8- or 9-inch cake layers.

1½ cups granulated sugar
¼ cup water
2 egg whites
2 tablespoons light corn syrup
¼ teaspoon salt
1 teaspoon vanilla

1. Combine sugar, water, egg whites, corn syrup and salt in top of double boiler; beat mixture until well blended.
2. Place over simmering water; cook, beating constantly, at high speed with an electric hand mixer or rotary beater, about 7 minutes, or until mixture triples in volume and holds firm peaks. Remove from heat; beat in vanilla. Spread, while still warm, on cooled cake.

Fluffy Brown Sugar Frosting: Follow Basic Recipe, substituting 1½ cups firmly packed light brown sugar for the granulated sugar.

SIMPLE GARNISHES

How to Make a "Cooky-Fruit" Tree

To make our "cooky-fruit" tree, shown on page 89, prepare CHRISTMAS SUGAR COOKIES. Make cooky cutters, using the fruit-shaped cooky cutter patterns on page 85. (The "orange" is made with a plain 2-inch round cutter.) If cookies are to be hung from a tree, cut a small hole at the top of dough with a drinking straw, for easy threading of ribbon or yarn. Make three disposable wax paper decorating bags (see page 13.)

To decorate, prepare ROYAL FROSTING (recipe page 75). Divide frosting into small custard cups; color red, yellow and green. Spread "apples" with red frosting; sprinkle one half with red sugar, while frosting is still wet. When frosting is dry, pipe green frosting through a paper cone to make a leaf. For "'cherries", spread two large circles with red frosting; sprinkle with red sugar; pipe green frosting through a wax paper cone to make stems and a leaf. Spread "lemons" with yellow frosting, sprinkle with yellow sugar; pipe a little green frosting on one end. Spread "oranges" with yellow frosting, sprinkle heavily with orange sugar, let dry; then pipe yellow frosting on top of sugar, spoke fashion, to resemble a cut orange; also pipe yellow frosting around edge. Mix a little yellow food coloring to green frosting to make a light green; spread on "pear" shapes. Spread a little red frosting on one side for a "blush". Pipe light green (or purple) frosting in small circles on "grape" shapes; pipe yellow or green bow or leaves at top. When frosting is dry, hang "cooky-fruits" on Christmas tree with red or green ribbons, or pieces of colored yarn.

MARZIPAN MUSHROOMS

These sweet, pretty mushrooms are made of almond paste and 10X sugar. From the same recipe, you can also make little green leaves.

Make 8 to 10 mushrooms with leaves.

½ **can (4 ounces) almond paste**
½ **cup 10X (confectioners') sugar**
1 **tablespoon light corn syrup**
 Green food coloring
 Cocoa

1. Break almond paste into smaller pieces, gradually knead in sugar and corn syrup.
2. Tint ⅓ of the marzipan a light green by kneading in a few drops of green food coloring. Roll out on a surface lightly dusted with 10X sugar; cut into leaf shapes with a cooky cutter.

3. Make 8 to 10 small balls of different sizes from remaining marzipan; flatten on side to shape "mushroom caps"; brush flat underside with cocoa. Make stems by rolling small balls of marzipan into cylindrical shapes. Attach stems to caps with drop of water or corn syrup.

Note: MARZIPAN MUSHROOMS are particularly attractive on top of cakes frosted with chocolate frosting.

Other Garnishes You Can Make:

See page 78 for directions, plus how-to drawings, for such beautiful garnishes as lemon roses, strawberry rosettes and chocolate curls. The following are still more simple-to-make garnishes, to give your cakes, cupcakes and pies a picture-perfect look!

Candied Orange Peel: Remove rind from 1 large orange, with a vegetable parer; cut into match-like strips. Simmer in water 5 minutes; drain. Combine ½ cup sugar with 3 tablespoons water in a small saucepan; bring to a boil, stirring constantly until sugar is melted. Boil 2 minutes; add orange rind; continue cooking 5 minutes. Cool completely. Drain when ready to use.

Toasted Coconut: Bake regular flaked coconut in a small cake pan or on a cooky sheet, in a moderate oven (350°) about 5 minutes. Be sure to watch, and shake it occasionally—otherwise coconut may burn. You'll need ¼ cup to decorate a 9-inch pie; 1 cup to cover the side and top of a 9-inch double-layer cake.

Chocolate Shavings: Prepare chocolate as for Chocolate Curls; use a vegetable parer to shave off small bits. In a pinch, for both chocolate curls and chocolate shavings, warm, but do not melt, a bar of milk chocolate. Make curls or shavings as directed.

Large Frosting Blossoms: Force frosting through star disc of your cooky press. Form round balls of frosting for centers of blossoms. Hollow centers with end of wooden spoon, or with your finger.

Glazed Fruit Slices: Brush fruit with melted apple jelly for a sweet, glossy coating. To keep banana slices white, dip in orange or pineapple juice before placing on pie or cake.

Sliced Nuts: Any nuts are attractive when placed on swirled frosting. To make slicing easier, warm nuts first.

Cupcake Garnishes: Arrange any of the following in patterns on top of cupcakes—semisweet chocolate pieces, jelly beans, gumdrops, sprinkles, candy corn, shoestring licorice, chopped nuts, or cinnamon heart candies. (Or why not let the kids decorate the cupcakes, themselves!)

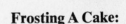

Splitting Layers:

To split any cake (butter or foam) into layers, measure vertically with a ruler; mark cake all around with wooden picks. Slice across tops of picks, using a long, serrated knife, cutting with a sawing motion.

Frosting A Cake:

1. Slice off any "hump" from each layer, with a sharp knife; place one layer upside-down on serving plate, so flat surface faces up; brush off crumbs.
2. Spread frosting on flat surface to the edge.
3. Place flat sides of layers together (anchoring with long metal skewers, if necessary, to prevent layers from sliding around). If using Butter Cream Frosting, spread a thin layer over entire assembled cake; let stand about 15 minutes.
4. Frost sides of cake, then top, swirling frosting with spatula. (Remove skewers; smooth frosting).
Note: For additional frosting tips, see page 000.

Cake Decorating—Easy and Elegant:

Plaid Design: Pull a table fork across the top of the cake at equally-spaced intervals. Turn cake one-quarter turn; repeat.

Feather Top: Drizzle melted chocolate (2 squares melted with ½ teaspoon shortening) across frosting, in thick lines about 1 inch apart. Draw edge of spatula at right angles to chocolate lines, to connect.

Shadow Design: Drizzle glaze or melted chocolate (prepared as for feather pattern) around edge of cake, with the tip of a teaspoon; let glaze or chocolate drip down side.

Candle Highlight: Pipe tinted frosting in "spokes" from center of cake. (You may wish to vary the lengths of the spokes, particularly if there are many candles going on the cake.) Place candle holders with candles at ends of spokes.

Sugar Snowflake: Place paper doily on top of cake. Sift 10X (confectioners') sugar over doily. Lift doily off, leaving snowflake design on cake. Important: Be sure cake is completely cooled before sprinkling with sugar; otherwise sugar may turn gray.

For Special Occasions

One of the nicest things about baking is that you can always add a personal touch to almost anything you make, with a simple, but pretty glaze, an attractive garnish, or an elaborate design. For special occasions, however, when you want something super-spectacular, create something entirely new! Combine shapes, try different and imaginative decorations; create a cake that says "Congratulations", "Happy Birthday" or simply "I Love You" in a most personal way. Here are some great ways to make cakes special, plus some of our favorite "Special Occasion" cakes.

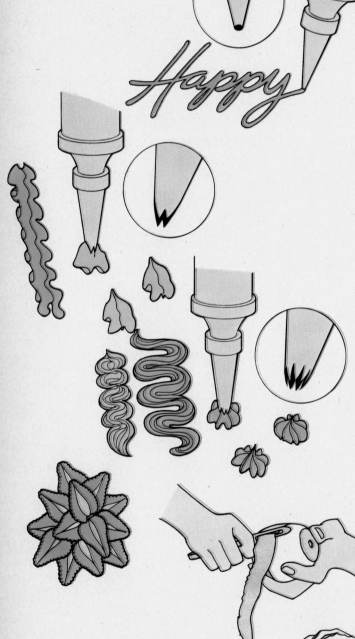

Writing Tip: For making letters, numerals, lattice designs and decorative borders.

Leaf Tip: To make small, delicate leaves, press a small amount of frosting through the tip, lifting quickly to make the point of the leaf. Make an overlapping ruffle by pressing frosting back and forth, in a line.

Notched Tip: To make small rosettes, press a bit of frosting through vertically-held decorating tube (or pastry bag) fitted with notched tip. Lift quickly. Also, use this tip to make more elaborate edgings.

Strawberry Rosette: Slice strawberries lengthwise; then outline a circle in center of cake or pie with some of the largest slices, points facing out. Continue making circles, overlapping the slices, toward the center; use smallest slices last. Finish with two half-slices, or a whole berry, if you wish.

Lemon Rose: Peel half a lemon in a continuous spiral, from one end to the widest part (using a slightly sawing motion, as you slice, to get a more natural "petal" effect). Take care to peel the yellow "zest" and only a tiny bit of the white. Form rose by rewinding the lemon peel—tightly in the center and slightly looser outside. Place finished rose on whipped cream or frosting, to hold it securely in place.

Chocolate Curls: To make enough to decorate a 9-inch double-layer cake: Melt 7 squares semisweet chocolate in a small bowl over hot water, stirring often. Turn out onto cold cooky sheet. Spread out to a 6x4-inch rectangle. Refrigerate just until set. Pull a long metal spatula across chocolate, letting the soft chocolate curl up in front of the spatula. Place curls on wax paper.

Valentine Cake: Prepare an 8-inch round and an 8-inch square cake layer. (They can be 9-inch layers, if you'd prefer; just make sure they're *both* 9 inches.) Cut round layer in half. To make heart, place halves on two adjacent sides of square cake, as shown. Decorate with pink frosting. Use a cake decorating set, or pastry bag fitted with a writing tip, or a disposable wax paper bag, to write a personal message on your cake.

Butterfly Cake: Cut an unfrosted 9-inch round cake layer, as indicated above. (The center diamond should be about 2 inches, from top to bottom.) Place narrow center strips end to end, in center of serving plate, to form "body"; place notched half-circles back to back, on either side of "body" to form "wings". Frost cake. (Light orange or yellow frosting will highlight decorations nicely.) Use 2-inch strips of black shoestring licorice to make "antennae". Decorate butterfly simply, with additional licorice, or make a more elaborate design, using brightly tinted frostings or different colored sugars.

(*Note:* For a double-layer butterfly, cut two unfrosted layers, as indicated. Spread frosting between layers; assemble; frost entire butterfly and decorate as above.)

Petal Cake: Bake any two 8- or 9-inch cake layers. Prepare any frosting recipe that makes enough for an 8- or 9-inch double-layer cake. (You may use whipped cream, instead, if you wish.) Place a small amount of frosting on the tip of a spatula. Starting at the bottom of the assembled cake, make small petals by pressing the spatula against the cake, drawing spatula up. Make a row around the cake; continue making overlapping rows, up the side. Make petals on top, starting from the outside. Garnish with a lemon rose, strawberry rosette or fresh flower in the center.

Meadow Flowers Wedding Cake: See Chapter 7 for the recipe for this simple, but lovely cake. Tint reserved frosting to match flowers. For example, make an orange lattice and place yellow and orange pompoms or small chrysanthemums on the top tier, cascading down to the bottom tier, as shown. Or make a yellow lattice and place fresh daisies on the cake. Other possibilities: chocolate lattice with Brown-eyed Susans; pink frosting and lattice with Sweetheart Roses; red lattice with poppies, Baby's Breath and blue Bachelor's Buttons.

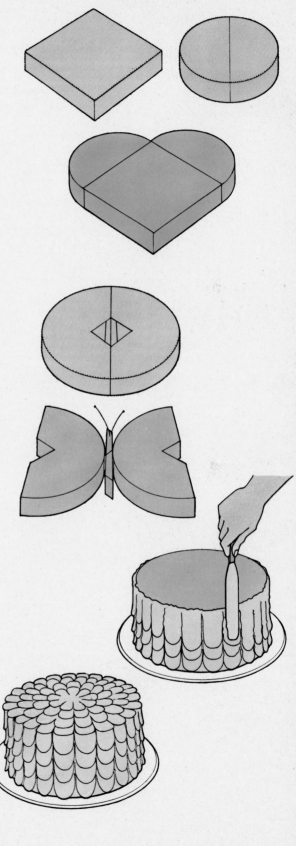

Chocolate Chip Cookies with an extra special crunch—chopped walnuts. Recipe in this chapter.

5

COOKIES

Bake a batch of the best cookies ever! Choose crisp, crunchy drop cookies, chewy bar cookies or pretty rolled or molded and pressed cookies. They're all in this chapter—along with an extra bonus for you—a baker's dozen of easy-to-trace cooky cutter patterns!

SPECIAL TIPS: No matter what type of cookies you plan to bake, always place cooky sheets in the *upper third* of the oven, to prevent the bottoms from baking too much.

• For best results, cookies should be baked one sheet at a time, on *cool* cooky sheets, so dough won't lose its shape. If you don't have two cooky sheets to use alternately, use an upside-down jelly roll pan. Another time-saver: Shape cookies on a piece of aluminum foil the size of the cooky sheet; when baked cookies come out of the oven, slide them off, and slide foil sheet of cookies onto cooky sheet.

• Always grease cooky sheets with solid vegetable shortening—*not* vegetable oil. The sheet will be much easier to clean.

• If your cooky sheet has become badly discolored, here's how to make it sparkle like new: Use spray or brush-on oven cleaner, just as you would in your oven; let it stand for the suggested amount of time. Rinse the sheet, using paper towels; then use a soap-filled steel wool pad to bring back the shine.

DROP COOKIES

NOEL WREATHS

Round cookies with a maple-walnut center. Candied cherries add the Christmas touch.

Bake at 350° for 12 minutes.
Makes 6 dozen cookies.

  1 cup (2 sticks) butter or margarine
½ cup sugar
  1 egg
  1 teaspoon vanilla
2½ cups sifted all-purpose flour
1⅓ cups walnuts, finely chopped
¼ cup maple syrup
    Red and green candied cherries

1. Beat butter or margarine with sugar in a large bowl until light and fluffy. Beat in egg and vanilla. Stir in flour, one third at a time, blending well to make a soft dough.
2. Measure out ⅓ cup of the dough and mix with walnuts and maple syrup in a small bowl; reserve for cooky centers in Step 3.
3. Fit a pastry bag with a small star tip; fill bag with remaining dough. Press out into 1½-inch rings on ungreased large cooky sheets, fill center of each cooky with about a teaspoonful of nut mixture.
4. Bake in moderate oven (350°) 12 minutes, or until lightly golden at edges. Remove carefully from cooky sheets to wire racks; cool completely. Decorate with sliced red and green candied cherries.

CHOCOLATE CHIP COOKIES

Chopped nuts, baked inside, make these favorite cookies extra special.

Bake at 350° for 8 minutes.
Makes 3½ dozen cookies.

1¾ cups sifted all-purpose flour
 ½ teaspoon baking soda
 ¼ teaspoon salt
 ¾ cup (1½ sticks) butter or margarine
 ½ cup granulated sugar
 ¼ cup firmly packed brown sugar
  1 egg
  1 teaspoon vanilla
  1 cup chopped walnuts
  1 package (6 ounces) semisweet chocolate pieces

1. Measure the flour, baking soda and salt onto a piece of wax paper.
2. Beat butter or margarine, brown sugar, egg and vanilla in a large bowl, until fluffy.
3. Add flour mixture, stirring until well blended. Stir in nuts and chocolate pieces.
4. Drop by rounded teaspoonfuls, 1 inch apart, onto greased cooky sheets.
5. Bake in a moderate oven (350°) 8 minutes or until golden brown. Remove from cooky sheets; cool on wire racks.

FLORENTINES

There's candied fruit inside these delicate chocolate-coated cookies.

Bake at 350° for 10 minutes.
Makes about 6 dozen cookies.

  1 cup sliced almonds
 ½ cup (4 ounces) candied orange peel, chopped
 ¼ cup candied red cherries, diced
  1 teaspoon grated lemon rind
 ¼ cup sifted all-purpose flour
 ¼ cup (½ stick) butter or margarine (for batter)
 ¼ cup sugar
 ¼ cup honey
 ¼ cup heavy cream
 12 squares (1½ packages) semisweet chocolate
  3 tablespoon butter or margarine (for coating)

1. Combine almonds, orange peel, cherries, lemon rind and flour in a small bowl; toss to coat thoroughly.
2. Combine the ¼ cup butter or margarine, sugar, honey and cream in a small saucepan. Heat slowly, stirring constantly, just until mixture bubbles. Remove from heat; carefully stir in almond mixture, just until well coated.

3. Drop by slightly rounded teaspoonfuls onto greased large cooky sheets; with a wide spatula, carefully spread cookies thin, to about 1½ inches in diameter.

4. Bake in a moderate oven (350°) 10 minutes, or until golden. Cool on cooky sheets 1 minute, or until firm. Lift with spatula and turn over, flat side up, onto a wire rack to cool completely.

5. Melt chocolate and the 3 tablespoons butter or margarine in top of double boiler over hot water; stir to blend.

6. Spread chocolate mixture thinly on flat sides almost to edges. Store in cool place until firm. Turn chocolate side down to serve.

SPECIAL TIP: The best way to store Florentines for a few days is to arrange them in a pan, with wax paper between the layers. Be sure to cover pan and store in a cool place.

ALMOND MACAROONS

Puffy, crunchy little cookies, chock-full of delicate almonds.

Bake at 325° for 20 minutes.
Makes about 3 dozen cookies.

  1 **can (8 ounces) almond paste**
  2 **egg whites**
    Dash of salt
  1 **teaspoon vanilla**
  1 **cup sifted 10X (confectioners') sugar**
    Granulated sugar
    Sliced almonds
    Candied red cherries, quartered

1. Grease a large cooky sheet; dust with flour; tap off excess.

2. Break up almond paste with fingers into medium-size bowl.

3. Add egg whites, salt and vanilla. Beat with electric mixer at low speed until mixture is smooth and well blended.

4. Slowly add confectioners' sugar, continuing to beat at low speed, until a soft dough forms.

5. Fit a pastry bag with a round tip. Fill bag with dough.

6. Pipe dough out in small rounds, or drop by teaspoonfuls onto prepared cooky sheet. (Macaroons will spread very little when they bake.)

7. For a crackly top: Dip fingertip into water; pat over tops; sprinkle with granulated sugar. Decorate tops with almonds and cherries.

8. Bake in slow oven (325°) 20 minutes, or until golden brown.

9. Remove to wire racks with a spatula; cool.

MOLASSES-SPICE COOKIES

Two of these with a glass of milk—what could be better for an after-school snack!

Bake at 350° for 10 minutes.
Makes about 3½ dozen cookies.

  2¼ **cups sifted all-purpose flour**
    1 **teaspoon baking soda**
  ½ **teaspoon salt**
  ½ **teaspoon ground ginger**
  ½ **teaspoon ground cinnamon**
  ½ **cup (1 stick) butter or margarine**
  ⅓ **cup firmly packed dark brown sugar**
    1 **egg**
  ½ **cup molasses**
  ¼ **cup orange juice**
  ½ **cup currants**

1. Sift flour, baking soda, salt, ginger, and cinnamon onto wax paper.

2. Beat butter or margarine in a large bowl; gradually add sugar and continue beating until mixture is well blended. Beat in egg; add molasses and orange juice, beating until well blended. Stir in dry ingredients, half at a time, blending well after each addition; fold in currants.

3. Drop by level tablespoonfuls, 3 inches apart, onto greased cooky sheets.

4. Bake at (350°) 10 minutes, or until firm. Remove from cooky sheets; cool on wire racks.

Low Calorie

32-CALORIE COCONUT MACAROONS

All the tasty goodness of rich macaroons without the costly calories.

Bake at 350° for 15 minutes.
Makes 3 dozen cookies at 32 calories each.

  2 **egg whites**
    Pinch of salt
    Pinch of cream of tartar
  1 **can (7 ounces) shredded coconut (2 cups)**
  2 **tablespoons cake flour**
  ¼ **teaspoon baking powder**

1. Beat the egg whites in small bowl of electric mixer until foamy. Add salt and cream of tartar; beat until stiff peaks form.

2. Combine coconut, cake flour and baking powder on wax paper. Fold into egg whites.

3. Use a measuring teaspoon to drop level spoonfuls of coconut mixture on nonstick cooky sheets.

4. Bake in a moderate oven (350°) 15 minutes, or until edges are browned. Cool on paper toweling.

A BAKER'S DOZEN:
EASY-TO-TRACE COOKY CUTTER PATTERNS

To make cooky cutters for any occasion, place a piece of tissue or tracing paper over patterns; trace outlines; cut out and glue onto cardboard. Cut around outlines, on cardboard, with scissors or razor blade. To use, place cardboard cutters on top of rolled dough; hold in place and cut around cooky cutter with a sharp knife. Transfer cookies to cooky sheet and bake according to recipe directions.

OATMEAL-DATE COOKIES

These sturdy cookies travel well as a lunch box treat or a pocket snack.

Bake at 350° for 12 minutes.
Makes about 5 dozen cookies.

- **1 cup <u>sifted</u> all-purpose flour**
- **1 teaspoon salt**
- **½ teaspoon baking soda**
- **⅛ teaspoon ground nutmeg**
- **½ cup (1 stick) butter or margarine**
- **1 cup firmly packed brown sugar**
- **½ cup granulated sugar**
- **1 egg**
- **½ cup dairy sour cream**
- **1 teaspoon vanilla**
- **3 cups quick-cooking oats**
- **1 cup pitted dates, chopped**

1. Sift flour, salt, baking soda, and nutmeg onto wax paper.
2. Beat butter or margarine in a large bowl; gradually add sugars and continue beating until mixture is well blended. Beat in egg, sour cream, and vanilla.
3. Stir in flour mixture. Add oats and dates, mixing until well blended.
4. Drop by level tablespoonfuls, 2 inches apart, onto greased cooky sheets.
5. Bake in moderate oven (350°) 12 minutes, or until golden brown. Remove from cooky sheets; cool completely on wire racks.

Low Calorie

21-CALORIE PEANUT BUTTER COOKIES

The diet trick here is to use sugar subsitute. Let the peanut butter provide the richness, so you can diet, and still enjoy dessert.

Bake at 375° for 8 minutes.
Makes 5 dozen cookies at 21 calories each.

- **⅔ cup <u>sifted</u> all-purpose flour**
- **½ teaspoon baking soda**
- **½ teaspoon baking powder**
- **3 tablespoons butter or margarine, softened**
- **4 tablespoons peanut butter**
- **2 tablespoons firmly packed brown sugar**
- **Sugar substitute to equal 4 tablespoons sugar**
- **1 teaspoon vanilla**
- **2 eggs, beaten**

1. Sift flour, baking soda and baking powder onto wax paper.
2. Beat butter or margarine, peanut butter, brown sugar and sugar substitute together. Add vanilla and

eggs; beat until light and fluffy.
3. Add sifted dry ingredients to peanut butter mixture; mix well.
4. Use a measuring teaspoon to drop level spoonfuls of cooky dough on nonstick cooky sheets.
5. Bake in moderate oven (375°) 8 minutes. Let the cookies cool on paper toweling.

MOLDED AND PRESSED COOKIES

MADELEINES

Shell-shaped morsels of lemony sponge cake you can savor at coffee-time as well as party-time. A quick sprinkle of 10X sugar before serving, makes these delicious cookies even more attractive.

Bake at 350° for 20 minutes.
Makes 4 dozen cookies.

- **1½ cups (3 sticks) butter or margarine**
- **3 eggs**
- **1 cup granulated sugar**
- **1 teaspoon grated lemon rind**
- **1 teaspoon vanilla**
- **1½ cups <u>sifted</u> cake flour**
- **10X (confectioners') sugar**

1. Clarify butter or margarine by melting over low heat in a small saucepan; remove from heat. Pour into a 2-cup measure; let stand until solids settle to bottom; then pour clear liquid into another cup; discard solids.
2. Measure ¾ cup of this clarified butter into a 1-cup measure.
3. Brush madeleine molds well with the remaining clarified butter or margarine; dust with flour; tap out excess.
4. Beat eggs with sugar and lemon rind in the top of a double boiler; place over simmering water. Beat mixture with an electric mixer at high speed 5 minutes, or until thick and light; remove from heat. Pour into a large bowl; stir in vanilla.
5. Fold flour into egg mixture, then fold in the ¾ cup clarified butter or margarine. Spoon into prepared molds, filling each half full. (Cover remaining batter and let stand at room temperature while baking first batch.)
6. Bake in moderate oven (350°) 20 minutes. Cool 5 minutes in molds on wire racks. Loosen around edges with tip of a small knife; turn out onto racks, tapping gently, if needed, to loosen from bottom. Cool completely. Repeat Steps 5 and 6, washing, buttering and flouring molds between bakings, to make 48 MADELEINES in all. Dust lightly with 10X sugar, if you wish.

BUTTERNUTS

Rum glaze plus pecans or candied cherries add a festive topping to these rich little treats.

Bake at 325° for 15 minutes.
Makes about 8 dozen 1-inch cookies.

¾ cup (1½ sticks) butter or margarine
½ cup <u>sifted</u> 10X (confectioners') sugar
¼ teaspoon salt
1¾ cups <u>sifted</u> all-purpose flour
1 package (6 ounces) butterscotch-flavor pieces (about 1 cup)
1 cup finely chopped pecans
Double recipe for Rum Glaze (recipe page 74)
Pecan halves
Candied red cherries, halved

1. Beat butter or margarine with 10X sugar and salt in a medium-size bowl; blend in flour until smooth. Stir in butterscotch pieces and pecans.
2. Shape dough, a scant teaspoonful at a time, into balls, between palms of hands; place balls, 1 inch apart, on large cooky sheets.
3. Bake in slow oven (325°) 15 minutes, or until firm but not brown. Remove from cooky sheets to wire racks; let cool completely.
4. Make double recipe for RUM GLAZE. Place cookies in a single layer on wire racks set over wax paper; spoon glaze over each to cover completely. (Scrape glaze that drips onto paper back into bowl and beat until smooth before using again.) Decorate each with a pecan or candied cherry half. Let cookies stand until glaze is firm.

Basic Recipe

SPRITZ SLIMS

Thin cookies tipped with melted chocolate. For a variation, you can color the dough and frost the tips, any color you wish.

Bake at 375° for 8 minutes.
Makes 12 dozen cookies.

1½ cups (3 sticks) butter or margarine
1 cup sugar
3 egg yolks
1 teaspoon vanilla
¼ teaspoon salt
3½ cups <u>sifted</u> all-purpose flour
4 squares (4 ounces) semisweet chocolate
1 tablespoon vegetable shortening
⅔ cup chopped pistachio nuts

1. Beat butter or margarine with sugar in a large bowl, until light and fluffy. Beat in egg yolks, vanilla and salt. Stir in flour, one third at a time, blending well to make a soft dough.
2. Fit rosette plate or star disk onto cooky press; fill press with dough (or fit pastry bag with a small star tip). Press dough out into 3-inch lengths on ungreased large cooky sheets.
3. Bake in a moderate oven (375°) 8 minutes, or until firm; remove from cooky sheets to wire racks; cool completely.
4. Melt semisweet chocolate with shortening in top of double boiler; cool completely.
5. Dip ends of slims into melted chocolate, then into chopped nuts. Place on wire racks until decoration is firm.

Spritz Bonbons: Tint SPRITZ SLIMS dough with red or green food coloring. Press through cooky press using rosette plate or star disk. Bake as directed. Decorate with ready-to-use frosting, coconut and colored sugars, if you wish.

CHOCOLATE-WALNUT WAFERS

Sugar-topped cookies with deep chocolate flavor; these are great for the holidays, or any days.

Bake at 350° for 12 minutes.
Makes 5 dozen cookies.

2 cups <u>sifted</u> all-purpose flour
1 teaspoon baking powder
½ teaspoon salt
¼ teaspoon baking soda
¾ cup (1½ sticks) butter or margarine
¾ cup firmly packed brown sugar
2 squares unsweetened chocolate, melted
1 egg
1 teaspoon vanilla
¼ cup milk
Granulated sugar
Walnut halves

1. Measure flour, baking powder, salt and baking soda into sifter.
2. Beat butter or margarine and brown sugar in a medium-size bowl, until fluffy; beat in melted chocolate, egg, vanilla and milk. Sift in dry ingredients, one third at a time, blending well to make a soft dough. Chill several hours, or until firm enough to handle.
3. Roll dough, one level teaspoonful at a time, between palms of hands, into round balls; roll in granulated sugar. Place, 3 inches apart, on ungreased cooky sheets; flatten to ¼-inch thickness with bottom of a glass. Top each with a walnut half.
4. Bake in moderate oven (350°) 12 minutes, or until firm. Remove the wafers carefully to wire racks with a spatula; cool.

THIMBLE COOKIES

Delicate little cookies with raspberry or strawberry preserves spooned in the center. Why not try different flavors the next time you bake them and make your own interesting variations?

Bake at 350° for 12 minutes.
Makes 3 dozen cookies.

2¼ cups <u>sifted</u> all-purpose flour
  1 cup (2 sticks) butter or margarine
  ½ cup firmly packed brown sugar
  2 eggs, separated
1½ teaspoons vanilla
1½ cups walnuts, finely chopped
     Raspberry or strawberry preserves

1. Sift flour onto wax paper.
2. Beat butter or margarine with brown sugar in a medium-size bowl until fluffy and light; beat in egg yolks and vanilla. Stir in flour, one half at a time, blending well to make a stiff dough.
3. Beat egg whites in a pie plate until foamy; sprinkle walnuts on wax paper.
4. Roll dough, 1 teaspoonful at a time, into balls, between palms of hands; roll each in egg white, then into walnuts to coat all over. Place, 2 inches apart, on large cooky sheets. Press down in center of each cooky with fingertip, or thimble, to make a little hollow.
5. Bake in a moderate oven (350°) 12 minutes, or until firm and lightly golden. Remove from cooky sheets to wire racks; cool completely. Spoon preserves into each hollow.

ALMOND MAZARINS

Little cooky pies with almond centers and chopped pistachio crowns.

Bake at 350° for 15 minutes.
Makes about 3 dozen cookies.

  1 cup <u>sifted</u> all-purpose flour
  ¼ teaspoon baking powder
  ⅓ cup butter or margarine, softened
  1 cup <u>sifted</u> 10X (confectioners') sugar
  3 eggs
  2 tablespoons butter or margarine, melted
  1 cup blanched almonds, ground
  1 teaspoon almond extract
     Sugar Icing (recipe page 74)
     Yellow food coloring
  ½ cup pistachio nuts, chopped

1. Measure flour and baking powder into a sifter.
2. Beat the ⅓ cup butter or margarine and ½ cup

of the 10X sugar in a medium-size bowl until well blended. Sift in flour mixture, blending well; stir in one of the eggs; blend to form a very stiff dough. Chill 30 minutes.
3. Pinch off dough, one teaspoonful at a time, and press over bottoms and sides of 1¼-inch tartshell pans to make shells. (Or press into tiny gem-pan cups.)
4. Beat remaining 2 eggs slightly in a medium-size bowl; stir in remaining 10X sugar, the melted butter or margarine, ground almonds and the 1 teaspoon almond extract.
5. Spoon 1 teaspoonful of filling into each pastry-lined pan, filling each about halfway. Set pans in a large shallow pan for easy handling.
6. Bake in a moderate oven (350°) 15 minutes, or until golden. Cool in pans on wire rack 10 minutes; remove tarts carefully from pans, easing out with the tip of a small knife, if needed.
7. Glaze with SUGAR ICING, tinted yellow. Sprinkle with pistachio nuts.

GLAZED LEMON ROUNDS

Bright yellow glaze baked onto these crisp cookies makes them smooth and lemony-good. They're a particularly nice finish to a heavy meal.

Bake at 400° for 8 minutes.
Makes about 3½ dozen cookies.

3½ cups <u>sifted</u> all-purpose flour
2¼ teaspoons baking powder
  ½ teaspoon salt
  1 cup (2 sticks) butter or margarine
1⅓ cups granulated sugar
  2 eggs
  2 tablespoons grated lemon rind
  1 tablespoon lemon juice
  6 tablespoons 10X (confectioners') sugar
  4 teaspoons water
     Yellow food coloring

1. Sift flour, baking powder, and salt onto a piece of wax paper.
2. Beat butter or margarine with granulated sugar in a large bowl, until light and fluffy; beat in eggs, one at a time, then lemon rind and juice. Stir in flour mixture, one third at a time, blending well to make a stiff dough.
3. Roll dough, one teaspoonful at a time, into balls; place, 2 inches apart, on large cooky sheets. Butter the bottom of a water glass; dip in granulated sugar. Press over cooky balls to flatten to ⅛-inch thickness.
4. Mix 10X sugar, water, and a drop of yellow food coloring in a cup, until smooth; brush over rounds.
5. Bake in hot oven (400°) 8 minutes, or until firm and golden around edge. Remove from cooky sheets; cool completely on wire racks.

Bring a touch of summer to the Holiday Season with our easy-to-make "cooky-fruit" tree. Recipe for Vanilla Sugar Cookies plus cooky cutter patterns in this chapter. Decorating directions in Chapter 4.

Who can resist a cooky jar filled
to the brim with goodies—especially
our jelly-filled Thimble Cookies,
dark Molasses-Spice Cookies,
shell-shaped Madeleines, speckled
Brown-Eyed Susans or chewy Peanut
Butter Bars! Recipes for
all are in this chapter.

Basic Recipe

VANILLA SUGAR COOKIES

Looking for a special cooky to add to your collection of favorite recipes? Here it is, a double find; it can be both a crunchy drop cooky and a crispy pressed cooky. Try it! And don't forget to note all of the fantastic variations that follow.

Bake at 400° for 10 minutes.
Makes either 3 dozen drop cookies or 6 dozen pressed cookies.

- 1 cup (2 sticks) butter or margarine, softened
- 1½ cups sugar
- 2 teaspoons vanilla
- 2 eggs
- 3 cups <u>sifted</u> all-purpose flour
- 2½ teaspoons baking powder
- ½ teaspoon salt

1. Beat butter or margarine, sugar, vanilla and eggs in a large bowl until light and fluffy.
2. Measure flour, baking powder and salt into sifter. Sift into creamed mixture; stir until well blended.
3. Drop by level tablespoonfuls onto greased cooky sheets (or, shape into 1-inch balls; press to a ¼-inch thickness with a glass that has been buttered on the bottom, then dipped in sugar).
4. Bake in a hot oven (400°) 10 minutes, or until edges are lightly browned. Remove from cooky sheets with spatula, to wire racks; cool.

Note: The following variations may either be dropped or pressed. Bake all of them according to the directions given in Step 4.

Almond Cookies: Reduce vanilla to 1 teaspoon; add 1 teaspoon almond extract.

Brown-eyed Susans: Follow recipe for VANILLA SUGAR COOKIES. Press cookies with glass dipped in yellow sugar. Put 3 or more semisweet chocolate pieces in center of each cooky.

Butterscotch-Walnut Cookies: Substitute ¾ cup firmly packed brown sugar for ¾ cup of the granulated sugar. Add 1 cup finely chopped walnuts.

Coconut Cookies: Add ½ cup flaked coconut. Shape into 1-inch balls.

Orange Cookies: Shape dough into 1-inch balls; roll in a mixture of 1 cup sugar and 4 tablespoons grated orange rind.

Raisin Cookies: Add 1 cup raisins.

Sugar and Spice Cookies: Reduce vanilla to 1 teaspoon. Add ½ teaspoon ground cinnamon and ¼ teaspoon ground nutmeg when sifting dry ingredients. Follow Basic Recipe for preparing cookies.

Giant jumbo cookies and a glass of milk—a great snack for kids of all ages. From top, down: Oatmeal Crunchies, Orange Rounds, and Chocolate-Mint Jumbos. Recipes in this chapter.

BAR COOKIES

DATE-PECAN CHEWS

Sugar-topped logs with dates and pecans rolled inside.

Bake at 350° for 25 minutes.
Makes about 6 dozen cookies.

  ¾ **cup** <u>sifted</u> **all-purpose flour**
  ½ **teaspoon baking powder**
  ¼ **teaspoon salt**
  3 **eggs**
  1 **cup sugar**
  2 **tablespoons orange juice**
  1 **package (8 ounces) pitted dates, chopped**
  1 **cup pecans, chopped**
  ¼ **cup candied orange peel, chopped**
    Sugar (for coating)

1. Sift flour, baking powder and salt onto wax paper.
2. Beat eggs in a large bowl until light and foamy; slowly beat in the 1 cup sugar; continue beating until mixture is thick and fluffy. Stir in orange juice.
3. Fold in flour mixture, dates, pecans and orange peel. Spread mixture evenly in a greased 13x9x2-inch baking pan.
4. Bake in a moderate oven (350°) 25 minutes, or until golden and top springs back when pressed with fingertip. Cool in pan on wire rack 15 minutes.
5. Cut lengthwise into 9 strips and crosswise into 8 to make 72 pieces, about 1x1½ inches each. Roll each in sugar in a pie plate to coat generously. (Cookies are soft and will roll into a log.)

RASPBERRY MERINGUE BARS

Here's a triple-layer treat: Cooky on the bottom; raspberry preserves in the middle; meringue on top. Smooth and sweet.

Bake at 350° for 15 minutes, then for an additional 25 minutes.
Makes 2 dozen bars.

  ¾ **cup (1½ sticks) butter or margarine**
  ¾ **cup sugar**
  2 **eggs, separated**
  1½ **cups** <u>sifted</u> **all-purpose flour**
  1 **cup chopped walnuts**
  1 **cup raspberry preserves**
  ½ **cup flaked coconut**

1. Beat butter or margarine with ¼ cup of the sugar in a medium-size bowl, until mixture is light and fluffy; beat in egg yolks.

2. Stir in flour until blended. Spread evenly in a 13x9x2-inch baking pan.
3. Bake in a moderate oven (350°) 15 minutes, or until golden; remove from oven.
4. While layer bakes, beat egg whites in a small bowl, until foamy white and double in volume; gradually beat in the remaining ½ cup sugar until meringue stands in firm peaks; fold the walnuts into meringue.
5. Spread raspberry preserves over layer in pan; sprinkle with coconut. Spread meringue over raspberry-coconut layer.
6. Bake in a moderate oven (350°) 25 minutes, or until lightly golden. Cool completely in pan on wire rack. Cut into bars. Carefully lift the cookies out of pan with a wide spatula. To keep cookies fresh, store in an airtight container.

PEANUT BUTTER BARS

These moist chewy bars are drizzled with a sugar glaze, then with chocolate. They're sure to be a favorite with the kids.

Bake at 350° for 35 minutes.
Makes 3 dozen bars.

  1 **cup crunchy peanut butter**
  ⅔ **cup butter or margarine, softened**
  1 **teaspoon vanilla**
  2 **cups firmly packed light brown sugar**
  3 **eggs**
  1 **cup** <u>sifted</u> **all-purpose flour**
  ½ **teaspoon salt**
    Sugar Icing (recipe page 74)
  ¼ **cup semisweet chocolate pieces (from a 6-ounce package)**
  1 **teaspoon vegetable shortening**

1. Combine peanut butter, butter or margarine and vanilla in a large bowl; beat with electric mixer until well blended; beat in sugar until light and fluffy; beat in eggs, one at a time.
2. Stir in flour and salt just until well blended; spread batter in a greased 13x9x2-inch baking pan.
3. Bake on moderate oven (350°) 35 minutes, or until center springs back when lightly touched with fingertip. Remove pan from oven to wire rack; cool slightly.
4. Drizzle SUGAR ICING from a spoon over still-warm cookies in pan; swirl with bowl of spoon to make a random pattern.
5. Melt chocolate with shortening in the top of a double boiler over simmering water. Drizzle chocolate over top of cookies to make a black-and-white pattern. When cool, use a sharp knife to cut into 36 rectangles. Carefully lift the cookies out of pan with a wide spatula.

OUR BEST-EVER BROWNIES

These are what Brownies are all about—moist, chewy and super-chocolate-y!

Bake at 350° for 30 minutes.
Makes 16 brownies.

 2 squares unsweetened chocolate
½ cup (1 stick) butter or margarine
 2 eggs
 1 cup sugar
 1 teaspoon vanilla
½ cup sifted all-purpose flour
⅛ teaspoon salt
¾ cup chopped walnuts

1. Melt chocolate and butter or margarine in a small saucepan over low heat; cool.
2. Beat eggs in a small bowl with electric mixer; gradually beat in sugar until mixture is fluffy and thick. Stir in chocolate mixture and vanilla.
3. Fold in flour and salt until well blended; stir in walnuts. Spread evenly in an 8x8x2-inch greased baking pan.
4. Bake in moderate oven (350°) 30 minutes, or until shiny and firm on top. Cool in pan on wire rack.

LEMON-DATE DIAMONDS

Tart lemon frosting contrasts pleasingly with the sweet chewy cooky base.

Bake at 325° for 35 minutes.
Makes 3 dozen bars.

1¼ cups sifted all-purpose flour
1½ teaspoons baking powder
 ½ teaspoon salt
 ½ teaspoon pumpkin-pie spice
 2 eggs
 1 cup sugar
 2 tablespoons vegetable oil
 1 package (8 ounces) pitted dates, chopped
 ½ cup pecans, chopped
    Lemon Glaze (recipe page 74)

1. Measure flour, baking powder, salt and pumpkin-pie spice into a sifter.
2. Beat eggs and sugar in a large bowl, until well blended; stir in vegetable oil, dates and pecans. Sift flour mixture over top, then blend in. Spread in a greased 13x9x2-inch baking pan.
3. Bake in a slow oven (325°) 35 minutes, or until golden and a wooden pick inserted in the center comes out clean. Cool in pan on wire rack.
4. Spread LEMON GLAZE over cookies. Let stand until frosting is firm. Cut into diamond shapes or bars.

BUTTERSCOTCH CHEWS

Make these ahead, if you wish; they keep well.

Bake at 350° for 25 minutes.
Makes 4 dozen bars.

 2 cups sifted all-purpose flour
 2 teaspoons baking powder
½ teaspoon salt
 1 package (1 pound) light brown sugar
½ cup (1 stick) butter or margarine
 2 eggs
 1 teaspoon vanilla
¼ teaspoon almond extract
 1 can (about 4 ounces) toasted sliced blanched almonds

1. Sift flour, baking powder, and salt into a large bowl; stir in brown sugar.
2. Melt butter or margarine in small saucepan; cool.
3. Beat eggs in a small bowl; stir in cooled butter or margarine, vanilla, and almond extract. Stir into flour mixture until well blended.
4. Spread in a greased 15x10x1-inch jelly roll pan. Sprinkle with almonds; press lightly into batter.
5. Bake in moderate oven (350°) 25 minutes, or until top springs back when lightly pressed with fingertip. Cool in pan on wire rack. Cut into bars.

JUMBO COOKIES

ORANGE SUGAR ROUNDS

A new angle on sugar cookies—the flavor of orange.

Bake at 400° for 8 minutes.
Makes sixteen 3-inch cookies.

2½ cups sifted all-purpose flour
 2 teaspoons baking powder
 1 teaspoon salt
 ¾ cup (1½ sticks) butter or margarine
1¼ cups sugar
 2 eggs
 1 tablespoon grated orange rind

1. Measure flour, baking powder and salt into sifter.
2. Beat butter or margarine with 1 cup of the sugar in a large bowl, until light and fluffy; beat in eggs and orange rind. Sift in flour mixture, one third at a time, blending well. Chill dough until firm.
3. Roll out dough to a ¼-inch thickness on a lightly floured surface; sprinkle with the remaining ¼ cup sugar. Cut into rounds with a floured 3-inch round cooky cutter. (*Note:* You may use an empty can as a cooky cutter, if you wish.) Place cookies, 1 inch

apart on large cooky sheets.

4. Bake in a hot oven (400°) 8 minutes, or until firm. Remove cookies to wire racks to cool. Leave plain, or drizzle with your favorite orange frosting.

JUMBO OATMEAL CRUNCHIES

Giant old-fashioned oatmeal cookies filled with good things—raisins, rolled oats, brown sugar and walnuts.

Bake at 375° for 12 minutes.
Makes about 2½ dozen cookies, 2½ inches in diameter.

    1½ cups **sifted** all-purpose flour
     ½ teaspoon baking soda
     ½ teaspoon salt
        Dash mace
     1 cup vegetable shortening
    1¼ cups firmly packed brown sugar
     1 egg
     ¼ cup milk
    1¾ cups quick-cooking rolled oats
     1 cup chopped walnuts
     1 cup raisins

1. Measure the flour, baking soda, salt and mace into a sifter.
2. Beat shortening with brown sugar in a large bowl, until light and fluffy; beat in egg and milk. Sift in flour mixture, blending well to make a thick batter; fold in rolled oats, walnuts and raisins.
3. Drop by heaping tablespoonfuls, 3 inches apart on greased cooky sheets (6 to a sheet). Spread each cooky to a 2½-inch round.
4. Bake in a moderate oven (375°) 12 minutes or until lightly golden. Remove from oven; let stand 1 minute on cooky sheet. Remove with wide spatula to wire rack. Cool completely.

CHOCOLATE-MINT JUMBOS

For a flower-shaped version of these cookies, follow the directions below.

Bake at 350° for 10 minutes.
Makes 1½ dozen 4-inch cookies.

     2 cups **sifted** all-purpose flour
     ⅓ cup unsweetened cocoa powder
    1½ teaspoons baking powder
     ½ teaspoon salt
    1¼ cups vegetable shortening
     1 cup sugar
     2 eggs
     ½ teaspoon peppermint extract

1. Measure flour, cocoa, baking powder and salt into sifter.
2. Beat shortening with sugar in a large bowl until light and fluffy; beat in eggs and pepperment extract. Sift in flour mixture, blending well. Chill until firm enough to handle.
3. Shape dough into 1¼-inch balls; place, 4 inches apart on greased large cooky sheets; flatten balls to ¼-inch thickness with the bottom of a glass, dipped in granulated sugar.
4. Bake in a moderate oven (350°) 10 minutes, or until firm. Remove cookies to wire racks to cool.

Chocolate-Mint Blossoms: Substitute the following for Step 3: Roll dough, one heaping teaspoonful at a time, into 1½-inch-long ovals; place in groups of four, pinwheel fashion, 3 inches apart, on greased large cooky sheets; flatten to ⅛-inch thickness as above. Bake according to Step 4.

ROLLED COOKIES

CHRISTMAS SUGAR COOKIES

A crispy vanilla cooky to cut and decorate. These are the cookies hung on the "Cooky-fruit Tree" shown on page 89. Use the fruit-shaped cutter patterns on page 85 (The "orange" is made with a 2-inch plain round cutter.) See page 76 for complete decorating directions.

Bake at 350° for 8 minutes.
Makes 3 dozen cookies.

    2½ cups **sifted** all-purpose flour
     ½ teaspoon salt
     ¾ cup (1½ sticks) butter or margarine
    1¼ cups sugar
     1 egg
     2 teaspoons vanilla
        Colored decorating sugar

1. Sift flour and salt onto wax paper.
2. Beat butter or margarine, sugar and egg in large bowl, with electric mixer at high speed 3 minutes, or until fluffy; blend in vanilla.
3. Stir in flour mixture to make a stiff dough; wrap in wax paper; chill 3 hours, or until firm enough to roll.
4. Roll dough, one quarter at a time, to a ¼-inch thickness on a lightly floured surface. Cut into rounds with a 3-inch cutter.
5. Place cookies, 1 inch apart, on ungreased cooky sheets. Sprinkle with colored sugar.
6. Bake in moderate oven (350°) 8 minutes, or until cookies are lightly browned at edges.
7. Remove to wire racks with spatula; cool.

Low Calorie

28-CALORIE BUTTERSCOTCH COOKIES

Diet butterscotch pudding mix keeps the calorie level low and the flavor high.

Bake at 375° for 8 minutes.
Makes 3 dozen cookies at 28 calories each.

- **1 cup sifted all-purpose flour**
- **½ teaspoon baking powder**
- **½ teaspoon salt**
- **3 tablespoons butter or margarine, softened**
- **2 tablespoons firmly packed brown sugar**
- **1 envelope (half a 2⅛-ounce package) low-calorie butterscotch pudding and pie filling mix**
- **1 egg**
- **½ teaspoon vanilla**

1. Sift flour, baking powder and salt onto wax paper.
2. Beat together butter or margarine and sugar. Add pudding mix; blend well. Add egg and vanilla; beat until fluffy. Blend in sifted dry ingredients.
3. Shape dough into a roll 1½ inches in diameter on wax paper. Wrap tightly in the wax paper. Chill in freezer 30 minutes, or until firm enough to slice.
4. Cut roll into ⅛-inch slices. Place slices on nonstick cooky sheets.
5. Bake in a moderate oven (375°) 8 minutes, or until cookies are browned on the edges. Cool on paper toweling.

SPRINGERLE

The pretty figures on these classic licorice-flavor cookies are made with a special rolling pin. Bake them ahead of time for Christmas giving.

Preheat oven to 375°; bake at 300° for 15 minutes.
Makes about 6 dozen cookies.

- **4 eggs**
- **2 cups sugar**
- **1 teaspoon anise extract**
- **4¼ cups sifted all-purpose flour**
- **1 teaspoon baking soda**
- **Anise seeds**

1. Beat eggs in a large bowl, with an electric mixer, until very thick (this takes about 10 minutes); gradually add sugar, continuing to beat 15 minutes, or until very light and fluffy.

2. Beat in anise extract, then add flour and baking soda to make a stiff dough.
3. Roll out dough, one quarter at a time, on a lightly floured surface, to ½-inch thickness. Then, using springerle rolling pin,* roll over dough only once, pressing designs into dough to a ¼-inch thickness. Cut cookies apart on dividing lines.
4. Grease large cooky sheets; sprinkle lightly with anise seeds. Carefully place cookies, 1 inch apart, on prepared cooky sheets. Let stand 24 hours, uncovered, in cool place (not refrigerator). Cookies will appear to have white frosting.
5. Place cookies in moderate oven (375°) and immediately lower heat to slow (300°). Bake 15 minutes, or until set but not browned.
6. Remove cookies to wire racks; cool completely. Store in tightly covered container about 2 weeks to season.

Note: Instead of a springerle rolling pin, you can use individual springerle blocks (see page 99). Most individual blocks, however, make larger cookies than do rolling pins, so your final yield will be less. (We got 21 cookies from ours.)

ISCHL TARTLETS

A favorite in Viennese pastry shops; we share our version of these double-layer cookies with you.

Bake at 350° for 8 minutes.
Makes about 3½ dozen cookies.

- **2¾ cups sifted all-purpose flour**
- **½ teaspoon baking powder**
- **1 cup (2 sticks) butter or margarine, softened**
- **1 package (3 ounces) cream cheese, softened**
- **1 cup granulated sugar**
- **1 egg**
- **½ cup almonds, ground**
- **1 tablespoon grated lemon rind**
- **1 jar (12 ounces) raspberry preserves**
- **10X (confectioners') sugar**

1. Sift flour and baking powder onto wax paper.
2. Beat butter or margarine, cream cheese, sugar and egg in a large mixing bowl until light and fluffy.
3. Add flour mixture, blending thoroughly. Stir in ground almonds and lemon rind. Turn dough out onto wax paper (mixture will be sticky). Shape into a ball. Chill several hours, or overnight.
4. Cut dough in half. (Refrigerate other half.) Roll out dough to a ⅛-inch thickness on a lightly floured surface, with a lightly floured rolling pin. With a 3-inch round cooky cutter, cut out as many circles from the dough as you can. Place circles on ungreased cooky sheets. Refrigerate scraps of dough for second rolling.

5. Repeat with other half of the dough, cutting out an equal number of 3-inch circles as from the first batch. Place on ungreased cooky sheets. With a ½-inch cooky cutter or thimble, cut out center of each of the second batch of circles. Use any scraps of dough for second rolling; cut out an equal number of solid circles, and circles with open centers.

6. Bake all in a moderate oven (350°) 8 minutes, or until edges of cookies are lightly browned. Remove cooky sheets from oven; let stand 1 minute. Remove cookies with a wide spatula to wire racks. Cool.

7. Heat raspberry preserves in a small saucepan. Spread each of the solid cookies completely with a thin layer of hot preserves. Top each with cutout cooky; press together gently to make a "sandwich". Place on wire rack. Sprinkle tops of tartlets with 10X sugar. Spoon a dab of preserves into the opening of each cooky; let preserves set slightly. To keep cookies fresh, store between wax paper-lined layers in an airtight tin.

PEPPARKAKOR

Here's the perfect gingerbread to cut out, and decorate as you wish. See our easy-to-trace cooky cutters on pages 84 and 85 and choose your favorites.

Bake at 350° for 7 minutes.
Makes about 8 dozen 2-inch cookies.

1⅔ cups <u>sifted</u> all-purpose flour
½ teaspoon baking soda
½ teaspoon salt
¾ teaspoon ground ginger
½ teaspoon ground cinnamon
¼ teaspoon ground cloves
¼ teaspoon ground cardamom
6 tablespoons (¾ stick) butter or margarine
⅓ cup sugar
¼ cup light molasses
1 teaspoon grated orange rind
¼ cup toasted almonds, finely chopped
   Royal Frosting (recipe page 75)

1. Sift flour, baking soda, salt, ginger, cinnamon, cloves and cardamom on wax paper.
2. Beat butter or margarine with sugar in a large bowl until light and fluffy; beat in molasses, orange rind and almonds. Stir in flour, one third at a time, blending well to make a stiff dough. Chill several hours, or overnight, until firm enough to roll.
3. Roll out dough, one third at a time, on a lightly floured surface, to a ⅛-inch thickness; cut into fancy shapes with floured 2-inch cooky cutters. Place cookies, 1 inch apart, on lightly greased large cooky sheets. Reroll and cut out all trimmings.
4. Bake in a moderate oven (350°) 7 minutes, or until firm. Cool cookies on wire racks.

5. Make ROYAL FROSTING. Fit a writing tip onto a cake decorating set or make your own disposable decorating bag (directions page 13); fill with frosting. Press out onto cookies in designs of your choice; let stand until frosting is firm.

LEBKUCHEN

Spicy Christmas cookies to make before the Christmas rush and enjoy throughout the holiday season.

Bake at 350° for 10 minutes.
Makes about 5 dozen cookies.

¾ cup honey
¾ cup firmly packed dark brown sugar
1 egg
2 teaspoons grated lemon rind
3 tablespoons lemon juice
3½ cups <u>sifted</u> all-purpose flour
1 teaspoon salt
1 teaspoon ground cinnamon
1 teaspoon ground nutmeg
½ teaspoon ground allspice
½ teaspoon ground ginger
¼ teaspoon ground cloves
½ teaspoon baking soda
1 container (8 ounces) citron, finely chopped
1 cup unblanched almonds, chopped
   Sugar Icing (recipe follows)
   Whole almonds
   Candied cherries

1. Heat honey to boiling in a small saucepan; pour into a large bowl; cool about 30 minutes.
2. Stir in brown sugar, egg, lemon rind and lemon juice, blending well.
3. Sift flour, salt, cinnamon, nutmeg, allspice, ginger, cloves and baking soda onto wax paper.
4. Stir flour mixture into honey mixture, one third at a time. Stir in citron and chopped almonds. Dough will be stiff, but sticky. Wrap in foil or plastic wrap; chill several hours, or until firm.
5. Roll out dough, one eighth at a time, on a lightly floured surface to a 6x5-inch rectangle. Cut into 8 rectangles, 2½ x 1½ inches each. Place rectangles, 1 inch apart, on greased large cooky sheets.
6. Bake in a moderate oven (350°) 10 minutes, or until firm. Remove cookies to wire racks.
7. Brush hot cookies with hot SUGAR ICING. Decorate with almonds and cherries; cool. Store in an airtight container at least two weeks.

Sugar Icing: Combine 1½ cups granulated sugar and ¾ cup water in a medium-size saucepan. Bring to boiling; reduce heat; simmer 3 minutes. Remove from heat; stir in ½ cup sifted 10X (confectioners') sugar. Makes about 2 cups.

SCOTCH SHORTBREAD

Crispy butter cookies to sprinkle with colored sugar.

Bake at 325° for 20 minutes.
Makes about 5 dozen cookies.

1 cup (2 sticks) butter or margarine
½ cup superfine granulated sugar
1 teaspoon vanilla
2¼ cups sifted all purpose flour

1. Beat butter or margarine with sugar in a large bowl, until light and fluffy; beat in vanilla.
2. Stir in flour, one third at a time, blending well to make a stiff dough. Knead 10 to 15 minutes, or until smooth. Chill several hours, or overnight, until firm enough to handle.
3. Roll or pat out dough, on a lightly floured surface, one quarter at a time, to a ¼-inch thickness. Cut into small rounds with a 1½-inch cutter. Place cookies, 1 inch apart, on large cooky sheets. Reroll and cut out all trimmings.
4. Bake in a slow oven (325°) 20 minutes, or until firm, but not brown. Remove from cooky sheet to wire racks; cool completely.

ALMOND-FILLED PASTRY CRESCENTS

From Morocco come these melt-in-your-mouth "Kab et Ghzal" (or Gazelle Horns).

Bake at 400° for 12 minutes.
Makes about 4 dozen cookies.

2¼ cups sifted all-purpose flour
½ teaspoon salt
1 cup (2 sticks) butter or margarine
4 tablespoons ice water
1 can (8 ounces) almond paste
2 tablespoons granulated sugar
1 egg
⅓ cup almonds, ground
⅔ cup 10X (confectioners') sugar

1. Combine flour and salt in a medium-size bowl. Cut in butter or margarine with a pastry blender until mixture is crumbly. Add ice water, one tablespoon at a time; combine with a fork until moistened.
2. Shape pastry into a ball; divide into 3 equal pieces; shape each piece into a round; flatten slightly. Wrap each third in plastic wrap. Refrigerate at least 1 hour.
3. Place almond paste in a small bowl; break up with a fork. Beat in egg, the 2 tablespoons of granulated sugar and ground almonds until mixture is thoroughly combined. (Mixture will be sticky.)
4. Turn almond mixture out onto a lightly floured

surface. Shape into a ball with floured hands. Divide into thirds. Shape each third into a rope ½-inch in diameter and 16 inches long. (If mixture sticks, flour hands and surface lightly.) Cut each rope into sixteen 1-inch pieces.
5. Roll out pastry, one third at a time, to a ⅛-inch thickness, on a lightly floured surface; roll to a 12x12-inch square. Trim off rough edges. With a sharp knife, cut into sixteen 3-inch squares.
6. Place one piece of almond paste diagonally across one corner of the pastry square. Lift the point over the paste and roll jelly roll fashion. Pinch the ends enclosing the almond filling. Curve the pastry into a crescent.
7. Place crescents, 1 inch apart, on an ungreased cooky sheet. Bake in a hot oven (400°) 12 minutes, or until edges of cookies just *begin* to brown.
8. Place 10X sugar in a pie plate or on large sheet of wax paper. Place warm cookies, a few at a time, upside down in sugar to coat; turn once or twice.
9. Place cookies on wire racks to cool thoroughly. Store in wax paper-separated layers in an airtight tin. Sprinkle with additional sugar before serving.

Low Calorie

32-CALORIE APRICOT PINWHEELS

So delicious, you'll never guess they're dietetic!

Bake at 375° for 12 minutes.
Makes 7 dozen cookies at 32 calories each.

1 cup apricots, finely chopped
½ cup boiling water
2½ cups sifted all-purpose flour
½ teaspoon baking powder
10 tablespoons butter or margarine, softened
¼ cup firmly packed brown sugar
Sugar substitute to equal 4 tablespoons sugar
6 tablespoons cold water

1. Combine apricots and boiling water in small bowl; allow to stand until most of water is absorbed. Drain.
2. Sift flour and baking powder into mixing bowl.
3. Beat butter or margarine, brown sugar, sugar substitute and water until well blended; add to flour mixture. Blend with fork until mixture forms a ball.
4. Place dough on wax paper; flatten slightly. Wrap in the wax paper; chill in freezer 20 minutes.
5. Roll out dough on a floured surface to form 24x10-inch rectangle. Spread drained apricots over dough. Roll up dough from the longer side to form a 24-inch long roll; cut in half. Wrap each roll in wax paper. Chill 3 hours or overnight.
6. Cut rolls into ⅜-inch-thick slices. Place on nonstick cooky sheets.
7. Bake in a moderate oven (375°) for 12 minutes. Let the cookies cool on paper toweling.

Old-fashioned Christmas cookies to give as gifts or to have on hand when family and friends stop by. Top right: molded Springerle. Center: spicy cut-out Pepparkakor. Also shown: chocolate-nut-tipped Spritz Slims and Noel Wreaths. Recipes in this chapter.

Country-fresh fruit pies to enjoy any time of the year. From top left, clockwise: Fresh Latticed Peach Pie, Nectarine Streusel Pie, Fresh Blueberry Pie, and Deep-Dish Rhubarb-Strawberry Pie. Recipes in this chapter.

6

PIES AND TARTS

It's easy to see why pie is such a big favorite. Few desserts are as versatile. A light, golden pastry shell can be filled with a bubbly fruit, a frothy chiffon, a smooth cream, custard or cheese filling. They're all delicious, and they're all in this chapter.

FLAKY PASTRY I

Makes enough for one 9-inch double-crust pie or lattice-top pie.

2 cups <u>sifted</u> all-purpose flour
1 teaspoon salt
⅔ cup vegetable shortening
4 or 5 tablespoons cold water

1. Sift flour and salt into a medium-size bowl; cut in shortening with a fork or pastry blender until mixture is crumbly.
2. Sprinkle water over mixture, 1 tablespoon at a time; mix lightly with a fork just until pastry holds together and leaves sides of bowl clean. Divide dough in half.
3. To make bottom crust, roll out half to a 12-inch round on a lightly floured surface. Fit into a 9-inch pie plate. Trim overhang to ½ inch.
4. To make top crust, roll out remaining pastry to an 11-inch round. Cut several slits or decorator cutouts near the center (to let steam escape).
5. Once pie is filled, place top crust over filling. Trim overhang to ½ inch, even with bottom pastry. Pinch to seal. Turn edge up and in, to seal in juices. Pinch again to make stand-up edge; flute, or try one of the other pie edgings shown on page 105.
6. Bake pie, and cool, following directions in individual recipes.

Lattice Top: For easy-to-follow directions on how to make a lattice top, see page 105.

SPECIAL TIPS: Here are a few pointers to help make your pastry flaky, light and easy to make.
• Handle pastry dough *as little as possible;* unlike bread dough, pastry dough that's overhandled will become tough. As soon as the dough holds together, form a ball; flatten the ball; then roll the dough out to the size specified.
• Always roll pastry dough from the center to the edge. That way, your crust will be even in size and thickness.
• Turn the dough gently as you roll it, to prevent it from sticking.
• For a good size marker, use your pie plate! Turn it upside down on the rolled dough. Then, you can judge how much more rolling to do.
• To help center the pastry dough in your pie plate, fold the rolled pastry in half over your rolling pin; lay one half over the pie plate. When the rolling pin is across the center, flip the other half over the rest of the pie plate.
• Be sure to fit the dough *loosely* in your pie plate. If the dough is stretched taut, it will shrink during baking.
• Trimmings from pastry can be re-rolled, cut and sprinkled with sugar and cinnamon for extra treats.

FLAKY PASTRY II

Make enough for one 9-inch pastry shell, for a single-crust pie.

1½ cups <u>sifted</u> all-purpose flour
1 teaspoon salt
½ cup vegetable shortening
4 tablespoons cold water (about)

1. Sift flour and salt in a medium-size bowl; cut in shortening with a fork or pastry blender, until mixture is crumbly.
2. Sprinkle water over mixture, 1 tablespoon at a time; mix lightly with a fork just until pastry holds together and leaves sides of bowl clean. Make a ball; flatten it.
3. Roll out to a 12-inch round on a lightly floured surface; fit into a 9-inch pie plate. Trim overhang to ½ inch. Turn edge under. Pinch to make a stand-up edge; flute, or try one of the other decorative pie edgings shown on page 105.

For baked pastry shells: Prick shell well all over with a fork. Bake in a very hot oven (450°) 5 minutes. Look at shell; if bubbles have formed, prick again. (After about 5 minutes of baking, pastry will have set and any bubbles formed will be permanent.) Continue to bake another 10 minutes, or until pastry is golden brown. Cool completely, in pie plate, on a wire rack.

SPECIAL TIPS: There's another way to bake your unfilled pastry shell smooth and bubble-free besides pricking all over with a fork. Fit a piece of foil or wax paper in bottom of plate over pastry; fill the shell with rice or beans (which can be reused); then bake 5 minutes, or until pastry is set. Remove rice or beans and foil or wax paper. Continue to bake until crust is golden brown.
• For lattice pies as well as pastry shells, turn edges of dough *under* and pinch to form a stand-up edge. Reason: There's no need to seal in juices, as there is with most two-crust pies; so the edge can be turned under for a neater appearance.

CRUMB CRUST

Makes one unbaked 9-inch crust.

1⅓ cups graham cracker crumbs (about 18 squares)
¼ cup sugar
¼ cup butter or margarine, softened

1. Mix graham cracker crumbs and sugar in a small bowl; blend in butter or margarine.
2. Press firmly over bottom and side of a buttered 9-inch pie plate; chill while making pie filling.

Vanilla Wafer-Pecan Crumb Crust: Combine 1 cup vanilla wafer crumbs with ½ cup ground pecans and ¼ cup softened butter or margarine in a small bowl. Press firmly over bottom and side of a lightly buttered 9-inch pie plate.

For baked crumb crusts: Bake in a moderate oven (350°) 8 minutes, or until set. Cool completely on a wire rack.

Low Calorie

SLIM-DOWN GRAHAM CRACKER CRUST

Bake at 400° for 5 minutes.
Makes one 9-inch crumb crust.
Total calories: 534.

3 tablespoons soft diet margarine
1 cup packaged graham cracker crumbs

1. Blend margarine and crumbs thoroughly, using a fork. Press onto bottom and side of a 9-inch pie plate, covering all surfaces except rim.
2. Bake in hot oven (400°) 5 minutes. Cool before filling.

SOUR CREAM PASTRY FOR TURNOVERS

Makes enough for 12 turnovers.

3 cups sifted all-purpose flour
2 tablespoons sugar
1 cup (2 sticks) butter or margarine
1 cup dairy sour cream

1. Measure flour and sugar into a medium-size bowl.
2. Cut in butter or margarine with a pastry blender until mixture is crumbly. Add sour cream.
3. Mix lightly with a fork until dough clings together and starts to leave side of bowl. Gather dough together with hands and knead a few times.
4. Wrap dough in plastic wrap or wax paper; chill several hours, or overnight.

COOKY CRUST PASTRY

Makes one 10-inch crust.

2 cups sifted all-purpose flour
½ cup sugar
¾ cup (1½ sticks) butter or margarine, softened
2 egg yolks, slightly beaten
1 teaspoon vanilla

Mix flour and sugar together in a medium-size bowl; cut in butter or margarine with a pastry blender

until mixture is crumbly. Add egg yolks and vanilla; mix lightly with a fork just until pastry holds together and leaves side of bowl clean. Chill until ready to use.

Note: For half the recipe, use 1 cup flour, ¼ cup sugar, 6 tablespoons butter or margarine, 1 egg yolk and ½ teaspoon vanilla.

FRUIT PIES

SPECIAL TIP: How many servings do you get from one pie? It all depends upon the richness. For fruit pies, figure 6 generous servings. For custard, cream and other rich pies, count on 8 servings. And for super-sweets such as Virginia Pecan Pie, smaller portions are usually sufficient.

FRESH LATTICED PEACH PIE

Fresh ripe peach pie with a see-through top. Enjoy this Southern favorite any time.

Bake at 425° for 15 minutes, then at 350° for 40 minutes.
Makes one 9-inch pie with lattice top.

½ cup sugar
2 tablespoons sifted all-purpose flour
½ teaspoon ground cinnamon
¼ teaspoon salt
6 ripe peaches (about 5 pounds)
1 tablespoon lemon juice
¼ teaspoon almond extract
Flaky Pastry 1 (recipe page 102)
OR: **1 package piecrust mix**
Milk or cream
Sugar

1. Mix sugar, flour, cinnamon and salt together.
2. Drop peaches, 3 or 4 at a time, into boiling water; leave in 15 to 30 seconds; lift out with slotted spoon. Peel off skins; cut in half; remove pits, then slice (you should have 10 cups).
3. Place peaches in a large bowl; sprinkle with lemon juice and almond extract; toss lightly. Sprinkle with sugar mixture; toss gently to mix.
4. Prepare pastry. Spoon filling into bottom crust; dot with remaining butter. Cover with lattice top (for easy directions, see page 105). Brush lattice top with milk or cream and sprinkle with sugar.
5. Bake in a hot oven (425°) 15 minutes; then lower heat to 350°; continue to bake 35 to 40 minutes longer, or until pastry is golden and juices bubble up near center. Cool on wire rack 1 hour.

SUGAR-FROSTED APPLE PIE

Packed with spiced and sugared apples, this is our version of one of America's favorites.

Bake at 425° for 35 minutes.
Makes one 9-inch double-crust pie.

Flaky Pastry I (recipe page 102)
OR: **1 package piecrust mix**
6 **medium-size apples, pared, quartered, cored and sliced thin (6 cups)**
1 **cup sugar**
2½ **tablespoons flour**
¾ **teaspoon ground cinnamon**
¼ **teaspoon ground nutmeg**
¼ **teaspoon ground mace**
¼ **teaspoon salt**
2 **tablespoons butter or margarine**
Milk or cream
1 **tablespoon sugar (for topping)**

1. Prepare pastry.
2. Mix sugar, flour, cinnamon, nutmeg, mace and salt in a large bowl; add apple slices; toss gently to mix; spoon into bottom crust; dot with butter or margarine. Cover with top crust. Pinch crust edges together; turn up and in. Pinch again to form a stand-up edge; flute.
3. Brush top with milk or cream. Sprinkle with sugar.
4. Bake in a hot oven (425°) 35 minutes or until golden brown and juices bubble through slits. Cool pie completely on a wire rack.

DEVONSHIRE APPLE PIE

Our favorite one-crust apple pie—thick apple filling with moist crumb topping. Superb!

Bake at 350° for 40 minutes.
Makes one 9-inch single-crust pie.

Flaky Pastry II (recipe page 102)
OR: **½ package piecrust mix**
¾ **cup granulated sugar**
¾ **cup firmly packed brown sugar**
2 **tablespoons flour (for filling)**
1 **teaspoon ground cinnamon**
¼ **teaspoon ground nutmeg**
1 **teaspoon lemon juice**
¾ **cup dairy sour cream**
6 **medium-size tart apples, pared, quartered, cored and sliced (6 cups)**
½ **cup flour (for topping)**
¼ **cup (½ stick) butter or margarine**

1. Prepare *unbaked* pastry shell.
2. Mix granulated sugar, ¼ cup of the brown sugar, the 2 tablespoons flour, cinnamon, nutmeg, lemon juice and sour cream in a large bowl; stir in apples. Spoon into prepared pastry shell.
3. Mix the ½ cup flour and remaining ½ cup brown sugar in a small bowl; cut in butter or margarine with a pastry blender until mixture is crumbly. Sprinkle over apple filling.
4. Bake in a moderate oven (350°) 40 minutes, or until apples are tender and topping is golden. Cool completely on a wire rack.

NECTARINE STREUSEL PIE

We've used nectarines in this fabulous butter and brown sugar-topped pie. You can use peaches or apricots instead—the result will be equally delicious.

Bake at 425° for 45 minutes.
Makes one 9-inch single-crust pie.

2½ **pounds nectarines (or peaches or apricots)**
½ **teaspoon grated lemon rind**
1 **teaspoon lemon juice**
¾ **cup granulated sugar**
3 **tablespoons quick-cooking tapioca**
½ **teaspoon ground cinnamon**
Flaky Pastry II (recipe page 102)
OR: **½ package piecrust mix**
1 **tablespoon butter or margarine**
¼ **cup firmly packed brown sugar**
½ **cup sifted all-purpose flour**
¼ **cup (½ stick) butter or margarine, cut up**

1. Drop nectarines, (or peaches or apricots), 3 or 4 at a time, into boiling water; leave in 15 to 30 seconds; lift out with slotted spoon. Peel off skins; cut in half; remove pits, then slice evenly into a large bowl. Sprinkle with lemon rind and juice, sugar, tapioca and cinnamon; toss gently to mix.
2. Prepare *unbaked* pastry shell. Spoon nectarine (or peach, or apricot) mixture into shell; dot with the 1 tablespoon butter or margarine.
3. Combine brown sugar, flour and the ¼ cup butter or margarine in a small bowl. Work in butter with fingers, until crumbly. Sprinkle over fruit, covering completely. Cover top of pie loosely with a piece of aluminum foil.
4. Bake in a hot oven (425°) 30 minutes. Remove foil. Continue baking 15 minutes, or until streusel is set and juices bubble up. Cool pie completely on wire rack.

SPECIAL TIPS: Don't forget to cover the top of this pie with aluminum foil; otherwise the top will brown too quickly, long before pie is done.
• To catch any syrup that may boil over during baking, slide a piece of aluminum foil on the rack below the pie.

Decorative Pie Edgings

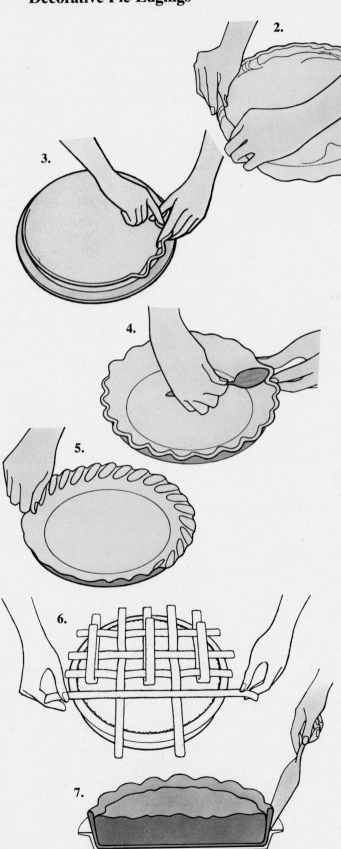

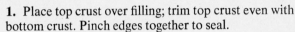

1. Place top crust over filling; trim top crust even with bottom crust. Pinch edges together to seal.

2. Turn sealed edge *up and in,* to seal in juices; pinch to form a stand-up edge. For one- or two-crust pies, try one of the decorative edges below.

3. Fluted edge: Place left thumb and forefinger along inside of rim. With right forefinger, pull pastry in, towards center of pie shell. Or place left thumb and forefinger outside rim. Press right forefinger on inside of rim, between fingers; push outward. Either way, repeat about every inch.

4. Scalloped edge: Place left thumb and forefinger on outside of rim. With a teaspoon, press inside of rim between fingers, forming a large, rounded scallop. Repeat about every inch.

5. Rope edge: Press pie rim firmly between thumb and forefinger of right hand, pushing down, towards the right, with thumb. Continue pressing, turning pie clockwise as you do.

Note: Left-handed people should reverse hands in directions for Steps 3, 4 and 5.

6. Lattice Top: Roll remaining half of FLAKY PASTRY I dough, or other dough being used, to a 12x8-inch rectangle. Cut lengthwise into ½-inch strips. Weave into a lattice over pie filling. Trim overhang even with bottom crust. Pinch to seal edge. Turn sealed edge *under*. Pinch again to make stand-up edge; flute.

Note: You may find it easier to weave the lattice on a piece of wax paper; then flip it over filling. Also, a pastry wheel will make pretty, unusually shaped lattice strips.

7. There are three reasons why a stand-up edge of any type is better than edges that are flush with the rim. First, a high edge is attractive. Second, a high edge allows you to put in more filling, making a really full pie. Most important though, you won't lose your lovely edge when serving each portion.

Sugar-Frosted Apple Pie—hot, juicy, bursting with apples. Recipe for the classic All-American favorite is in this chapter.

FRESH BLUEBERRY PIE

When it comes to Blueberry Pie, summer is almost worth waiting for—that's when fresh, popping-sweet blueberries are in season. To rush the season, use frozen or canned berries—always in plentiful supply.

Bake at 425° for 15 minutes, then at 350° for 35 minutes.
Makes one 9-inch double-crust pie.

   4 cups fresh blueberries (or equivalent frozen, or canned, drained blueberries)
   1 cup sugar
   ¼ cup <u>sifted</u> all-purpose flour
   ¼ teaspoon salt
   ¼ teaspoon ground cloves
   ¼ teaspoon ground cinnamon
   Flaky Pastry I (recipe page 102)
   OR: **1 package piecrust mix**
   3 tablespoons butter or margarine
   Milk or cream
   Sugar

1. Wash berries gently; drain well; place in a large bowl. Sprinkle with sugar, flour, salt, cloves, cinnamon; toss to mix.
2. Prepare pastry. Spoon blueberry mixture into bottom crust; dot with butter. Cover with top crust. Pinch crust edges together; turn up and in. Pinch again to form a stand-up edge; flute. Brush crust with milk or cream; sprinkle with sugar.
3. Bake in a hot oven (425°) 15 minutes; then lower oven temperature to 350° and continue to bake 35 minutes longer, or until pastry is golden and juices bubble up. Cool at least 1 hour on wire rack.

COUNTRY CHERRY PIE

Here's a delicious cherry pie your family will love. Cut out a pretty design in the top crust, so the bright, red filling shows through.

Bake at 425° for 30 minutes.
Makes one 9-inch double-crust pie.

   Flaky Pastry I (recipe page 102)
   OR: **1 package piecrust mix**
   2 cans (1 pound each) pitted sour cherries
   1 cup sugar
   3 tablespoons cornstarch
   ¼ teaspoon salt
   Red food coloring
   Milk or cream
   Sugar

1. Prepare pastry.
2. Drain cherries; reserve ½ cup of the juice.
3. Combine sugar, cornstarch and salt in a sauce-

pan; stir in the ½ cup reserved juice. Cook over medium heat, stirring constantly, until mixture thickens and bubbles 1 minute. Add cherries and a few drops of red food coloring.
4. Spoon filling into bottom crust. Cover with top crust. Trim overhang to ½ inch, even with bottom crust. Pinch edges together. Turn sealed edge up and in. Pinch again to form stand-up edge; flute. Brush top with milk or cream and sprinkle with sugar.
5. Bake in a hot oven (425°) 30 minutes or until pastry is golden and filling is bubbly. Cool completely on a wire rack.

DEEP-DISH CHERRY PIE

Here's the traditional deep-dish cherry pie with plenty of juicy fruit under a blanket of golden pastry.

Bake at 425° for 50 minutes.
Makes one deep 6-cup pie.

   3 cans (1 pound each) pitted tart red cherries, drained
   1¾ cups sugar
   ⅓ cup quick-cooking tapioca
   1 teaspoon grated lemon rind
   ⅛ teaspoon salt
   Flaky Pastry II (recipe page 102)
   OR: **½ package piecrust mix**
   2 tablespoons butter or margarine

1. Place cherries in a large bowl; sprinkle with sugar, tapioca, lemon rind and salt; toss lightly to mix. Let stand while making pastry.
2. Prepare pastry. Roll out on a lightly floured surface; roll enough to cover a 6-cup shallow baking dish. (*Note:* To make sure pastry top will fit, turn your baking dish upside down over rolled-out pastry and measure, allowing an extra inch all around.) Cut several slits near center to let steam escape.
3. Spoon cherry mixture into baking dish; dot with butter or margarine. Cover with pastry; fold edges under, flush with sides of baking dish. (Pastry should be *inside* dish.) Pinch to make a stand-up edge; flute.
4. Bake in a hot oven (425°) 50 minutes, or until pastry is golden and juices bubble up. Cool at least 1 hour on a wire rack. The best way to serve deep-dish pies is in individual bowls. Pass around pour cream, or serve with vanilla ice cream.

SPECIAL TIP: *Don't* cover the outside rim of your baking dish with pastry. The advantages of preparing a deep-dish pie with the pastry *inside* the baking dish are that your pie will have an attractive appearance when you bring it to the table; also, you won't lose part of the crust when you serve each portion.

DEEP-DISH RHUBARB-STRAWBERRY PIE

Everyone will love the tart-sweet taste of this attractive, baked fruit dessert.

Bake at 425° for 40 minutes.
Makes one deep 8-inch pie with lattice top.

¾ cup sugar
⅓ cup sifted all-purpose flour
1 teaspoon ground cinnamon
½ teaspoon ground cloves
1 pound fresh rhubarb
1 pint strawberries
2 tablespoons butter or margarine
Flaky Pastry II (recipe page 102)
OR: ½ package piecrust mix
Milk or cream
Sugar

1. Mix sugar, flour, cinnamon and cloves in bowl.
2. Wash rhubarb; trim ends; cut into 1-inch pieces (you should have 6 cups); wash strawberries; hull and halve (you should have 4 cups). Place both in a large bowl. Sprinkle with sugar mixture; toss lightly to mix. Let stand 15 minutes. Toss again.
3. Spoon rhubarb-strawberry filling into an 8x8x2-inch baking dish; dot with butter or margarine.
4. Prepare pastry. Roll out to a 10-inch square on a lightly floured surface. Cut in ½-inch strips with a pastry wheel or knife. Weave strips into a lattice. Cover filling. Turn ends under just enough so that strips touch sides of baking dish. Brush lattice top lightly with milk or cream; sprinkle with sugar.
5. Bake in a hot oven (425°) 40 minutes, or until pastry is golden and juices bubble up. Cool. Serve warm with vanilla ice cream, if you wish.

CHIFFON PIES

CHOCOLATE CHIFFON PIE

Light, elegant chocolate pie topped with whipped cream. Try chocolate curls for the perfect garnish (recipe page 78).

Makes one 9-inch single-crust pie.

Flaky Pastry II (recipe page 102)
OR: ½ package piecrust mix
1 envelope unflavored gelatin
¾ cup sugar
2 cups milk
4 squares unsweetened chocolate, cut up
4 eggs, separated
1 teaspoon vanilla
1 cup heavy cream

1. Prepare *baked* pastry shell.
2. Mix gelatin and sugar in a medium-size saucepan; stir in milk until well blended; add chocolate.
3. Cook, stirring constantly, until gelatin dissolves and chocolate melts. Remove saucepan from heat.
4. Beat egg yolks with fork in a small bowl; gradually pour a generous ½ cup of the hot chocolate mixture into eggs. Stir back into saucepan.
5. Cook, stirring constantly, 3 minutes, or until mixture thickens. Remove from heat; stir in vanilla. Pour into a bowl. Chill 1 hour or until cold.
6. Beat egg whites in a small bowl with electric mixer at high speed until stiff, but not dry.
7. Fold egg whites into cold chocolate mixture until well blended. Pour into baked pastry shell.
8. Chill at least 4 hours, or overnight. Just before serving, beat cream in a small bowl until stiff. Top pie with whipped cream. Either chocolate curls or chocolate shavings (see page 76) make nice garnishes.

Low Calorie

SKINNY CHOCOLATE CHIFFON PIE

Here's a trimmed-down version of our Chocolate Chiffon Pie—with calories cut every step of the way.

Makes one 8-inch crumb-crust pie; 8 servings at 198 calories each, or 10 servings at 158 calories each.

Slim-Down Graham Cracker Crust
(recipe page 103)
1 envelope unflavored gelatin
½ cup nonfat dry milk powder
⅓ cup unsweetened cocoa powder
½ teaspoon salt
1⅓ cups water
3 eggs, separated
¼ cup sugar
2 teaspoons vanilla
Sugar substitute to equal ¼ cup sugar

1. Prepare SLIM-DOWN GRAHAM CRACKER CRUST.
2. Combine gelatin, nonfat dry milk powder, cocoa, salt and water in a medium-size saucepan. Cook over medium heat, stirring constantly, until gelatin is dissolved and mixture is smooth. Cool slightly.
3. Beat egg yolks slightly; stir into warm mixture. Cook over low heat, stirring constantly, just until mixture comes to a boil. Remove from heat. Refrigerate; stir occasionally.
4. Beat egg whites until soft peaks form. Gradually beat in sugar. Beat until stiff.
5. Stir vanilla and sugar substitute into cool chocolate mixture; beat at high speed for 1 minute; fold into egg whites. Turn mixture into graham cracker crumb crust. Refrigerate 3 hours, or until firm. Garnish with prepared low-calorie whipped cream topping and toasted, sliced almonds, if you wish.

STRAWBERRY CHIFFON PIE

What better dessert is there than a beautiful and refreshing strawberry chiffon pie? Absolutely delicious!

Makes one 9-inch single-crust pie.

    Flaky Pastry II (recipe page 102)
    OR: ½ package piecrust mix
4 cups (2 pints) strawberries
1 cup sugar
2 envelopes unflavored gelatin
½ cup water
3 egg whites
1½ cups heavy cream

1. Prepare *baked* pastry shell.
2. Wash strawberries and hull. Slice enough to make 3 cups; reserve the remainder for garnish.
3. Combine sliced strawberries and ½ cup of the sugar in a medium-size bowl; let stand 5 minutes; mash well or press through a sieve into a large bowl.
4. Soften gelatin in water in a small saucepan. Heat slowly until gelatin dissolves; cool slightly, then stir into strawberry mixture. Place bowl in a pan of ice and water to speed setting; chill, stirring several times, until mixture begins to thicken.
5. While gelatin mixture chills, beat egg whites in a medium-size bowl until foamy white; slowly beat in remaining ½ cup sugar, until meringue stands in firm peaks. In a medium-size bowl, beat 1 cup of the cream until stiff. Fold meringue, then whipped cream into strawberry mixture until no streaks of white remain. Pour into cooled pastry shell. Chill several hours, or until firm.
6. Just before serving, beat remaining cream in a small bowl until stiff; spoon on center of pie. Garnish with remaining strawberries.

BLACK BOTTOM PIE

Rich chocolate on the bottom; light rum-flavored filling above. Top with whipped cream and garnish with chocolate curls for a picture-perfect pie.

Makes one 9-inch single-crust pie.

    Flaky Pastry II (recipe page 102)
    OR: ½ package piecrust mix
2 tablespoons cornstarch
1¼ cups sugar
3 cups milk
6 egg yolks, well beaten
1½ teaspoons vanilla
2 squares unsweetened chocolate, melted
1 envelope unflavored gelatin
¼ cup cold water
3 tablespoons golden rum
4 egg whites

1. Prepare *baked* pastry shell.
2. Combine cornstarch and ¼ cup of the sugar in a medium-size saucepan; slowly stir in milk. Cook over low heat, stirring constantly, until thickened. Blend in a small amount of the hot mixture into beaten egg yolks; return mixture to saucepan. Cook 2 minutes longer, stirring constantly, until custard coats spoon. Remove from heat; stir in vanilla.
3. Measure out 2 cups of the custard into a medium-size bowl; stir in chocolate; cool. Pour into baked pastry shell. Chill.
4. Soften gelatin in water in a custard cup; add to remaining hot custard; stir until dissolved. Stir in rum. Place bowl in a pan of ice and water to speed setting. Chill, stirring often, until slightly thickened.
5. Beat egg whites in a medium-size bowl until foamy white and double in volume; slowly beat in ½ cup sugar until meringue stands in firm peaks.
6. Fold meringue into chilled gelatin mixture; chill until mixture mounds. Spoon over chocolate layer.
7. Chill several hours, preferably overnight, until firm. Garnish with whipped cream and chocolate curls (recipe page 78), if you wish.

Low Calorie

LEMON CHIFFON PIE

A well-chilled bowl and beaters and plenty of patience are all it takes to turn skim milk powder into the "whipped cream" that gives this luscious lemon filling its body. The calorie savings are worth it!

Makes one 9-inch single-crust pie; 8 servings at 129 calories each or 10 servings at 103 calories each.

    Slim-Down Graham Cracker Crust
    (recipe page 103)
1 envelope unflavored gelatin
½ cup cold water
2 eggs, separated
1 tablespoon grated lemon rind
4 tablespoons lemon juice
    Pinch of salt
¼ cup sugar
    Sugar substitute to equal ⅓ cup sugar
⅓ cup ice water
⅓ cup nonfat dry milk powder

1. Prepare SLIM-DOWN GRAHAM CRACKER CRUST.
2. Soften envelope of unflavored gelatin in the ½ cup cold water.
3. Combine egg yolks, lemon rind, 3 tablespoons of the lemon juice, salt and sugar in the top of a double boiler. Cook over boiling water, stirring constantly, until mixture is thickened, about 5 minutes.
4. Remove from heat; stir in softened gelatin and sugar substitute. Cool the mixture just until it reaches room temperature.

5. Beat egg whites until stiff peaks form (use a non-plastic bowl). Measure ice water, remaining 1 tablespoon of lemon juice and nonfat dry milk powder into small bowl. Beat with electric mixer at high speed until mixture is the consistency of stiffly whipped cream, about 8 to 10 minutes.
6. Fold the beaten egg whites and whipped nonfat dry milk into gelatin mixture; turn into cooled pie shell. Refrigerate about 4 hours, or until set.

PEACH MELBA CHIFFON PIE

This spectacular looking pie combines all of the features of luscious Peach Melba—creamy filling, raspberry sauce, peach slices on top!

Makes one 9-inch single-crust pie.

Flaky Pastry II (recipe page 102)
OR: ½ **package piecrust mix**
1 **can (1 pound, 14 ounces) sliced peaches, drained**
¾ **cup sugar (for filling)**
2 **envelopes unflavored gelatin**
4 **eggs, separated**
⅔ **cup milk**
1 **package (10 ounces) frozen raspberries, thawed**
1 **tablespoon cornstarch**
1 **tablespoon sugar (for topping)**
½ **cup frozen whipped topping, thawed (from a 4½-ounce container)**

1. Prepare *baked* pastry shell.
2. Chop peaches very fine, saving 6 slices for top.
3. Combine ½ cup of the sugar and gelatin in a medium-size saucepan; beat egg yolks with milk in a small bowl; stir into gelatin mixture. (Save egg whites and remaining ¼ cup sugar for Step 5.)
4. Cook gelatin mixture over low heat, stirring constantly, about 10 minutes, or until mixture coats a spoon. Cool slightly; stir in peaches. Place pan in a bowl of ice and water to speed setting; chill, stirring often, until mixture starts to thicken.
5. While peach mixture chills, beat egg whites in a medium-size bowl until foamy white; slowly beat in remaining ¼ cup sugar until meringue stands in firm peaks. Fold meringue into peach mixture until no streaks of white remain. Spoon into cooled pastry shell. Chill at least 2 hours, or until set.
6. Drain raspberries; reserve syrup. In a small saucepan, combine ½ cup syrup, cornstarch and 1 tablespoon sugar. Cook, stirring constantly, until mixture thickens and comes to a boil; let bubble 1 minute. Cool, then combine with raspberries. Spoon over top of pie, leaving about a 2-inch border all around. Refrigerate about 1 hour longer.
7. Just before serving, spoon the whipped topping in the center of the pie. Place reserved peaches around the topping, pinwheel fashion.

CUSTARD AND CREAM PIES

COCONUT CUSTARD PIE

One of America's favorite pies—crunchy coconut and vanilla in a smooth custard filling.

Bake shell at 425° for 3 minutes, then bake pie at 325° for 40 minutes.
Makes one 9-inch single-crust pie.

Flaky Pastry II (recipe page 102)
OR: ½ **package piecrust mix**
3 **cups milk**
4 **eggs**
⅓ **cup sugar**
¼ **teaspoon salt**
1 **can (3½ ounces) flaked coconut**
1 **teaspoon vanilla**

1. Prepare *unbaked* pastry shell.
2. Bake in a hot oven (425°) 3 minutes. Remove shell; cool; lower oven temperature to 325°.
3. In a medium-size saucepan, heat milk slowly until bubbles appear around edge.
4. In a large bowl, beat eggs slightly; stir in sugar and salt; slowly stir in milk. Strain into another bowl; stir in coconut and vanilla. Pour into partly baked pastry shell.
5. Bake in a slow oven (325°) 40 minutes, or until center is almost set, but still soft. (Do not overbake; custard will set as it cools.) Cool on a wire rack. Serve warm or chilled.

VIRGINIA PECAN PIE

This Southern treat is luscious and rich. Serve it in small portions with a drift of softly whipped cream.

Bake at 350° for 45 minutes.
Makes one 9-inch single-crust pie.

Flaky Pastry II (recipe page 102)
OR: ½ **package piecrust mix**
3 **eggs**
½ **cup sugar**
½ **teaspoon salt**
1 **cup dark corn syrup**
¼ **cup butter or margarine, melted**
1 **teaspoon vanilla**
1 **cup pecan halves**
1 **cup heavy cream, whipped**

1. Prepare *unbaked* pastry shell.
2. Beat eggs slightly in a medium-size bowl; blend in sugar, salt, corn syrup, butter or margarine and vanilla. Pour into prepared shell; arrange pecan

Lemon desserts—always refreshing, whether simple or elegant. Shown here, from top down: Lemon-Date Torte (recipe, Chapter 7); Lemon Meringue Pie (recipe, this chapter); and Lemon Pound Cake (recipe, Chapter 4).

Photographer: Bill McGinn

*Cool, summery Strawberry Chiffon Pie—
as pretty as it is delicious.
Recipe in this chapter.*

halves in pattern on top.

3. Bake in moderate oven (350°) 45 minutes, or until center is almost set, but still soft. (Do not overbake; filling will set as it cools.) Cool on wire rack. Spoon whipped cream around edge just before serving.

SPECIAL TIP: To tell if a custard pie is set, hold edge and jiggle ever-so-slightly. If pie still has large ripples, it's not ready. It should just "shiver" a bit.

LEMON MERINGUE PIE

Smooth, fresh-lemon flavor; dreamy cloud-like topping, and a neat serving every time.

Makes one 9-inch single-crust pie.

Flaky Pastry II (recipe page 102)
OR: ½ **package piecrust mix**
1⅓ **cups sugar (for filling)**
½ **cup cornstarch**
¼ **teaspoon salt**
2¼ **cups water**
4 **eggs, separated**
2 **tablespoons butter or margarine**
1 **tablespoon grated lemon rind**
½ **cup lemon juice**
¼ **teaspoon cream of tartar**
½ **cup sugar (for meringue)**

1. Prepare *baked* pastry shell.
2. Combine 1⅓ cups sugar, cornstarch and salt in a medium-size saucepan; gradually stir in water.
3. Cook over medium heat, stirring constantly, until mixture thickens and bubbles. Cook 1 minute. Remove from heat.
4. Beat egg yolks lightly in a small bowl; slowly blend in about ½ cup of the hot cornstarch mixture; stir back into remaining mixture in a saucepan. Cook over low heat, 2 minutes, stirring constantly; remove from heat. (Do not overcook.)
5. Stir in butter, lemon rind and juice; pour into cooled pastry shell. Press a piece of plastic wrap directly on filling to prevent formation of a skin. (Remove before topping pie.) Refrigerate.
6. Beat egg whites with cream of tartar in a medium-size bowl, until foamy white. Slowly add remaining sugar, continuing to beat until meringue stands in firm peaks.
7. Fit a pastry bag with a large notched tip. Fill with the meringue; press meringue into 6 to 8 large puffs on a greased and lightly floured cooky sheet. (You can also spoon meringue into puffs.)
8. Bake in a hot oven (425°) 3 to 5 minutes, or just until peaks turn golden. Cool on cooky sheet. When the puffs are cool, carefully place on the chilled pie with a small spatula.

SPECIAL TIP: The secret to good meringue is having as much sugar dissolve as possible. For best results, add sugar *only* after egg whites are foamy white.

HAWAIIAN COCONUT CREAM PIE

You don't have to visit the palm-thatched huts of Hawaii to enjoy wonderful coconut pie. You can make it in your own home—in almost no time at all.

Makes one 9-inch single-crust pie.

Flaky Pastry II (recipe page 102)
OR: ½ **package piecrust mix**
½ **cup sugar**
4 **tablespoons cornstarch**
¼ **teaspoon salt**
2¼ **cups milk**
3 **egg yolks**
1 **tablespoon butter or margarine**
2 **teaspoons vanilla**
¾ **cup flaked coconut**
1 **cup heavy cream, whipped**

1. Prepare *baked* pastry shell.
2. Combine ½ cup of the sugar, the cornstarch and salt in a medium-size saucepan. Stir milk in slowly.
3. Cook over low heat, stirring constantly, until mixture thickens and bubbles. Cook 1 minute.
4. Beat egg yolks slightly in a small bowl. Stir in ½ cup of the hot mixture, then stir back into saucepan. Cook, stirring 1 minute more. Stir in butter or margarine, vanilla and ½ cup of the coconut. Cool; pour into cooled pastry shell. Press a piece of plastic wrap directly on filling to prevent formation of a skin. Chill at least 1 hour.
5. Meanwhile, toast remaining coconut in a shallow pan in a moderate oven (350°). When pie is chilled, remove plastic wrap. Spread whipped cream over chilled filling. Sprinkle with the toasted coconut.

NEW ENGLAND PUMPKIN-NUT PIE

A dessert that's always in demand, even more appealing with golden candy-like topping. This recipe makes a very full pie!

Bake at 425° for 15 minutes, then at 375° for 30 minutes.
Makes one 9-inch single-crust pie.

Flaky Pastry II (recipe page 102)
OR: ½ **package piecrust mix**
2 **eggs**
1 **can (1 pound) pumpkin**
½ **cup granulated sugar**
½ **cup firmly packed brown sugar**

1 teaspoon salt
1 teaspoon ground cinnamon
¼ teaspoon ground cloves
¼ teaspoon ground nutmeg
1 tall can (1⅔ cups) evaporated milk
  Nut Topping (recipe follows)

1. Prepare *unbaked* pastry shell.
2. Beat eggs slightly in a large bowl; stir in pumpkin, granulated and brown sugars, salt, cinnamon, cloves and nutmeg; stir in evaporated milk.
3. Place pastry shell on middle shelf of oven. Pour pumpkin filling into shell.
4. Bake in a hot oven (425°) 15 minutes; lower oven temperature to moderate (375°). Continue baking 20 minutes.
5. Spoon NUT TOPPING around edge of pie. Bake 10 minutes longer, or until custard is almost set, but still soft in center. (Do not overbake; custard will set as it cools.) Cool pie completely on a wire rack. Leave plain or garnish with whipped cream, if you wish.

Nut Topping: Beat 3 tablespoons butter or margarine with ⅔ cup firmly packed brown sugar in a small bowl; stir in ⅔ cup coarsely chopped pecans until well blended.

CHEESE PIES

LATTICE CHERRY-CHEESE PIE

For a speedy and delicious dessert, cover this creamy cheese pie with a sweet cherry topping and bake a cheese lattice on top.

Bake at 350° for 30 minutes, then at 450° for 10 minutes.
Makes one 9-inch pie with lattice top.

    Cooky Crust Pastry (recipe page 103)
4 packages (3 ounces each) cream cheese
1 container (8 ounces) cottage cheese
¾ cup sugar
1 teaspoon vanilla
⅛ teaspoon ground nutmeg
2 eggs
¼ teaspoon ground cinnamon
1 can (1 pound, 5 ounces) cherry pie filling

1. Prepare pastry. Roll out to an 11-inch round on a lightly floured surface, or between 2 sheets of wax paper; fit into a 9-inch pie plate. Trim overhang to ½ inch; turn under. Pinch to form stand-up edge; flute.
2. Combine 3 packages of the cream cheese and cottage cheese in medium-size bowl; beat with electric beater until smooth; beat in sugar, vanilla and nutmeg. Add eggs, one at a time, beating well after

each addition; reserve ⅓ cup of mixture. Pour remaining cheese mixture into pastry shell.
3. Bake in moderate oven (350°) 30 minutes. Meanwhile, combine reserved cheese mixture and remaining 1 package cream cheese in bowl; beat until smooth. Fit a pastry bag with a plain round tip (about ¼ inch in diameter); fill with cream cheese mixture. Stir cinnamon into cherry pie filling.
4. Remove pie from oven; turn oven temperature to 450°. Spread cherry filling over top of pie. Pipe cheese mixture over pie in a lattice pattern and around edge. Bake in very hot oven (450°) 10 minutes longer, or until lattice is nicely browned. Cool completely on wire rack. Serve at room temperature.

STRAWBERRY CHEESE TART

Mellow cream cheese in a short, sweet crust, topped with fresh, red berries and bright green grapes—a large tart that's almost too pretty to eat!

Bake crust at 400° for 10 minutes, then at 350° for 5 minutes.
Makes one 10-inch single-crust tart.

½ recipe Cooky Crust Pastry (recipe page 103)
1 package (8 ounces) cream cheese, softened
¼ cup sugar
1 tablespoon heavy cream
1½ tablespoons orange juice
1 pint strawberries
½ pound green grapes
¼ cup apple jelly
2 tablespoons sliced almonds, toasted

1. Prepare COOKY CRUST PASTRY.
2. Butter removable bottom of a 9½-inch round fluted quiche pan. Roll out pastry to an 11-inch round on a lightly floured surface. Carefully slip bottom of quiche pan under pastry; lift bottom, with pastry, into pan; press firmly against sides, turning pastry under to make a stronger edge. Prick bottom and side well with a fork. Refrigerate 30 minutes.
3. Bake in a hot oven (400°) 10 minutes; lower heat to 350°. Bake 5 minutes longer, or until pastry is golden. Cool thoroughly on a wire rack.
4. Carefully remove side of pan, leaving pastry on removable pan bottom. Place on serving platter.
5. In a small bowl, beat cream cheese with an electric mixer until fluffy. Gradually beat in sugar, cream and orange juice. Spread over pastry. Refrigerate 1 hour.
6. Hull and halve enough strawberries to make 1 cup. Halve and seed (if necessary) enough grapes to make ¾ cup. Arrange strawberry and grape halves on filling.
7. In a small saucepan, melt jelly over low heat;

bring just to boiling. Cool slightly. Brush over fruit to glaze. Refrigerate until ready to serve. Just before serving, sprinkle with almonds.

TURNOVERS, TARTS, DUMPLINGS

NECTARINE-RASPBERRY TURNOVERS

Great to prepare now and freeze for later. Pop frozen turnovers in the oven for a snack for the kids; also, a company-good dessert for special occasions.

Preheat oven to 400°; bake at 375° for 25 minutes. Makes 12 turnovers.

    Sour Cream Pastry (recipe page 103)
¼ **cup sugar**
1 **cup nectarines, peeled, pitted and thinly sliced (about ½ pound)**
1 **package (10 ounces) quick-thaw frozen raspberries, thawed and drained**
    Water
    Sugar

1. Prepare pastry; chill as directed.
2. Make filling just before baking: Sprinkle sugar over nectarines in a small bowl; toss with a fork to mix well; add the well-drained raspberries. Preheat oven to hot (400°).
3. Divide dough in half. Keep one half refrigerated until ready to use. Roll out the other half on a lightly floured surface to a 15x10-inch rectangle; trim edges evenly with a pastry wheel or sharp knife. Cut into six 5-inch squares. Place about 2 tablespoons filling on each square; moisten edges with water; fold over to make triangles. Crimp edges with a fork to seal. Lift onto ungreased cooky sheet.
4. Reroll trimmings; cut into small leaves and rounds with a truffle cutter or pastry wheel. Brush tops of pastries with water; decorate with pastry cutouts; make 1 or 2 small gashes in top of each turnover to let steam escape. Sprinkle each turnover with sugar.
5. Lower oven temperature to moderate (375°) as soon as you put turnovers in. Bake 25 minutes, or until puffed and rich brown in color; remove to wire rack to cool. Serve warm. Repeat with remaining pastry and filling.

SPECIAL TIPS: If you wish to bake only 6 turnovers, fill and shape second half of pastry. Place turnovers in a single layer on a cooky sheet; freeze. When frozen, wrap in foil or transparent wrap. When ready to use, bake as directed, increasing baking time by about 5 minutes. There is no need to defrost.
• When baking either frozen or unfrozen turnovers,

remember to place the cooky sheet on the *upper third* of your oven—otherwise the bottoms may overbake.

DOUBLE APPLE TURNOVERS

Spicy apple turnovers are doubly good when applesauce gives a flavor bonus.

Preheat oven to 400°; bake at 350° for 25 minutes. Makes 12 turnovers.

    Sour Cream Pastry (recipe page 103)
2 **cups (about 2 small) apples, pared, cored**
¾ **cup applesauce**
¼ **cup firmly packed light brown sugar**
½ **teaspoon ground cinnamon**
¼ **teaspoon mace**
2 **tablespoons raisins**

1. Prepare pastry; chill as directed.
2. Combine apples, applesauce, sugar, cinnamon, mace and raisins in a small bowl. Mix well with a fork.
3. Roll out dough. Fill and bake turnovers following directions for NECTARINE-RASPBERRY TURNOVERS.

CHESS TARTS

An old English culinary masterpiece—tiny tarts chock full of fruits and nuts.

Bake at 450° for 10 minutes, then at 350° for 25 minutes.
Makes ten 3-inch tarts.

    Flaky Pastry I (recipe page 102)
    OR: **1 package piecrust mix**
½ **cup (1 stick) butter or margarine, softened**
1 **cup firmly packed brown sugar**
2 **eggs**
1 **teaspoon grated lemon rind**
½ **cup dairy sour cream**
¾ **cup walnuts, chopped**
¾ **cup dates, cut up**
½ **cup raisins**
    Sour cream
    Walnut halves

1. Prepare pastry. Roll out half the pastry on a lightly floured surface. Cut into five 5-inch rounds. Fit into foil tart pans (3-inch diameter, ⅓ cup capacity). Turn pastry under and pinch to make stand-up edge; flute. Repeat with remaining pastry.
2. Beat butter or margarine and brown sugar in a medium-size bowl. Beat in eggs, one at a time. Stir in lemon rind, sour cream, chopped walnuts, dates and raisins.

3. Place tart shells in jelly roll pan; spoon filling into each one.

4. Bake in a very hot oven (450°) 10 minutes. Lower heat to 350°; bake 25 minutes longer, or until filling is firm. Remove tarts from oven; cool on wire rack.

5. Carefully remove each tart from its pan. Serve topped with sour cream and garnish with walnut halves, if you wish.

SPECIAL TIP: For best results, don't remove cooled tarts from their pans until you're actually ready to serve them. For easy removal, gently hold the edge of each tart with one hand. With the other hand, use a small paring knife and very carefully lift the tart from the pan.

LEMON TARTLETS VERONIQUE

Cookylike shells hold mellow lemon filling—with glazed grapes on top. Pretty fruits to use another time: Strawberries, peach slices.

Bake shells at 375° for 22 minutes.
Makes one dozen 3-inch tarts.

  2 cups <u>sifted</u> all-purpose flour
  3 tablespoons sugar
  ½ teaspoon salt
  ½ cup (1 stick) butter or margarine
  ¼ cup shortening
  6 tablespoons water
     Lemon filling (recipe follows)
  1 pound seedless green grapes, stemmed
     and halved
  1 cup apple jelly, melted and cooled
  1 cup heavy cream

1. Sift flour, sugar and salt into a medium-size bowl. Cut in butter or margarine and shortening with a pastry blender until mixture is crumbly.

2. Sprinkle water over top; mix lightly with a fork until pastry holds together and leaves side of bowl clean. Turn out onto a lightly floured surface; knead just until smooth; divide dough into 12 even pieces. Chill dough 1 hour for easier handling.

3. Press each piece of dough into a 3-inch metal or foil tart-shell pan; cover bottom and side evenly. Fit a small piece of wax paper over pastry in each pan; pour uncooked rice or beans on top to hold pastry in place during baking. Set pans in a large shallow pan for easy handling.

4. Bake in a moderate oven (375°) 10 minutes; remove from oven. Lift out beans or rice and wax paper; return pans to oven. Bake 12 minutes longer, or until pastry is golden. Cool shells completely, in their pans, on wire racks.

5. Spoon LEMON FILLING into each shell; arrange grape halves, cut side up, on top, to form rosettes; brush grapes with apple jelly; chill.

6. Just before serving, beat cream in a medium-size bowl, until stiff. Attach a fancy tip to a pastry bag; fill bag with whipped cream; press out tiny rosettes on top of tartlets. (For directions on how to make your own disposable decorating bag, see page 13.) Chill until serving time.

Lemon Filling: Beat 6 eggs slightly in the top of a large double boiler; stir in 1 cup sugar, ½ cup (1 stick) butter or margarine, 2 teaspoons grated lemon rind, and ⅓ cup lemon juice. Cook, stirring, constantly, over hot, not boiling water, 15 minutes, or until very thick. Pour into a medium-size bowl; cover bowl with plastic wrap; chill until ready to use. Makes 3 cups.

PEACH DUMPLINGS

Luscious peaches, wrapped in flaky, light pastry. An old-fashioned dessert your family will love.

Bake at 425° for 30 minutes.
Makes 6 dumplings.

  ¾ cup water
  ½ cup granulated sugar (for syrup)
  ½ cup bottled grenadine syrup
     Flaky Pastry II (recipe page 102)
     OR: **1 package piecrust mix**
  ¼ cup firmly packed brown sugar
  ¼ teaspoon ground cinnamon
  1 tablespoon butter or margarine
  6 large peaches, peeled, halved and pitted
     Milk or cream
     Granulated sugar (for topping)

1. Combine water, the ½ cup granulated sugar, and grenadine syrup in a medium-size saucepan. Heat to boiling, then simmer 5 minutes; remove from heat.

2. Prepare pastry. Roll out on a lightly floured surface to an 18x12-inch rectangle; cut into six 6x6-inch squares.

3. Blend brown sugar, cinnamon and butter or margarine in a small bowl. Spoon into hollows in peach halves; press 2 halves back together.

4. Place a filled peach in center of each pastry square; fold pastry up and around fruit; pinch edges to seal. Place in a 13x9x2-inch baking pan. Brush dumplings lightly with milk or cream; sprinkle with granulated sugar.

5. Bake in a hot oven (425°) 30 minutes, or until pastry is golden and peaches are tender. (Test fruit with a long thin metal skewer.)

6. Cool slightly in pan on a wire rack. Serve warm, with cream or ice cream, if you wish.

Custard and cream pies—favorites from all sections of the country. Clockwise, from left: Virginia Pecan Pie, New England Pumpkin-Nut Pie and Hawaiian Coconut Cream Pie. Recipes for all are in this chapter.

Sliced nuts and meringue between the layers give this Almond Blitz Torte interesting texture—as well as delicate flavor. Recipe in this chapter.

7

SPECIALTIES

Our "Specialties" chapter is filled with spectacular desserts; luscious, fruit-filled strudel, rich cream puffs and eclairs, creamy cheesecakes, elegant tortes and a selection of delicately baked meringues. They're all so good, you won't know which to try first.

PASTRIES

APPLE-NUT STRUDEL

Enjoy making your own paper-thin strudel dough to roll up with a buttery apple-nut filling. Dough may also be used in place of *phyllo* in Baklava.

Bake at 400° for 35 minutes.
Makes one large strudel; 8 servings.

3 cups sifted all-purpose flour
¼ teaspoon salt
1 egg
¾ cup lukewarm water
2 tablespoons vegetable oil
¾ cup (1½ sticks) butter or margarine, melted
2 cups soft white bread crumbs (4 slices)
7 to 8 cups sliced, pared and cored cooking apples
¾ cup raisins
½ cup chopped walnuts
1¼ cups sugar
1½ teaspoons ground cinnamon
10X (confectioners') sugar

1. Sift flour and salt into a large bowl. Make a well in center of flour and add egg, water and vegetable oil. Stir to make a sticky dough.
2. Place dough on a lightly floured surface. Slap dough down onto board; pick up; continue to slap down and pick up the dough for 10 minutes to develop the gluten (as in bread, which gives the elasticity necessary for stretching the dough.) Cover dough with a bowl and allow to rest, undisturbed, for about 30 minutes.
3. Measure 4 tablespoons butter into large skillet; add bread crumbs and stir over medium-high heat. until crumbs are golden.
4. Place a clean fabric cloth or sheet on a kitchen or card table about 30 inches square. Sprinkle cloth with flour and rub in.
5. Roll out dough to as large a square as possible on floured cloth. Place hands, palm-side down, under dough and begin, gently, to stretch dough, moving around table until dough has stretched over all sides of the table. (*Note:* Be sure to remove rings and your watch to prevent holes in the dough.)
6. Sprinkle dough with about 4 tablespoons of the melted butter. Sprinkle crumbs over entire surface of dough.
7. Combine apples, raisins, nuts, sugar and cinnamon in a large bowl. Spoon apple mixture in an even row down one side of dough, 2 inches in from the edge.
8. Trim off thick parts of dough on all four overhanging sides with kitchen scissors.
9. Using the overhanging cloth to lift dough, roll dough over filling. Fold the two adjacent sides of the dough toward center, in order to completely enclose the filling.
10. Lift the cloth at filling end to allow dough to roll over and over on itself until completely rolled. (*Note:* If you'd prefer to make two smaller strudels, cut pastry in half on table. Fill both and roll simultaneously, using cloth as guide.)
11. Line a large cooky sheet with a double thickness of heavy-duty aluminum foil. Ease filled roll onto cooky sheet, shaping roll into horseshoe shape. Or, place two smaller rolls 2 inches apart on cooky sheet. Turn up end of foil 1 inch all around cooky sheet, to keep oven clean, in case of spill-over.
12. Bake in hot oven (400°) 35 to 40 minutes, brushing several times with remaining butter, or until pastry is golden.
13. Allow pastry to cool 15 minutes and then slide onto serving board. Sprinkle with 10X sugar.

SPECIAL TIPS: The secret to light, flaky strudel is in stretching the dough paper-thin. (It should be so thin that you could slip a piece of newspaper underneath and be able to read it.) You may use either your fingers or fists to stretch dough—whichever is easier.
- Once the edge of the dough is covering the filling, and the two adjacent sides are flipped over, roll up the strudel, exactly as you would a jelly roll.
- Here's the best way to freeze and reheat strudel: Wrap cooled strudel in foil or plastic wrap; then freeze. To reheat, place frozen strudel on cooky sheet; cover loosely with foil. Place in moderate oven (350°) for 30 minutes; remove foil and heat 10 to 15 minutes longer.

BAKLAVA

The fabulous pastry that Greece has contributed to the world of good eating. If you can't find phyllo or strudel pastry leaves, use a double recipe of strudel dough.

Bake at 325° for 50 minutes.
Makes one 13x9x2-inch pastry; 3½ dozen pieces.

3 cups walnuts (about ¾ pound), shelled
½ cup sugar
1½ teaspoons ground cinnamon
2 packages (8 ounces each) phyllo or strudel leaves or double recipe strudel dough (recipe at left)
½ cup (1 stick) unsalted butter or margarine, melted
1 tablespoon water
Honey Syrup (recipe follows)

1. Place walnuts on a 15½x10½x1-inch jelly roll pan; toast in a moderate oven (350°) 10 minutes. Whirl walnuts, while still warm, one-half cup at a time, in container of electric blender, until finely ground. (You may use a food grinder if you wish.) Remove ground walnuts to a medium-size bowl. Repeat this procedure until all of the walnuts are ground. Mix in sugar and ground cinnamon; set sugar-nut mixture aside.

2. Brush bottom of a 13x9x2-inch baking pan with melted butter. Fold two phyllo leaves in half; place on bottom of pan. (Or cut out and place two thicknesses of strudel dough in bottom of pan.) Brush with butter. Place two more folded leaves, or two layers of strudel dough, in pan; brush with butter. (Keep the rest of the pastry leaves, or strudel dough, covered with a clean damp kitchen towel to prevent pastry from drying out.)

3. Sprinkle top with ½ cup nut mixture. Add two more folded leaves; brush with butter.

4. Repeat Step 3 five more times. Stack remaining pastry leaves, brushing every other one. Brush top leaf with remaining butter; sprinkle with the 1 tablespoon water.

5. With a sharp knife, mark off the Baklava. Cut through the top layer *only* of the phyllo, making 5 lengthwise cuts, 1½-inches apart (you will have 6 equal strips). Then cut diagonally at 1½-inch intervals, making diamonds (9 strips). This is the traditional shape of the Baklava.

6. Bake in a slow oven (325°) 50 minutes, or until top is golden. Remove pan to wire rack. Cut *all the way* through the diamonds, separating slightly. Pour *cooled* honey syrup over. Cool thoroughly in pan on rack. Cover with foil; let stand overnight for syrup to be absorbed. No refrigeration necessary.

Honey Syrup: Makes 2 cups.

- **1 small lemon**
- **1 cup sugar**
- **1 cup water**
- **1 two-inch piece stick cinnamon**
- **2 whole cloves**
- **1 cup honey**
- **1 tablespoon brandy (optional)**

1. Remove rind (thin yellow, no white) from lemon; squeeze out 1½ teaspoons of lemon juice into a small cup; reserve.

2. Place lemon rind, sugar, water, cinnamon stick and cloves in a heavy medium-size saucepan. Bring to boiling; lower heat, continue to cook, without stirring, 25 minutes, or until mixture is syrupy (230° on a candy thermometer).

3. Stir in honey; pour the syrup through a strainer into a 2-cup measure. Stir in the reserved lemon juice and brandy.

LUTECE'S TARTE A L'ORANGE

A showcase for the full zesty flavor of fresh oranges; simple but possessing great elegance.

Preheat oven to 450°; bake at 400°, 35 minutes. Makes one 9-inch tart.

- **1 package (12 ounces) frozen patty shells, thawed**
- **6 medium-size oranges**
- **4 egg yolks**
- **⅓ cup sugar**
- **¼ cup flour**
- **1 teaspoon grated lemon rind**
- **6 packaged ladyfingers**
- **½ cup apricot preserves**
- **1 tablespoon sugar**
- **6 tablespoons Grand Marnier**

1. Heat oven to very hot (450°).

2. Arrange patty shells in a circle, just touching, on a floured surface. Roll out, keeping circular shape, to a 12-inch round. Fit into a 9-inch layer-cake pan with removable bottom or a 9-inch fluted quiche pan. Turn edge under; crimp. Fit a piece of foil into shell; fill shell with beans or rice.

3. Put shell into preheated oven; immediately turn heat down to 400°. Bake shell 15 minutes; remove beans and foil. Sprinkle bottom with sugar; prick lightly with a fork. Bake 20 minutes longer, or until golden and crisp and sugar starts to caramelize. Cool on wire rack.

4. Grate rind from 1 orange; reserve rind. Squeeze enough oranges to yield 1½ cups juice.

5. Beat egg yolks slightly in top of double boiler. Beat in sugar and flour; stir in orange juice. Cook over hot, not boiling, water until very thick, about 7 minutes, or until mixture mounds when dropped from spoon; cool. Add orange and lemon rinds.

6. Split ladyfingers in half. Slice each half lengthwise in half again.

7. Simmer apricot preserves and the 1 tablespoon sugar with 2 tablespoons of the Grand Marnier in a small saucepan, 2 minutes; rub through a fine sieve; cool slightly.

8. Slice the two remaining oranges in *paper-thin* slices; remove any seeds. (Notch edges, if you wish.) Put on a large plate; sprinkle with remaining 4 tablespoons Grand Marnier. Let stand 10 minutes.

9. Spoon orange cream into shell. Arrange the thin slices of ladyfingers over cream to cover completely (a chef's secret to absorb excess juice from orange slices). Fill in spaces with pieces cut to fit. Drain oranges. Sprinkle ladyfingers with liqueur drained from oranges.

10. Arrange orange slices over ladyfingers, slightly overlapping, in a circular pattern. Brush oranges and pastry with the preserves. Cool slightly. Refrigerate, unless serving at once.

121

CREAM HORNS PARISIENNE

This simplified version of puff pastry takes very little time and effort, yet it becomes a most elegant dessert, when completed.

Bake at 400° for 20 minutes.
Makes sixteen 5-inch horns.

3 cups <u>sifted</u> all-purpose flour
1½ cups (3 sticks) butter or margarine
1 cup dairy sour cream
Water
Sugar
Pink Cream Filling (recipe follows)

1. Measure flour into a medium-size bowl. Cut in butter or margarine with a pastry blender until mixture is crumbly; add sour cream. Knead lightly with hands just until pastry holds together and leaves side of bowl clean. Wrap dough in wax paper; chill overnight.
2. To make your own cream horn molds: Tear off eight 9-inch pieces heavy-duty foil from an 18-inch-wide roll. Cut each piece in half to make a square; Fold each square crosswise to make a triangle. Using center of longest side of triangle as tip of cone, start at one side and roll up to form a slim cone. (Fold tip down to secure the mold, or fasten with paper clip.)
3. Divide pastry in half. Keep one half refrigerated until ready to use. Roll out evenly to an 18x10-inch rectangle on floured surface. Cut pastry lengthwise into 8 strips, each 1¼ inches wide.
4. Moisten each strip lightly with water. Starting at pointed end, wrap around cone-shaped foil, overlapping slightly. Place on ungreased cooky sheet. Chill 30 minutes; brush each horn with water; sprinkle with sugar.
5. Bake in hot oven (400°) 20 minutes or until puffed and a rich brown color.
6. Remove horns to wire rack to cool. As each horn is cool enough to handle, carefully remove from mold. Cool completely before filling. Use same molds for baking second half of pastry.
7. Fill horns just before serving.

Pink Cream Filling: Beat 2 cups heavy cream, 2 tablespoons sugar and ½ teaspoon almond extract in medium-size bowl, until stiff. Fold in 2 tablespoons finely chopped maraschino cherries and 2 teaspoons syrup from cherries. Add a drop of red food coloring. Makes enough to fill 16 horns.

Note: If you wish to make only 8 horns, use only ½ of filling recipe. Shape second half of horns on molds. Place in a single layer in a pan; freeze. When frozen, wrap in foil or plastic wrap. When ready to use, fill horns and bake as directed. No need to defrost horns before baking them.

Basic Recipe

CREAM PUFF PASTE (Paté à Chou)

This recipe makes 12 large cream puffs or 12 large eclairs or 2 Viennese Mocha-Nut Crowns.

1 cup water
½ cup (1 stick) butter or margarine
¼ teaspoon salt
1 cup <u>sifted</u> all-purpose flour
4 eggs

1. Heat water, butter or margarine and salt to a full rolling boil in a large saucepan.
2. Add flour all at once. Stir vigorously with a wooden spoon until mixture forms a thick, smooth ball that leaves the side of pan clean (about 1 minute). Remove from heat; cool slightly.
3. Add eggs, one at a time, beating well after each addition, until paste is shiny and smooth. (Paste will separate as you add each egg, but with continued beating, it will smooth out.)
4. Shape, following recipe instructions.

VIENNESE MOCHA-NUT CROWN

A regal dessert that would have pleased the Emperor Franz Joseph himself; truly a royal treat.

Bake at 400° for 40 minutes.
Makes one ring; 6 servings.

½ recipe Basic Cream Puff Paste (recipe above)

Chocolate Praline Filling:
½ cup hazelnuts or almonds, unblanched
⅓ cup granulated sugar
2 cups heavy cream
⅓ cup unsweetened cocoa
½ cup 10X (confectioners') sugar

Chocolate Glaze (recipe follows)
Coffee Butter Cream (recipe follows)

1. Make BASIC CREAM PUFF PASTE. Draw a 7-inch circle on an ungreased cooky sheet. Spoon paste in 6 mounds, just inside circle. Or, press paste through a pastry bag. Puffs should almost touch.
2. Bake in a hot oven (400°) 40 minutes, or until puffed and golden brown. With a small knife, make slits in ring to let steam escape. Turn off heat; leave ring in oven 5 minutes longer. Remove to wire rack, then cool completely.
3. Make CHOCOLATE PRALINE FILLING: Combine nuts, sugar and water in a small heavy skillet. Bring to a boil, stirring constantly. Boil rapidly, uncovered, until nuts make a popping sound, about 10

This regal Viennese Mocha-Nut Crown pulls apart into six perfect chocolate cream puffs. Recipe in this chapter.

1.

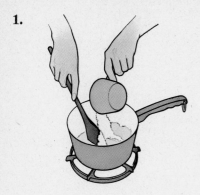

1. Be sure to add flour *all at once* to the boiling water and butter in the saucepan. Begin stirring with a wooden spoon as soon as flour is added.

2. Stir until the mixture forms a mass or ball that leaves the side of the pan and follows the spoon around.

2.

3.

3. Remove pan from heat. Beat in eggs, *one at a time*. Keep over heat one more minute, stirring constantly. (Paste will break apart and slide around, but don't worry—vigorous beating will blend it again. This will happen after each egg is added.) When last egg is beaten in, cool slightly. Now paste is ready to be shaped as the individual recipe directs.

4. You can shape cream puffs with a teaspoon. Just remember that the paste will puff up to three times its size, so be sure to allow enough room in between. For eclairs, spoon small mounds in a line, then connect with the swirl of a spatula.

4.

5.

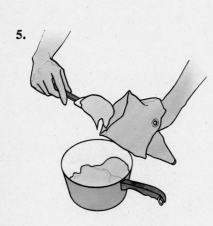

5. The easiest way to shape both cream puffs with eclairs is with a pastry bag fitted with a large round tip. Fold the top of the bag down, and slip your hand under the fold. You now have a good grip on the bag so you can pinch off each spoonful of paste as you fill the bag.

6. Squeeze out small mounds for the cream puffs, or tiny fingers for eclairs.

6.

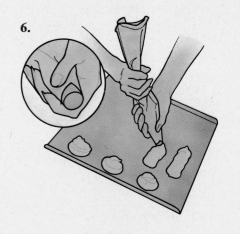

7. Make a small pilot hole in the end of the baked eclair, or side of baked puff, with a paring knife. Press filling through pastry bag fitted with a small round tip, inserted into pilot hole; fill hollow center.

8. For the VIENNESE MOCHA-NUT CROWN: The ring of puffs is easily formed with the pastry bag. Have swirls of paste almost touching on cooky sheet. When baked, they will be joined together in a ring. Complete according to recipe directions.

7.

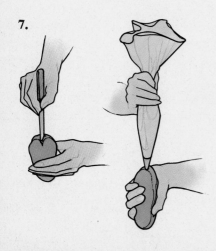

8.

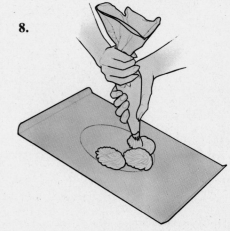

minutes. Remove from heat; stir with a wooden spoon until sugar crystallizes and becomes dry. Return pan to heat; cook over low heat until sugar starts to melt and form a glaze on nuts. Turn out onto a cooky sheet; separate with a fork; cool completely. Crush with a rolling pin, or whirl in a blender until almost powdery. Beat cream with cocoa and 10X sugar in a large bowl until stiff; fold in crushed nuts; chill.

4. To assemble: Split ring in half horizontally. Scoop out any filaments of soft dough.

5. Place bottom half of ring on serving plate. Spread with CHOCOLATE PRALINE FILLING. Place top of ring in place. Spoon CHOCOLATE GLAZE over each puff. Decorate top with small rosettes of COFFEE BUTTER CREAM. Garnish with whole nuts, if you wish. Refrigerate 1 hour, or until ready to serve.

Chocolate Glaze: Combine 1 square unsweetened chocolate, 1 tablespoon butter or margarine, 2 teaspoons brandy and 2 tablespoons water in a small bowl. Place in a pan of simmering water, stirring occasionally, until chocolate is melted. Remove from heat; stir in ½ cup 10X sugar. (If glaze is too thick, add more hot water.) Keep warm.

Coffee Butter Cream: Dissolve ¼ teaspoon instant coffee in ½ teaspoon water in a small bowl. Add 1 tablespoon soft butter or margarine and ¼ cup 10X sugar. Beat with a fork until smooth. Spoon into a cake decorating set or pastry bag fitted with a small notched tip. Press out into rosettes.

CHOCOLATE ECLAIRS

Luscious custard-cream-filled delights, shiny-bright with an easy chocolate glaze.

Bake at 400° for 40 minutes.
Makes 12 eclairs.

> 1 recipe Basic Cream Puff Paste (recipe page 122)
> Vanilla Custard Cream Filling (recipe follows)
> Chocolate Glaze (see Viennese Mocha-Nut Crown, above)

1. Make BASIC CREAM PUFF PASTE.
2. Attach a large plain tip to a pastry bag; spoon paste into bag. Press paste out into twelve 4-inch strips, 1½ inches apart, on an ungreased large cooky sheet (Or, spoon into finger-length strips.)
3. Bake in a hot oven (400°) 40 minutes, or until puffed and golden brown. Remove from cooky sheet to wire rack; cool completely.
4. Prepare VANILLA CUSTARD CREAM FILLING.
5. To fill eclairs: Make a small hole in the end of each eclair with a small knife. Fit pastry bag with plain tip; fill with VANILLA CUSTARD CREAM FILLING. Press filling into eclairs. Or, you may split eclairs

lengthwise, then spoon in filling. Spoon CHOCOLATE GLAZE over each eclair.

Vanilla Custard Cream Filling: For 12 eclairs.

> ¾ cup sifted all-purpose flour
> 1 cup sugar
> 3 cups milk
> 6 egg yolks
> 1 teaspoon vanilla

1. Combine flour and sugar in a medium-size saucepan. Slowly stir in milk. Heat to boiling, stirring constantly; lower heat. Continue cooking 2 to 3 minutes, stirring constantly, or until mixture is quite thick; remove from heat.
2. Beat egg yolks slightly in a medium-size bowl. Gradually beat in about 1 cup of the hot milk mixture. Pour all back into saucepan. Cook over medium heat, 1 minute, stirring constantly. Remove from heat; stir in vanilla. Place a piece of wax paper directly on surface of filling to prevent a skin from forming. Chill at least 2 hours.

STRAWBERRY CREAM PUFFS

Fresh strawberry filling in these golden puffs brings a welcome taste of spring to a dreary winter.

Bake at 400° for 40 minutes.
Makes 6 puffs.

> ½ recipe Basic Cream Puff Paste (recipe page 122)
> 1 pint fresh strawberries
> ¼ cup granulated sugar
> 1 cup heavy cream
> ½ teaspoon almond extract
> 10X (confectioners') sugar

1. Make BASIC CREAM PUFF PASTE.
2. Drop paste by rounded tablespoonfuls into 6 even mounds, 2 inches apart, on an ungreased large cooky sheet.
3. Bake in a hot oven (400°) 40 minutes, or until puffed and golden brown. Remove to wire rack; cool completely.
4. To make filling: Wash strawberries; set aside 6 for garnish. Hull remaining berries; slice into a medium-size bowl; stir in 3 tablespoons of the granulated sugar. Chill at least 30 minutes.
5. Beat cream with remaining granulated sugar and the almond extract in a medium-size bowl until stiff. Chill.
6. Just before serving, cut a slice from top of each puff; remove any filaments of soft dough. Fold sliced berries into cream, spoon about ⅓ cup into each puff; replace tops. Sieve 10X sugar over top. Arrange on a serving plate and garnish with strawberries and mint leaves, if you wish.

CAKES AND CHEESECAKES

MEADOW FLOWERS WEDDING CAKE

Here's a spectacular looking two-tier cake to bake for a wedding, anniversary, bridal shower—or any super-special occasion. The cake is simple to make, thanks to pound cake mix. Decorate it as you wish, with a tinted frosting lattice and your favorite fresh flowers. See page 79 for decorating suggestions.

Bake at 325° for 1 hour and 5 minutes.
Makes one 2-tier cake; about 30 servings.

**3 packages (16 to 17 ounces each) pound
   cake mix
   Apricot Glaze (recipe follows)
   Rich Butter Cream Frosting (recipe follows)**

1. Grease a 13x9x2-inch baking pan; line bottom with wax paper; grease again.
2. Prepare 2 packages of pound cake mix following label directions. Pour into pan.
3. Grease an 8x8x2-inch baking pan. Line bottom with wax paper; grease paper.
4. Prepare third package of pound cake mix following label directions. Pour into pan. Stagger pans on oven racks as near center of oven as possible.
5. Bake both cakes in a slow oven (325°) 1 hour and 5 minutes, or until centers spring back when lightly pressed with fingertip. Cool cakes 10 minutes on wire racks; loosen around edges with a knife; turn out onto wire racks; cool completely.

Putting The Cake Together:

1. Prepare APRICOT GLAZE and RICH BUTTER CREAM FROSTING. Trim off all brown edges of cakes. Trim tops of layers, if humped, so they will stack evenly.
2. Split each cake into two layers. Spread a thin layer of frosting in between the layers. Put layers together again to form two cakes.
3. Stack the small cake on the large cake with a thin layer of frosting.
4. Brush all surfaces of cakes with APRICOT GLAZE; let glaze set, about 15 minutes.
5. Spread a thin layer of frosting on sides and top of assembled cake, to secure any stray crumbs; let set, about 15 minutes.
6. Reserve about 1½ cups of the RICH BUTTER CREAM FROSTING for decorating. Tint with food coloring, if you wish. Frost the entire cake smoothly with the remaining RICH BUTTER CREAM FROSTING.

Decorating the Cake: (See drawing on page 79.)

1. For lattice, mark off design in frosting (with a wooden pick). Make several disposable wax paper cones (directions on page 13), or else use a cake decorating set fitted with a plain writing tip. Fill cone with frosting; cut ⅛-inch off point for opening. Pipe frosting in lattice design, as pictured. Discard cone as it wears thin; squeeze any frosting into another cone.
2. For border (if you wish): Cut tip of wax paper cone in an inverted "V". (Or fit cake decorating set with a leaf tip.) Fill cone with frosting. Make overlapping leaf design. Shortly before serving, decorate with fresh flowers. (For several suggestions, see page 79.) Cut stems short. Wrap stems in wet cotton and foil to keep fresh.

Apricot Glaze: Combine 1 jar (12 ounces) apricot preserves, 2 tablespoons sugar and 2 tablespoons water in a small saucepan. Simmer, stirring occasionally, 5 minutes. Sieve into a small bowl. Stir in 2 tablespoons rum or brandy.

Rich Butter Cream Frosting: Beat 1¼ pounds (5 sticks) butter or margarine with 1 egg yolk in a large bowl until soft. Beat in three packages (1 pound each) 10X (confectioners') sugar alternately with ¼ cup orange liqueur until mixture is smooth.

SAVARIN WITH CREAM & STRAWBERRIES

A marvelous brandy-soaked, yeast-leavened dessert baked in a ring mold, that is equally good by itself, or served with fruit.

Bake at 375° for 35 minutes.
Makes one cake; about 10 servings.

**1 envelope active dry yeast
¼ cup very warm water
2 tablespoons sugar
¼ teaspoon salt
3 eggs
2½ cups sifted all-purpose flour
6 tablespoons butter or margarine, softened
   Brandy Syrup (recipe follows)
¾ cup apricot preserves
   Whipped cream
   Strawberries**

1. Grease a 6-cup ring mold.
2. Sprinkle yeast into very warm water in a 1-cup measure. ("Very warm water" should feel comfortably warm when dropped on wrist.) Stir in ½ teaspoon of the sugar; dissolve yeast. Let stand until bubbly and double in volume, about 10 minutes.
3. Combine yeast mixture, remaining sugar, salt, eggs and 2 cups flour in a large bowl; beat with electric mixer at medium speed, 2 minutes, scraping side of the bowl often. Add butter or margarine, 1 tablespoon at a time, beating well after each addition. Stir in remaining flour. Turn dough into prepared ring mold.
4. Let rise in a warm place, away from drafts,

45 minutes, or until double in bulk. (Dough should rise about 1 inch above edge of pan.)

5. Bake in moderate oven (375°) 35 minutes, or until top is brown and loaf sounds hollow when tapped. Remove from pan to wire rack; cool.
6. Make BRANDY SYRUP.
7. Prick cake all over with a skewer or two-tined fork; place on a deep plate. Baste several times with BRANDY SYRUP, reserving ¼ cup, until cake is thoroughly soaked. Place on serving plate.
8. Heat apricot preserves in small saucepan; press through sieve; stir in reserved BRANDY SYRUP. Brush all over cake to glaze evenly.
9. Fill center with whipped cream and garnish with strawberries.

Brandy Syrup: Makes 2 cups.

1¼ cups sugar
1¼ cups water
 1 three-inch piece stick cinnamon
½ teaspoon anise seeds, crushed
⅛ teaspoon ground mace
½ cup brandy (or rum)

Combine sugar, water, cinnamon, anise seeds and mace in a small suacepan; bring to boiling, stirring constantly, until sugar dissolves. Simmer, uncovered, 15 minutes; strain into a small bowl. Stir in brandy or rum. Use while still warm.

PINEAPPLE CHEESECAKE

The King of Cheesecakes. Velvety-smooth and rich. Try garnishing with pineapple slices and cherries.

Bake crust at 400° for 8 minutes; bake cheesecake at 475° for 12 minutes, then at 250° for 1½ hours. Makes one 10-inch cheesecake.

½ recipe Cooky Crust (recipe page 103)
   Pineapple Filling (recipe follows)
 5 packages (8 ounces each) cream cheese
1¾ cups sugar
 3 tablespoons flour
 1 teaspoon vanilla
 5 eggs
 2 egg yolks
¼ cup heavy cream

1. Roll one third of chilled COOKY CRUST dough to cover bottom of a 10-inch spring-form pan.
2. Bake in hot oven (400°) 8 minutes, or until crust is lightly browned; cool. Grease side of the spring-form pan; roll remaining dough into 2 strips, each about 15 inches long and 2½ inches wide; press onto side of pan and fit side of pan together with bottom. Refrigerate.
3. Let cream cheese soften in a large bowl; blend

in sugar, flour and vanilla. Beat with electric mixer until light and fluffy. Add eggs and egg yolks, one at a time, beating well after each addition; stir in heavy cream; spoon PINEAPPLE FILLING into crust; pour cream cheese mixture over.
4. Bake in a very hot oven (475°) 12 minutes; lower temperature to 250° and bake 1½ hours longer. Turn off oven; let cake remain in oven for about 1 hour.
5. Remove from oven; cool in pan on a wire rack; loosen around edge with a knife; release spring and remove side of pan.

Pineapple Filling: Combine 3 tablespoons sugar and 1 tablespoon cornstarch in a small saucepan. Slowly stir in contents of a 1-pound, 4-ounce can of crushed pineapple. Cook, stirring constantly, over medium heat, until mixture thickens and bubbles 1 minute; cool.

SOUR CREAM-WALNUT CHEESECAKE

Smaller, yet no less rich than larger cakes, with a crunchy walnut crust and topping.

Bake at 350° for 40 minutes, then 5 minutes longer to set topping.
Makes one 8-inch cheesecake.

 1 cup zwieback crumbs
 2 tablespoons sugar
¼ cup walnuts, finely chopped
 2 tablespoons butter or margarine, melted
 2 packages (8 ounces each) cream cheese, softened
½ cup sugar
1½ teaspoons vanilla
 3 eggs, well beaten
 1 cup dairy sour cream
 1 tablespoon sugar

1. Combine zwieback crumbs, the 2 tablespoons sugar and 2 tablespoons of the walnuts; blend in butter or margarine. Press mixture evenly on bottom and side of an 8-inch spring-form pan. Chill.
2. Beat cream cheese with electric mixer at medium speed, in a large bowl, until fluffy. Gradually beat in sugar and 1 teaspoon of the vanilla. Beat in eggs, one third at a time. Turn into prepared pan.
3. Bake in moderate oven (350°) 40 minutes, or until center is firm. Remove from oven. Cool on wire rack 5 minutes, away from drafts.
4. Combine sour cream, remaining sugar and vanilla. Spread over top of cake; sprinkle with remaining walnuts.
5. Return to moderate oven (350°) 5 minutes, or until topping is set. Remove from oven; cool in pan on wire rack, away from drafts. Remove side of pan. Refrigerate several hours before serving.

PETITS BABAS AU RHUM

A European confection thought to be named, whimsically, after Ali Baba. Moist and fragrant, a gift for that special friend.

Bake at 425° for 8 to 10 minutes.
Makes 4 dozen babas.

    ½ cup milk
     2 tablespoons sugar
    ⅛ teaspoon salt
    ½ cup (1 stick) butter or margarine
     1 envelope active dry yeast
    ¼ cup water
     2 eggs
     2 cups <u>sifted</u> all-purpose flour
     3 tablespoons dried currants
        Rum Syrup (recipe follows)
        Candied red cherries
        Angelica

1. Combine milk, sugar, salt and butter or margarine in a small saucepan. Heat slowly, until butter or margarine melts; cool to lukewarm.
2. Sprinkle yeast into very warm water in a large bowl. ("Very warm water" should feel comfortably warm when dropped on wrist.) Stir until yeast dissolves; stir in milk mixture.
3. Beat in eggs and flour to make a very soft dough. Beat vigorously with a wooden spoon at least 5 minutes, or until dough is shiny and elastic. Scrape dough down from side of bowl. Cover with plastic wrap. Let rise in a warm place, away from drafts, 45 minutes, or until double in bulk.
4. Beat dough well; stir in currants.
5. Spoon into greased tiny muffin-pan (gem pan) cups (less than 2″ across), placing a scant tablespoon in each. (If you do not have enough pans to bake all tiny cakes at once, cover dough and refrigerate while first batch rises and bakes, then stir down before spooning into pans.) Cover; let rise in a warm place, away from drafts, 45 minutes, or until almost triple in bulk.
6. Bake in hot oven (425°) 8 to 10 minutes, or until babas are a rich, golden brown. Remove from pans; place, top sides down, in a single layer in a jelly roll pan.
7. Pour warm RUM SYRUP over Babas; keep basting until all syrup is absorbed. Garnish each BABA AU RHUM with a half candied red cherry and slivers of angelica, if you wish.

Rum Syrup: Combine 1 cup sugar, 2 cups water and 1 jar (12 ounces) apricot preserves in a medium-size saucepan. Heat to boiling, stirring constantly; lower heat; simmer, uncovered, 5 minutes. Press through a sieve. Cool 15 minutes, stir in ¾ to 1 cup golden rum to taste. Makes 4 cups; enough for 4 dozen babas.

TORTES

CHOCOLATE-WALNUT TORTE

An unusually rich and moist cake that uses ground walnuts and breadcrumbs in place of the usual flour.

Bake at 350° for 15 minutes.
Makes one 8-inch cake.

     6 eggs, separated
    ¾ cup sugar
    ¼ cup water
     1 teaspoon vanilla
     1 cup broken walnuts, ground
    ⅓ cup packaged bread crumbs
    ½ teaspoon salt
        Chocolate Sour Cream Frosting (recipe follows)
        Chocolate Rum Glaze (recipe follows)
        Whole walnuts

1. Line three 8x1½-inch layer-cake pans with a double thickness of wax paper. (Do not grease.)
2. Beat egg whites in a large bowl at high speed with electric mixer, until foamy white and double in volume. Gradually beat in ¼ cup of the sugar, until meringue stands in soft peaks.
3. Beat egg yolks in a small bowl at high speed with electric mixer until thick and lemon-colored. Gradually beat in remaining sugar until mixture is very light and fluffy and falls in ribbons from beaters when beaters are lifted (about 5 minutes). Lower speed; beat in the water and vanilla.
4. Fold walnuts, bread crumbs, and salt into egg yolk mixture; blend completely. Fold egg yolk mixture into meringue until no streaks of yellow or white remain. Pour into pans, dividing equally.
5. Bake in moderate oven (350°) 15 minutes, or until centers spring back when lightly pressed with fingertip.
6. Invert pans over wire rack; let cool 20 minutes. Loosen cakes around edges with a knife; carefully loosen cakes from bottom with small spatula, being careful not to tear cakes (cakes are very delicate). Turn out of pans; peel off wax paper.
7. Reserve 1 cup CHOCOLATE SOUR CREAM FROSTING. Put layers together with part of remaining frosting. Spread CHOCOLATE RUM GLAZE on top and side of cake. Pipe reserved frosting decoratively on top and side of cake. Decorate with whole walnuts.

Chocolate Sour Cream Frosting: Makes enough to fill and frost one 8-inch cake.

    ¾ cup (1½ sticks) butter or margarine
     4 squares semisweet chocolate, melted
     1 package (1 pound) 10X (confectioners') sugar
     4 tablespoons dairy sour cream
    1½ teaspoons vanilla

Make any day a special occasion with one of these creamy cheesecakes. Shown here from top down: Pineapple Cheesecake, Sour Cream Walnut Cheesecake (recipes in this chapter) and Lattice Cherry-Cheese Pie (recipe, Chapter 6).

The moist fruit filling and
flaky-light pastry make this Apple-Nut
Strudel a sensational dessert.
Recipe in this chapter.

Combine butter or margarine and chocolate in a small bowl. Beat until thoroughly blended. Add sugar alternately with sour cream and vanilla, beating until mixture is spreadable.

Chocolate Rum Glaze: Combine 1 square semi-sweet chocolate, 1 tablespoon butter or margarine, 1 tablespoon 10X (confectioners') sugar and 1 tablespoon rum or brandy in a small bowl; set bowl in a small saucepan partly filled with water. Heat, stirring often, until chocolate is melted; cool slightly. If glaze separates, add a few drops of cold water or milk; then stir until it is smooth.

LEMON-DATE TORTE

There are chopped dates and walnuts in the delicate layers of this torte, and smooth lemon filling between. A dollop of whipped cream and a pretty lemon rose on top make the perfect garnish.

Bake at 350° for 40 minutes.
Makes one 8-inch cake.

    1½ cups sifted all-purpose flour
    1½ teaspoons baking powder
    ½   teaspoon ground cinnamon
    ¼   teaspoon salt
    ⅛   teaspoon ground cloves
     1 package (8 ounces) pitted dates, chopped
    ½   cup walnuts, chopped
     4 eggs, separated
     1 cup sugar
     5 tablespoons butter or margarine
     1 teaspoon vanilla
    ⅓   cup milk
        Lemon Filling (recipe page 74)

1. Grease two 8x1½-inch round layer-cake pans; dust with flour; tap out excess.
2. Sift flour, baking powder, cinnamon, salt and cloves into a large bowl; stir in dates and walnuts.
3. Beat egg whites in a medium-size bowl until foamy white and double in volume. Gradually beat in ½ cup of the sugar, 1 tablespoon at a time, until sugar dissolves, and meringue stands in firm peaks.
4. Beat butter or margarine with remaining ½ cup sugar in a large bowl; beat in 2 of the egg yolks and vanilla until light and fluffy. Beat in flour mixture, one half at a time, alternately with milk, until blended; fold in meringue. Spread evenly into prepared pans.
5. Bake in a moderate oven (350°) 40 minutes, or until centers spring back when lightly pressed with fingertip. Cool in pans on wire racks 10 minutes. Turn out onto racks; cool completely.
6. Prepare LEMON FILLING. (Use remaining 2 yolks from torte recipe.)

7. Split cake layers to make 4 thin layers; spread each of 3 layers with ⅓ cup of the LEMON FILLING; stack together on a serving plate. Top with plain layer. Garnish with whipped cream and a lemon rose (directions page 78). Chill at least 4 hours to mellow. Cut in thin wedges.

ALMOND BLITZ TORTE

A light-as-air torte featuring frothy meringue, almonds and whipped cream between the layers.

Bake at 350° for 30 minutes.
Makes one 9-inch cake.

     2 cups sifted cake flour
     2 teaspoons baking powder
     1 teaspoon salt
     5 eggs, separated
    1¾ cups sugar
    ⅓   cup vegetable shortening
     1 teaspoon vanilla
    ½   teaspoon almond extract
    ½   cup milk
    ¾   cup almonds, sliced
     1 cup heavy cream
     2 tablespoons sugar

1. Grease two 9x1½-inch layer-cake pans; dust with flour; tap out excess.
2. Sift flour, baking powder and salt onto wax paper; reserve.
3. Beat egg whites in small bowl with electric mixer at high speed until foamy white and double in volume. Gradually beat in ¾ cup of the sugar, until meringue stands in firm peaks; reserve.
4. With same beater (don't wash) beat remaining 1 cup sugar, shortening, egg yolks, vanilla and almond extract in large bowl with electric mixer at high speed, 3 minutes.
5. Stir in flour mixture by hand, alternately with milk, beating after each addition, until batter is smooth. Spread into pans. Carefully spread reserved meringue over batter; sprinkle with almonds.
6. Bake in moderate oven (350°) 30 minutes, or until meringue is golden brown and cake begins to pull from sides of pan. (Meringue may crack in baking, but don't worry, it will settle while cooling).
7. Cool cake layers in pans on wire rack 30 minutes, or until cool enough to handle. Loosen around edges with a knife; turn out onto your hand, then gently place, meringue sides up, on wire racks; cool.
8. At least 2 hours before serving, beat cream and 2 tablespoons sugar in a small bowl, until stiff.
9. Put layers together on serving plate with part of the whipped cream; decorate top of cake with remaining cream and garnish with strawberries, if you wish. Refrigerate until serving time.

LINZER TORTE

One of the best Linzers we have tested was given to us by Mrs. Elizabeth (Max) Steidell, the mother of one of our staff members.

Bake at 350° for 50 minutes.
Makes one 10-inch cake.

1¾ cups <u>sifted</u> all-purpose flour
 ¾ cup sugar
  2 teaspoons unsweetened cocoa
  1 teaspoon baking powder
 ¾ teaspoon ground cinnamon
 ¼ teaspoon salt
 ¼ teaspoon ground cloves
 ½ cup (1 stick) butter or margarine, softened
  1 egg, beaten
  1 can (3½ ounces) whole blanched almonds, ground (1 cup)
  2 tablespoons kirsch or cherry brandy
 ½ teaspoon grated lemon rind
  2 tablespoons lemon juice
  1 jar (10 ounces) red raspberry jam
    10X (confectioners') sugar

1. Sift flour, sugar, cocoa, baking powder, cinnamon, salt and cloves into a medium-size bowl. Cut in butter or margarine with a pastry blender.
2. Stir in egg, ground almonds, kirsch, lemon rind and juice until mixture is well blended. Chill 1 hour, or until dough gets firmer.
3. Cut the dough in half and press one half to fit the bottom of a 10-inch greased and floured springform pan. Spread ½ cup jam over dough.
4. Sprinkle your work surface lightly with flour and roll remaining dough into finger-thick strips. Arrange strips, lattice-fashion, over preserves.
5. Bake in moderate oven (350°) 50 minutes, or until pastry is firm. Cool in pan on wire rack. Remove cake from pan. Fill lattices with additional raspberry jam, if you wish. Sprinkle with 10X sugar.
Note: You may use a 9x9x2-inch pan if you prefer.

DOUBLE-CHOCOLATE TORTE

Four dark layers with a double filling and Chocolate Butter Cream Frosting make this delectable beauty a super-rich dessert.

Bake at 350° for 35 minutes.
Makes one 9-inch torte.

  1 recipe Devil's Food Cake (recipe page 63), for cake layers only
  1 jar (12 ounces) apricot preserves
    Chocolate Butter Cream Frosting (recipe page 75)

1. Prepare chocolate cake layers, according to directions in DEVIL'S FOOD CAKE recipe. Follow recipe through Step 5.
2. Bake in a moderate oven (350°) 35 minutes, or until tops spring back when lightly pressed with fingertip. Cool in pans on wire racks 10 minutes; loosen around edges with a knife; turn out onto wire racks; cool completely.
3. Prepare CHOCOLATE BUTTER CREAM FROSTING.
4. When ready to put torte together, heat apricot preserves slowly in a small saucepan, stirring constantly, just until hot; press through a sieve into a small bowl; cool.
5. Split cake layers to make 4 thin layers. (For directions on how to split layers, see page 77.) Spread each of 3 layers with ⅓ cup of the CHOCOLATE BUTTER CREAM FROSTING, then with ⅓ cup of the apricot preserves; stack together on a serving plate. Top with plain layer.
6. Frost side and top of torte with remaining chocolate frosting; chill. Garnish with sliced almonds or chopped walnuts, if you wish. To serve, cut in thin wedges.

Note: If you'd prefer a bit less chocolate, frost with VANILLA BUTTER CREAM FROSTING.

MERINGUES

MEGEVE CAKE

Three meringue layers with a rich chocolate filling— all covered with chocolate curls.

Bake at 300° for 30 minutes.
Makes one 10-inch cake.

Meringue:
  3 egg whites
  1 cup less 1 tablespoon superfine granulated sugar

Whipped Chocolate Filling:
 ⅔ cup heavy cream
  7 squares (1 ounce each) semisweet chocolate
3½ squares (1 ounce each) unsweetened chocolate
  4 tablespoons (½ stick) butter or margarine
  4 egg whites
  1 cup less 1 tablespoon superfine granulated sugar
    Chocolate Curls (recipe page 78)
    10X (confectioners') sugar

1. Grease 1 large and 1 small cooky sheet; dust with flour, tapping off excess. Using an 8-inch layer-cake pan as a guide, draw 2 circles on large cooky sheet and one on small cooky sheet.
2. Beat the 3 egg whites in a large bowl, with an electric mixer, until foamy white and double in volume. Sprinkle in the 1 cup less 1 tablespoon sugar.

1 tablespoon at a time, beating all the time, until sugar dissolves completely and meringue stands in firm peaks, about 15 minutes. Spoon mixture evenly into the 3 circles; spread out to edges.

3. Bake in slow oven (300°) 30 minutes, or until layers are firm and lightly golden. Cool 5 minutes on cooky sheets on wire racks, then loosen meringue layers carefully from brown paper with a wide spatula and slide onto racks; cool.

4. Make CHOCOLATE CURLS.

5. Heat cream in top of double boiler; add semisweet and unsweetened chocolate. Stir often with a wooden spoon until chocolate is completely melted. Stir in butter or margarine.

6. Beat the 4 egg whites in large bowl, until foamy white; gradually add remaining sugar, beating well after each addition; continue beating until meringue is glossy and stands in firm peaks; reserve.

7. Fill bottom of double boiler partly with ice and water; set top of boiler with chocolate mixture in ice water. Beat chocolate mixture at high speed with electric hand mixer or rotary hand beater, until light and fluffy and almost double in volume; scrape down sides of double boiler often. Fold chocolate into meringue, until no streaks of white or brown remain.

8. Place 1 meringue layer on a serving plate; spread with about 1½ cups chocolate filling; repeat with another layer and ½ cup filling. Place third layer on top. Frost sides and top with remaining filling. Place prepared CHOCOLATE CURLS on sides and piled high on top of cake; chill. Thirty minutes before serving, remove cake from refrigerator; sprinkle with 10X sugar. Cut in wedges with sharp serrated knife.

COFFEE MERINGUE GLACE

Crisp coffee meringue shell is filled with vanilla ice cream, topped with a mocha sauce.

Bake at 275° for 1½ to 2 hours.
Makes one 11-inch cake.

  4 egg whites
  1 cup sugar
  3 tablespoons instant coffee
⅛ teaspoon salt
  1 quart vanilla ice cream
  2 tablespoons walnuts, finely chopped
    Mocha Sauce (recipe follows)

1. Beat egg whites until stiff, but not dry. Mix sugar with coffee and salt; gradually beat into egg whites.

2. Cover cooky sheet with aluminum foil; mark off a 9-inch circle on foil. Spread meringue within circle, building up the edge to about 2 inches.

3. Bake in slow oven (275°) 1½ to 2 hours, or until crisp and dry. Remove from oven; cool. Carefully

peel away foil; place meringue on serving plate.

4. Fill shell with ice cream; drizzle with the MOCHA SAUCE. Sprinkle with chopped walnuts. Cut in wedges to serve; spoon more sauce over each serving.

Mocha Sauce: Makes about 2 cups.

  1 package (6 ounces) semisweet chocolate pieces
¼ cup (½ stick) butter or margarine
  1 cup sifted 10X (confectioners') sugar
½ cup light corn syrup
  2 teaspoons instant coffee
    Dash of salt
½ cup hot water
  1 teaspoon vanilla

1. Melt chocolate pieces with butter or margarine in top of a double boiler over simmering water.

2. Stir in sugar, corn syrup, instant coffee, salt, hot water and vanilla until sauce is smooth and slightly thickened. Cool. Serve at room temperature.

PEACHES AND CREAM MERINGUE

Delicately decorated meringue shell to fill with ice cream and sliced peaches. Top with a fruit glaze for a lovely version of the French Vacherin.

Bake twice at 250° for 45 minutes.
Makes one 9-inch cake.

  6 egg whites
1¾ cups sugar
  1 quart vanilla ice cream
  3 large ripe peaches, peeled, halved, and pitted
    Almond Peach Glaze (recipe follows)

1. Line a cooky sheet with brown paper; draw a 7-inch circle in center.

2. Make meringue in two batches: Beat 3 egg whites in a medium-size bowl, until foamy white and double in volume. Sprinkle in 1 cup of the sugar *very slowly,* 1 tablespoon at a time, beating all the time until sugar dissolves completely and meringue stands in firm peaks.

3. Spread mixture inside the circle on brown paper, build up a 2-inch rim around edge.

4. Bake in very slow oven (250°) 45 minutes, or until firm. Let cool on paper while making second batch of meringue.

5. Beat remaining 3 egg whites with remaining ¾ cup sugar, following directions in Step 2.

6. Fit a large star tip onto a pastry bag and fill bag with meringue mixture. Pipe rings around side and on top of baked meringue shell; make swirls around top with remaining meringue.

7. Bake "decorated" meringue in very slow oven (250°) 45 minutes, or until firm. Cool completely on paper, then loosen shell with a spatula. (This

can be done several days before serving; simply store meringue shell in an airtight container.

8. One hour before serving: Place meringue shell on a serving plate. Scoop ice cream with large spoon to make "petals" and fill meringue shell. Arrange peach halves over ice cream; top with ALMOND PEACH GLAZE.

Almond Peach Glaze: Mash 1 peeled, halved, and pitted ripe peach in a small saucepan; stir in ½ cup light corn syrup. Heat to boiling; lower heat; simmer 5 minutes. Remove from heat; stir in ½ teaspoon almond extract. Cool. Makes about 1 cup.

LEMON ANGEL PIE

This is a make-ahead dessert. It needs long chilling to mellow to perfection.

Bake shell at 275° for 1 hour.
Makes one 9-inch pie.

> Butter or margarine
> 4 eggs, separated
> ¼ teaspoon cream of tartar
> ½ teaspoon salt
> ½ teaspoon vanilla
> 2 cups sugar
> 4 tablespoons cornstarch
> 1½ cups water
> ½ cup lemon juice
> 2 tablespoons butter or margarine
> 1 cup heavy cream

1. Generously butter a 9-inch pie plate.
2. Beat egg whites with cream of tartar, ¼ teaspoon of the salt and vanilla in a large bowl, until foamy white and double in volume. Using an electric mixer, gradually beat in 1 cup of the sugar, until sugar dissolves completely and meringue stands in stiff peaks (about 25 minutes).
3. Spoon meringue into pie plate. Spread almost to side of plate, hollowing center and building up edge slightly to form a shell.
4. Bake in a very slow oven (275°) 1 hour, or until firm and lightly golden. Cool completely in pie plate on wire rack.
5. While shell bakes, mix remaining 1 cup sugar, cornstarch, and ¼ teaspoon salt in a medium-size saucepan. Stir in water, then beat in egg yolks and lemon juice.
6. Cook, stirring constantly, until mixture thickens, and boils, 3 minutes; remove from heat. Stir in butter or margarine, until melted; pour into medium-size bowl; cover. Chill until completely cold.
7. Beat cream in a medium-size bowl until stiff. Layer lemon filling, alternately with whipped cream, into meringue shell. Chill about 5 hours, or overnight, before cutting.

RASPBERRY MERINGUE CAKE

A towering beauty—five meringue layers are stacked with raspberry cream and topped with fresh berries. A super dessert!

Bake shells at 300° for 30 minutes.
Makes one 10-inch meringue.

> 6 egg whites
> ¼ teaspoon cream of tartar
> 1½ cups sugar (for meringue)
> ½ cup almonds, ground
> ½ cup cornstarch
> ¼ cup red raspberry jelly
> 2 cups heavy cream
> 1 tablespoon sugar (for cream)
> Fresh red raspberries

1. Grease 2 large and 1 small cooky sheets. Dust with flour; tap out excess. Using an 8-inch round layer-cake pan as a guide, draw 2 circles on each of the large cooky sheets and 1 on the smaller one. Set aside for Step 3. (If you do not have enough cooky sheets or oven space to bake all of the meringue layers at once, shape meringues on greased, floured foil, and let stand at room temperature until first batch is baked. Then simply slide foil onto cooky sheets.
2. Beat egg whites with cream of tartar in a large bowl with an electric mixer until foamy white and double in volume. Gradually add the 1½ cups sugar, 1 tablespoon at a time, beating all the time, until sugar dissolves and meringue stands in firm peaks (about 25 minutes).
3. Mix almonds and cornstarch in a small bowl; fold into meringue until completely blended. Spoon meringue evenly into the five circles; spread out to the edges.
4. Bake in a slow oven (300°) 30 minutes, or until layers are firm and lightly golden. Cool 5 minutes on cooky sheets on wire racks, then loosen meringues carefully with a wide spatula, and slide onto racks; cool completely.
5. Three hours before serving, whip jelly with a fork, in a cup. Beat 1½ cups of the cream in a medium-size bowl until thick; beat in jelly; continue beating until stiff.
6. Place 1 meringue layer on a serving plate; spread with one-fourth of the cream mixture; repeat with remaining layers and cream, leaving top layer plain.
7. Beat remaining ½ cup cream with the 1 tablespoon sugar in a small bowl until stiff; spoon in puffs on top layer; garnish with red raspberries. Chill until serving time. To serve, cut in wedges.
Note: If meringues are made a day ahead, stack layers with wax paper between them, and store in a cool, dry place.

Whether you're giving a lavish dinner party or just having a few friends over for a casual evening of cards and games, you're sure to delight your guests with this fantastic Chocolate Walnut Torte. Recipe in this chapter.

Peaches, pineapple, grapes, strawberries—choose any fruit you wish. They're all beautiful and delicious when glazed atop our Easy Cheese Fruit Tarts. Recipe in this chapter.

8

TERRIFIC TIME SAVERS

Even when time is short, you can still turn out delicious cakes and pastries. The trick is to use convenience foods and cut preparation time to a minimum. In this chapter you'll see how to do it, and how to create sensational baked desserts in almost no time at all.

CAKES, CUPCAKES AND PASTRY

WALNUT COFFEE CAKE

Refrigerated rolls make a quick coffee cake, when butter, cinnamon, brown sugar and nuts are rolled up inside, and the crescents are placed in layers.

Bake at 375° for 35 minutes.
Makes one 9x5x3-inch coffee cake.

- **2 packages refrigerated crescent dinner rolls**
- **2 tablespoons butter or margarine, softened**
- **½ cup firmly packed brown sugar**
- **2 teaspoons ground cinnamon**
- **¼ cup chopped walnuts**

1. Unroll dough; separate into triangles. Spread each triangle with part of the butter or margarine.
2. Combine brown sugar, cinnamon and walnuts in a small bowl. Sprinkle about 1 tablespoon of the mixture over each dough triangle. Roll up as label directs.
3. Place rolls, point sides down, in a greased 9x5x3-inch pan, in two layers. Brush top of loaf with remaining butter or margarine; sprinkle with remaining topping.
4. Bake in moderate oven (375°) 35 minutes, or until golden brown. Turn cake out onto wire rack; cool completely before serving.

ISLANDS BANANA CAKE

Ripe bananas and tender coconut in a buttery topping—poured over yellow cake, then quick-broiled for a yummy warm dessert.

Bake at 350° for 30 minutes.
Makes one 9-inch square cake.

- **2 cups biscuit mix**
- **½ cup granulated sugar**
- **½ teaspoon ground mace**
- **2 eggs**
- **½ cup milk**
- **1 teaspoon vanilla**
- **6 tablespoons (¾ stick) butter or margarine**
- **¼ cup firmly packed brown sugar**
- **½ cup flaked coconut**
- **½ cup chopped walnuts**
- **3 medium-size ripe bananas**

1. Combine biscuit mix, granulated sugar, mace, eggs, milk, vanilla and 3 tablespoons of the butter or margarine in a large bowl. Beat with electric mixer at low speed ½ minute to blend ingredients.

Increase speed to medium-high; beat 4 minutes. Scrape side of bowl often with rubber spatula.
2. Turn batter into a buttered 9x9x2-inch baking pan; spread evenly.
3. Bake in a moderate oven (350°) 30 minutes, or until center of cake springs back when lightly pressed with fingertip. Cool cake a few minutes on wire rack.
4. Set oven temperature to broil.
5. Combine brown sugar and remaining 3 tablespoons butter or margarine in a small bowl; stir in coconut and walnuts.
6. Peel bananas; slice diagonally and arrange petal fashion, overlapping, on top of cake. Sprinkle with brown sugar mixture.
7. Broil, with top 3 inches from heat, just until topping is bubbly and lightly browned, about 2 minutes (watch cake carefully while browning). Cool cake on wire rack. Cut into squares while still warm.

ORANGE SWEET CAKE

Orange juice and rind provide the tangy taste in this easy cake; walnuts add the crunch, and biscuit mix makes it simple!

Bake at 350° for 30 minutes.
Makes one 9-inch square cake.

- **2 cups biscuit mix**
- **½ cup granulated sugar**
- **2 eggs**
- **1 tablespoon grated orange rind**
- **½ cup orange juice**
- **6 tablespoons butter or margarine, softened**
- **1 teaspoon vanilla**
- **⅓ cup firmly packed brown sugar**
- **½ cup chopped walnuts**
- **1 tablespoon cream**

1. Combine biscuit mix, granulated sugar, eggs, orange rind, orange juice, vanilla and 3 tablespoons of the butter in a large mixing bowl. Beat at low speed with electric mixer ½ minute to blend ingredients. Increase speed to medium-high; beat 4 minutes. Scrape bowl often with rubber spatula.
2. Turn the batter into a buttered 9x9x2-inch baking pan.
3. Bake in moderate oven (350°) 30 minutes, or until center of cake springs back when lightly pressed with finger. Cool cake a few minutes on a wire rack.
4. Combine brown sugar, chopped walnuts, remaining butter and cream; beat until well mixed. Spread on cake. Broil, with top 3 inches from heat, just until topping is bubbly and lightly browned, about 2 minutes. Cool cake on wire rack. Cut cake in squares. Remaining cake may be covered and stored in the pan.

COCONUT-JELLY CUPCAKES

Fancy cupcakes with colorful cut-out tops.

Bake at 350° for 15 minutes.
Makes 30 cupcakes.

1 package yellow cake mix
1 can (16½ ounces) vanilla frosting
1 jar (12 ounces) currant, raspberry or strawberry jelly
   Flaked coconut

1. Line 30 medium-size muffin-pan cups with pleated muffin-pan liners.
2. Prepare cake mix, following label directions. Spoon batter into prepared liners. Bake, following label directions.
3. Remove cupcakes from pans to wire racks. Cool. Leave paper liners on for easy handling.
4. Use a small sharp knife to cut a small cone-shaped piece from the top of each cake. Carefully set pieces aside. Spoon a little vanilla frosting into the hole in each cupcake; replace cone-shaped pieces. Spread entire top of each cupcake with jelly; sprinkle with coconut, pressing slightly into jelly.

QUICK CHERRY STRUDEL

This elegant strudel is surprisingly easy to make.

Preheat oven to 450°; bake at 400° for 25 minutes.
Makes 1 large strudel.

1 package (10 ounces) frozen patty shells
1 can (1 pound, 5 ounces) cherry pie filling
2 teaspoons grated lemon rind
¼ cup packaged bread crumbs
1 tablespoon milk
¼ cup sliced unblanched almonds
2 tablespoons sugar

1. Preheat oven to 450°.
2. Let patty shells soften at room temperature for 20 minutes.
3. Combine cherry pie filling and lemon rind in a small bowl; reserve.
4. On a *well-floured cloth-covered surface,* overlap patty shells in a straight line. Using a *floured stockinette covered* rolling pin, press down onto the patty shells. (*Note:* You may use a floured rolling pin without the stockinette, but flour the rolling pin frequently to prevent the patty shells from sticking.) Roll out from center of patty shells to a 22x16-inch rectangle, being careful not to tear pastry.
5. Sprinkle pastry with bread crumbs.
6. Spoon cherry pie filling down length of pastry closest to you into a 2-inch strip and within 2 inches

of ends. Fold in sides; keep filling in.
7. Using the floured cloth, grasp at both ends and gently lift the cloth up and let the strudel roll itself up. Carefully slide onto a cooky sheet, keeping seam side down, and form into a horseshoe shape.
8. Brush top generously with milk; sprinkle almond slices on top, pressing well in order to keep in place. Then sprinkle with sugar.
9. Lower oven heat to (400°); bake 25 minutes or until golden brown; let cool on baking sheet 10 minutes. Serve the strudel warm.

GLAZED APPLE JALOUSIE

A flaky glazed apple pastry, so like its counterpart that's found in Viennese confection shops.

Preheat oven to 450°; bake at 400° for 30 minutes.
Makes one 13x5-inch pastry; about 6 servings.

¼ cup currants or raisins
2 teaspoons grated lemon rind
⅓ cup sugar
¼ teaspoon ground cardamom
2 tablespoons butter or margarine
1 package (10 ounces) frozen patty shells, thawed
1 can (1 pound, 4 oz.) pie-sliced apples, drained
1 egg, beaten
⅓ cup apple or crab apple jelly, melted

1. Preheat oven to 450°. Combine currants. lemon rind, sugar and cardamom in a small bowl. Blend in butter or margarine with a fork.
2. Overlap 3 patty shells on a lightly floured surface; overlap remaining 3 patty shells next to them so that all are overlapped. Roll out to a 13x12-inch rectangle.
3. Place a double thickness of 12-inch aluminum foil on a cooky sheet. Cut a 13x5-inch piece of pastry; place on foil. Cover center of pastry with ⅓ of the apples; sprinkle with ⅓ of the sugar mixture. Add more apples and sugar mixture; repeat for top layer.
4. From remaining pastry cut 4 strips, each 13x½ inches; cut each in half. Brush edges of pastry base with beaten egg. Place strips in 4 crisscross patterns over apples, pressing ends onto base.
5. Cut remaining pastry into 1-inch strips; place along all 4 edges of pastry base to fasten down the crisscrosses and seal in filling. Press firmly into place. Brush all surfaces with beaten egg. Carefully fold edges of foil to contain pastry. This will help keep the shape of the pastry.
6. Place in very hot oven (450°). Immediately lower heat to 400°. Bake 30 minutes, or until pastry is golden. Cool a few minutes on cooky sheet. Carefully remove from foil to wire rack. While still hot, brush entire jalousie with melted jelly.

PETALED HONEY RING

Butterflake dinner rolls can make a lovely coffee cake when you arrange them in a pan, drizzle with butter and honey, then bake until golden.

Bake at 350° for 25 minutes.
Makes one 7-cup ring.

 2 **packages refrigerated butterflake dinner rolls**
 ¼ **cup raisins**
 3 **teaspoons grated lemon rind**
 3 **tablespoons honey**
 ¼ **cup (½ stick) butter or margarine, melted**

1. Separate each package of rolls to make 24 even pieces. Place 12 pieces in a well-buttered 7-cup ring mold to make an even layer. Sprinkle one-third of the raisins and 1 teaspoon of the lemon rind over layer; then drizzle 1 tablespoon each of the honey and melted butter or margarine over top.
2. Make two more layers the same way; place remaining rolls on top. Drizzle remaining butter or margarine over all.
3. Bake in moderate oven (350°) 25 minutes, or until firm and golden. Loosen at once around edge with knife; invert onto a serving plate. Let stand 10 minutes. To serve, pull off layers with two forks; serve warm.

NO-BAKE "BAKED" DESSERTS

PUMPKIN PARTY TARTS

These fluffy light tarts can be made the day ahead and garnished just before serving.

Makes twelve 3-inch tarts.

 1 **envelope unflavored gelatin**
 ½ **cup sugar**
 1 **can (1 pound) pumpkin**
 ¾ **teaspoon ground cinnamon**
 ¼ **teaspoon ground nutmeg**
 ¼ **cup orange juice**
 1 **pint vanilla ice cream**
 2 **packages (5 ounces each) pastry tart shells, (6 to a pack)**

1. Combine gelatin and sugar in a medium-size saucepan. Stir in pumpkin, cinnamon, nutmeg and orange juice.
2. Cook, stirring constantly, until mixture bubbles and gelatin dissolves. Remove from heat and add ice cream, a few spoonfuls at a time.
3. Spoon pumpkin mixture into tart shells. Chill 4 hours, or overnight. Swirl whipped cream on the top of each tart, if you wish.

EASY CHEESE-FRUIT TARTS

Tiny nibbles of delicious fruit and cheese—so easy, you can put them together in no time; so good, no one will ever guess you didn't make them from scratch.

Makes six 3-inch tarts.

 2 **packages (3 ounces each) cream cheese**
 ½ **cup milk**
 1 **can (9¾ ounces) raspberry or pineapple dessert mix**
 1 **package (5 ounces) pastry tart shells (6 to a package)**
   Fresh or canned fruits for garnish
 6 **tablespoons apple jelly**
   Chopped pistachio nuts or almonds

1. Beat cream cheese in a small bowl until soft. Gradually beat in milk; continue beating until completely smooth. Add dessert mix; stir with spoon 30 seconds, or until thickened.
2. Spoon into tart shells, dividing evenly. Decorate with fruits of your choice. Melt apple jelly in a small saucepan; cool slightly, brush over fruits to glaze. Sprinkle with nuts, if you wish. Chill.

BRANDIED APRICOT TARTS

Here's another fabulous dessert you can serve when time's a problem. Cook the vanilla pudding and add a bit of brandy for a touch of elegance.

Makes six 3-inch tarts.

 1 **package (3¼ ounces) vanilla pudding and pie filling**
 1½ **cups milk**
 2 **tablespoons brandy**
 1 **can (8 ounces) apricot halves, drained**
 1 **package (5 ounces) pastry tart shells (6 to a package)**
 2 **tablespoons sugar**

1. Prepare vanilla pudding and pie filling following label directions, using 1½ cups milk. Remove from heat. Add brandy.
2. Set saucepan in a pan of ice and water to speed setting. Chill, stirring often, 5 minutes, until mixture begins to mound. Or, you may press wax paper on surface of pudding, then chill in refrigerator.
3. Place 1 apricot half in bottom of each tart shell. Spoon filling into shells. Refrigerate tarts until ready to serve.
4. Just before serving, place sugar in a small skillet. Over low heat, melt sugar until it begins to caramelize. With spoon, drizzle over top of tart in a tic-tac-toe pattern.

Our tropical Islands Banana Cake is both quick and easy. Cake mix and a broiled topping cut preparation time to a minimum. Recipe in this chapter.

INDEX

142

INDEX

ACKNOWLEDGMENTS

Pages 66-67: "Molinillo" hot
chocolate mixers, courtesy of the
Chocolate Manufacturers
Association of the United States;
"Windmills and Landscapes of
Holland", Dutch tiles courtesy of
Country Floors, Inc., 300 East 61st
Street, New York, N.Y. 10021.
Page 112: Dolly Arm Wicker Chair
and Pedestal Table courtesy of
Walters Wicker Wonderland, 991
Second Avenue, New York, N.Y.
10022.
Page 121: Tarte à l'Orange courtesy
of Lutece, New York, New York.
Page 124: "Sax Pink" china courtesy
of Ginori Fifth Avenue, 711 Fifth
Avenue, New York, N.Y. 10022.